**W9-BHD-966**

# Public Choice and Environmental Regulation

**General Editor:** Wallace E. Oates, *Professor of Economics,*
*University of Maryland*

This important series is designed to make a significant contribution to the development of the principles and practices of environmental economics. It includes both theoretical and empirical work. International in scope, it addresses issues of current and future concern in both East and West and in developed and developing countries.

The main purpose of the series is to create a forum for the publication of high quality work and to show how economic analysis can make a contribution to understanding and resolving the environmental problems confronting the world in the late twentieth century.

Recent titles in the series include:

Global Environmental Change and Agriculture
Assessing the Impacts
*Edited by George Frisvold and Betsey Kuhn*

Fiscal Policy and Environmental Welfare
Modelling Interjurisdictional Competition
*Thorsten Bayindir-Upmann*

Designing Institutions for Environmental and Resource Management
*Edited by Edna Tusak Loehman and D. Marc Kilgour*

The International Yearbook of Environmental and Resource Economics
1998/1999
A Survey of Current Issues
*Edited by Tom Tietenberg and Henk Folmer*

The Economic Approach to Environmental Policy
The Selected Essays of A. Myrick Freeman III
*A. Myrick Freeman III*

Economic Integration and the Environment
A Political–Economic Perspective
*Rolf Bommer*

Public Choice and Environmental Regulation
Tradable Permit Systems in the United States
and $CO_2$ Taxation in Europe
*Gert Tinggaard Svendsen*

Environmental Policy Analysis with Limited Information
Principles and Applications of the Transfer Method
*William H. Desvousges, F. Reed Johnson and H. Spencer Banzhaf*

Environmental Transition in Nordic and Baltic Countries
*Edited by Hans Aage*

Biodiversity, Conservation and Sustainable Development
Principles and Practices with Asian Examples
*Clem Tisdell*

Green Taxes
Economic Theory and Empirical Evidence from Scandinavia
*Edited by Runar Brännlund and Ing-Marie Gren*

# Public Choice and Environmental Regulation

Tradable Permit Systems in the United States and $CO_2$ Taxation in Europe

Gert Tinggaard Svendsen

*The Aarhus School of Business, Aarhus, Denmark*

NEW HORIZONS IN ENVIRONMENTAL ECONOMICS

**Edward Elgar**

Cheltenham, UK • Northampton, MA, USA

Published by
Edward Elgar Publishing Limited
8 Lansdown Place
Cheltenham
Glos GL50 2HU
UK

Edward Elgar Publishing, Inc.
6 Market Street
Northampton
Massachusetts 01060
USA

A catalogue record for this book
is available from the British Library

**Library of Congress Cataloguing in Publication Data**

Svendsen, Gert Tinggaard, 1963–
        Public choice and environmental regulation: tradable permit
    systems in the United States and $CO_2$ taxation in Europe / Gert
    Tinggaard Svendsen.
        Includes index.
            1. Emissions trading.  2. Emissions trading—United States.
        3. Carbon taxes—Denmark.  4. Environmental impact charges.
    I. Title.
    HC79.P55S86    1998
        363.738'7—dc21                                                98–24873
                                                                              CIP

ISBN 1 85898 628 1

Printed and bound in Great Britain by Biddles Ltd, Guildford and King's Lynn

For Kristina and Lars Kjartan.

# Contents

# Figures

# Tables

# Abbreviations

| | |
|---|---|
| APS | Ambient Permit System |
| APPA | American Public Power Association |
| ARP | Acid Rain Program |
| BACT | Best Available Control Technology |
| BAT | Best Available Technology |
| BCT | Best Conventional Technology |
| BOD | Biological Oxygen Demand |
| BPT | Best Practicable Technology |
| BMP | Best Management Practices |
| CAA | Clean Air Act |
| CAC | Command-And-Control |
| CBOT | Chicago Board of Trade |
| CEMS | Continuous Emissions Monitoring System |
| CFC | Chlorofluorocarbon |
| CO | Carbon Monoxide |
| $CO_2$ | Carbon Dioxide |
| CPMS | Continuous Process Monitoring Systems |
| CPUC | California Public Utilities Commission |
| DEF | Association of Danish Electric Utilities |
| DI | Confederation of Danish Industries |
| DN | Danish Society for Conservation of Nature |
| EDF | Environmental Defense Fund |
| EEI | Edison Electric Institute |
| ELSAM | Danish Electricity Consortium (West of the Great Belt) |
| ELKRAFT | Danish Electricity Consortium (East of the Great Belt) |
| EMEP | European Monitoring and Evaluation Programme |
| ETP | Emissions Trading Program |
| EPA | US Environmental Protection Agency |
| EPAct | Energy Policy Act |
| EPS | Emission Permit System |
| ERC | Emission Reduction Credit |
| EU | European Union |
| FERC | Federal Energy Regulatory Commission |
| GDP | Gross Domestic Product |
| GJ | Gigajoule ($10^9$ joule) |

| | |
|---|---|
| HC | Hydro-Carbon |
| IPPs | Independent Power Producers |
| LAER | Lowest Achievable Emission Reduction |
| MW | Mega Watt |
| MPO | Modified Pollution Offset |
| NAAQS | National Ambient Air Quality Standards |
| NAM | National Association of Manufacturers |
| NATO | The North Atlantic Treaty Organization |
| NIEP | National Independent Energy Producers |
| NRCA | The National Rural Cooperative Association |
| NRDC | Natural Resources Defense Council |
| NSPS | New Source Performance Standard |
| NO | Non-degradation Offset |
| $NO_x$ | Nitrogen Oxide |
| NUGs | Non-Utility Generators |
| OPEC | Organization of Petroleum Exporting Countries |
| PO | Pollution Offset |
| POTW | Publicly Owned Treatment Work |
| PUCs | Public Utility Commissions |
| RACT | Reasonable Available Control Technology |
| RECLAIM | Regional Clean Air Incentives Market |
| ROG | Reactive Organic Gases |
| SCAQMD | South Coast Air Quality Management District |
| SIP | State Implementation Plans |
| $SO_2$ | Sulphur Dioxide |
| $SO_x$ | Sulphur Oxide |
| UN | United Nations |
| US | United States of America |
| VOC | Volatile Organic Compound |

# Preface

I recall the sense of revelation when first reading about tradable permits. Ten years ago, Tom Tietenberg's pioneering work, *Emissions Trading* (1985), put me on the track.

Caught by the idea, I wrote a master thesis about tradable permit systems in political science at the University of Aarhus, followed by a dissertation in economics and public choice at the Aarhus School of Business. This book has grown out of the latter. It tries, for the first time, to give a systematic review of the US experience on tradable permit systems. Because the study encompasses several disciplines, such as economics, political science and law, it aims to shed a new and fresh light on future environmental regulation. In general, it is proposed that well-organized interests should be regulated by a tradable permit system (based on the US experience) and that non-organized interests should be taxed (based on the European experience). This mix of design may ensure the best outcome in practice, because it is cost-effective, and, at the same time, politically and administratively feasible.

The interdisciplinary approach and the resulting policy recommendations make the book relevant to policy makers and academics in all social sciences. Moreover, the book is intended for upper-level undergraduate and graduate courses in public choice and environmental economics. It can be used both as main text and as supplementary reading.

I can mention but only a few of those who helped me with this book. Significant contributions to the book originated from a stay in 1994-95 as visiting scholar at the University of Maryland, United States. With respect to that visit, I am particularly grateful to Wallace E. Oates and Mancur Olson. Their brilliant courses in environmental economics and public choice were to me like the 'sound of music'. Furthermore, the favourable location of the university made it easy for me to interview the central policy makers in Washington D.C. In the United States, I also benefited greatly from the help of Tom Tietenberg (Colby College); Dallas Burtraw (Resources for the Future); Robert H. Nelson and Thomas C. Schelling (University of Maryland); Robert W. Hahn (AEI), Robert N. Stavins (Harvard University), Toula Tavlarides (University of Georgetown); David Gray (University of Ottawa); Daniel Seligman (Sierra Club); Claire Schary, Melanie Dean, and Renée Rico (Acid Rain Division, EPA).

Denmark is one of the leading countries within the area of environmental protection. This has fostered vivid and high-skilled academic discussions. My special thanks go to my PhD supervisors: Christian Hjorth-Andersen (University of Copenhagen) and Hans Linderoth (The Aarhus School of Business), and my master thesis supervisor: Niels Chr. Sidenius (University of Aarhus). Also thanks to Jesper Jespersen (University of Roskilde); Niels Nannerup (University of Odense); Martin Paldam, Carsten Daugbjerg, Ellen Margrethe Basse, Mikael Skou Andersen, Toke Aidt, and Peter Nannestad (University of Aarhus); Peder Andersen, Nina Smith and Niels Kjærgaard (Danish Economic Council); Erik Strøjer Madsen, Tor Eriksson, Valdemar Smith, Jan Bentzen, Urs Steiner, Judith Ugelow, Erik Maaløe, Bodil Rasmussen and Susan Stilling (Aarhus School of Business); Dirk Hansen (Danish Ministry of the Environment); Jørgen Abildgaard (Danish Ministry of Energy); Jan Lien Christensen (The Institute of Local Government Studies); Flemming Nissen and Søren Warming (ELSAM); Claus Kastberg Nielsen (Danish Ministry of Business and Industry); Peter Nedergaard (Consumers' Advisory Council), and Erling Olsen (Speaker of the Danish Parliament). I am indebted to the Danish Ministry of Energy who readily provided financial support for this book.

I also met many helpful social scientists in European countries other than Denmark. My special thanks go to Ger Klaassen (Commission of the European Communities); Michael Hoel (University of Oslo); Lasse Ringius (CICERO); Jan T. Boom and Bouwe Dijkstra (University of Groningen); Joachim Hensel (University of Freiburg); Bo Persson (Linkoping University); Atli Midtun (BI, Sandvika), Arild Vatn (NLH, Ås); Michael Grubb (The Royal Institute of International Affairs); Oliver Fromm and Bernd Hansjürgens (University of Marburg), and Dennis Mueller (University of Vienna).

I deeply appreciate all those not mentioned here who helped and supported me in this work. Needless to say, I alone am responsible for the content.

In producing the final manuscript, I owe co-editor Karen Dunn a warm note of thanks for her excellent comments. Also thank you very much to Ann-Marie Gabel, who kindly provided secretarial assistance and a beautiful layout.

The book is dedicated to my wife, Kristina, and our 2-year-old son, Lars Kjartan.

# 1 Introduction

## 1.1 STATEMENT OF THE PROBLEM

What is the appropriate design of environmental policy? Economic instruments have the capacity to achieve optimal and cost-effective outcomes in theory but meet critical distortions when applied in practice. In this second-best world of reality, one must ask what kind of design allows society to achieve environmental objectives cost-effectively. The criterion of cost-effectiveness will be used in this discussion of potential carbon dioxide ($CO_2$) abatement policies in the European Union (EU) and the United States (US).

A number of target levels have been established politically for $CO_2$ abatement. Both the EU and the US aim to stabilize $CO_2$ emissions by the year 2000 at the 1990 level. Within the EU, Denmark maintains an even more ambitious target level of 20% $CO_2$ reduction from the 1988 level by the year 2005. How can these $CO_2$ target levels be achieved cost-effectively in practice?

Denmark has implemented a $CO_2$ tax, but the policy design has not been adequate to achieve the target level. The EU has not yet succeeded in implementing a proposed $CO_2$ tax. In contrast, the newest US experience with permit markets has been successful. This suggests there may be something in the permit market system that could benefit both the US and the EU. How, then, should the tax and/or the permit market system be designed?

To answer this question, three categories of real-world distortions are considered: political, economic, and administrative. Political distortions are those that occur whenever policies are changed during the decision-making process away from their cost-effective design. The two other distortions mainly apply to the permit market. Economic distortions are those that occur if the market structure is not competitive and cannot generate a price signal. Administrative distortions are those associated with administering the regulation. They will be higher the more complex the regulation is and the less well-defined and enforceable property rights to permits are.

These three distortions are analysed theoretically using both public choice theory and neo-classical economic theory. Public choice theory is used to analyse the political distortions. Hypotheses are generated regarding which kind of regulation the State and the main political actors will seek. This analysis is important in order to identify policies in which political consensus can be reached. Neo-classical economic theory is used to analyse the other two distortions. It enables a characterization and comparison of the tax and permit market systems. Empirically, the investigation draws on the US experience with permit markets and auctions and on the European experience with $CO_2$ taxes.

It will be shown that tax and permit systems both have merits. Permit markets have been politically successful, but they involve higher transaction costs than taxation does. $CO_2$ taxation has failed politically; the EU members have not been able to agree on such a policy, and in Denmark it has not been politically possible to set the tax high enough for the Danish $CO_2$ target to be reached. Understanding European and Danish experiments with $CO_2$ taxation and the US experience with permit markets is, therefore, of utmost importance for the design of effective environmental regulation in the future. Mutually valuable lessons for the choice and use of economic instruments can be drawn from this analysis. European policy makers can learn from the use of permit markets in the US, and US policy makers can learn from European experience with $CO_2$ taxation.

## 1.2 CONTRIBUTION

An interdisciplinary approach enables the book to address a wide range of social scientists and policy makers. The book intends to fill two gaps.

The first gap is the traditional split between the disciplines of economics and political science. Economists have been criticized for ignoring the reality of political and administrative friction when doing 'blackboard economics'. Economic literature has often made the implicit assumption that this friction is correctable at zero costs: 'the government is seen as an omniscient and benevolent institution dictating taxes, subsidies and quantities so as to achieve a Pareto-optimal allocation of resources'.[1] Such optimal results are not typical in reality, where second-best solutions must be applied. On the other hand, political science has sought to incorporate this friction, but has often focused on decision-making without taking into consideration the cost-effectiveness and overall economic consequences for society of a given policy.

The second gap is the missing application of public choice theory and environmental economic theory. Only lately has this gap between theory and practice been recognized. As Green and Shapiro (1994:ix) note, public choice theory has in general not been successfully applied yet. Hahn and Stavins (1992) note that, with respect to environmental regulation, the debate has until now rested largely on economic theory without regard to the political-administrative reality. The strength of the public choice approach, compared to that of political science, is its one-dimensional focus on economic performance and its parsimonious behavioural assumption. It focuses on the rational utility maximization of the agent, whereas political science focuses on structure. The public choice approach offers significant predictive power, in this case the power to predict outcomes of future environmental regulation in Denmark, the EU and

1.  Mueller (1989:4)

the US.[2]

The main contribution is therefore the addition of the political and administrative contexts to the traditional analysis of economic instruments used in environmental regulation. The book combines environmental economics and public choice theory to uncover new knowledge about the appropriate mix of design. Economic theory is used to explain why a given design of an economic instrument has or has not been cost-effective. The theoretical starting points for this part of the study are Baumol and Oates (1988) and Tietenberg (1985). Public choice theory is used to explain how the political decision-making process shaped actual policy and how the State and organized and non-organized interests influenced the political outcome. The theoretical starting point for this part of the study is Olson (1965). Finally, the choice and use of methodology are considered. In relation to the public choice approach, the starting points are Mueller (1989) and Green and Shapiro (1994). Yin's work (1989) is used in relation to the comparative method and the transfer of experiences from one country to another.

In this way, the book is an attempt to reveal how organized groups influence the choice of policy design in environmental regulation. A most important distinction in the political arena is the one between organized and non-organized groups. In society, organized groups will have a strong economic incentive to influence political decision-makers so that their narrow interests are favoured. Interest groups will lobby for redistribution and a design of policies that maximize their share of the national income pie. Similarly, the State has a strong economic incentive to maximize its tax collections. This general theoretical perspective – known from public choice theory – is applied here to the case of environmental regulation. The aim is to design environmental regulation in recognition of organized and non-organized interests. The book's central question is the following: what economic instruments should be applied in practice if the State's incentive to maximize state revenue and the behaviour of special interest groups are kept in mind?

The general contention of this book is that Denmark and the EU should apply a 'grandfathered' $CO_2$ permit market to organized interests. Whenever the term 'permit market' is used, it refers to a grandfathered permit market. Grandfathering means that the regulated parties are given emission rights for free, typically according to their historical emissions.

It is suggested that a grandfathered $CO_2$ permit market is a more effective policy than a $CO_2$ tax in relation to organized interests such as industry, electric utilities and environmental organizations. The tax alternative offers less precise environmental results and presents the problem that tax revenue is difficult to refund in a politically acceptable way where these interests are concerned.

In contrast, this study finds that a $CO_2$ tax should be applied to non-organized

---

2.   These points are linked to the deductive method applied in economics and the inductive method used in political science. They are further developed in Chapter 2.

interests, such as households and the transportation sector. These interests are not well-represented in the political arena, and the revenue generated from such a tax could be refunded in the form of a lower income tax so that a double dividend would be achieved from improved environmental quality and less distortion elsewhere in the economy. Green taxation may therefore also increase production and create more tax revenue.

The focus on the potential use of permit markets in the EU is new.[3] So far, taxes have been considered and applied rather than permit markets.[4] The whole range of experience with permit markets and $SO_2$ auctions in the eight US programs has not yet been systematically evaluated.[5] That will be done here. An answer to the important question of whether a permit market can be cost-effective in practice is sought by evaluating those eight US programs. Failed attempts to incorporate source location and changes in political attitudes are found to be important factors explaining the performance of these programs.

## 1.3  OVERVIEW

The methodology of public choice and the framework for analysing political distortions are further developed in Chapter 2. First, the disciplines of economics and political science are compared. Second, the economic incentives to define property rights and provide collective goods in autocracies and democracies are traced. This provides a framework for understanding and predicting the behaviour of the State and the main interest groups influencing environmental regulation. Public goods, such as environmental quality and security, are,

3. Data are available on US permit markets, all of which have been initiated with grandfathering. Dales (1968a–b) and Crocker (1966) revived the theoretical interest in tradable permit systems for pollution control. The origins of the concept may be traced back to Alfred Marshall and Henry George. The literature is extensive. See, for example, Baumol and Oates (1988); Tietenberg (1996; 1990a and b;1989a and b;1985;1980;1974); Oates (1995;1994); Cropper and Oates (1992); Klaassen (1996); Koutstaal (1997); Dijkstra (1998); Hahn (1990; 1989a and b); Hahn and Hester (1989a and b;1987); Stavins (1995); Atkinson (1994); Bromley (1995); Pearce and Turner (1990); Congleton (1996); Montgomery (1972); Bohm and Russel (1985); Cook (1988); Hecq and Kestemont (1991); Heggelund (1991); Helm (1991); Helm and Pearce (1990); Joeres and David (1983); Raufer (1992); Liroff (1980); Majone (1976); OECD (1992a and b;1991;1989); Roberts (1982); Roberts and Spence (1976); Rose (1973); Rose-Ackerman (1977); Rosencrantz (1981); Seskin and Anderson and Reid (1983); Shapiro and Warhit (1983); Tripp and Dudek (1989); Yandle (1978); Helm (1991); and Raufer and Feldman (1987). In Danish literature is found: Andersen (1987;1984); Bolwig and Jeppesen (1973); Georg (1993); Hjorth-Andersen (1989;1982;1975); Jespersen and Brendstrup (1994); Mortensen (1992); Mortensen and Sørensen (1991); Skou Andersen (1989); and Svendsen (1995a and c;1994a and f;1993a and b;1992;1991).

4.   Hahn (1989b) and Howe (1994).

5.   See Klaassen (1996), Tietenberg (1985), and Hahn (1989a and b). Three cases of environmental regulation with some elements similar to those of 'permit markets' are known in the EU (in Denmark, the Netherlands and Germany). However, they have been applied in over-regulated and severely restricted command-and-control settings where few data are available. Still, the Danish $SNO_x$ bubble has some valuable features, as discussed in Section 6.3.

surprisingly, provided because of economic rationality. Interest groups evolve and organize gradually, in spite of free-rider incentives, when the right circumstances are present. The redistribution of national income to special interest groups is traced to lobbyism in modern western democracies and the notion of rational ignorance.

Chapter 3 first introduces and compares the similarities and differences between taxation and permit markets. It then examines the political argument for using a free initial distribution of permits and a revenue-neutral auction. Taxation and permit markets are shown to have very different financial consequences for the polluters affected by these policies. The relevant economic and administrative distortions are then discussed. The vulnerability of permit markets to incomplete competition and missing information, which lead to market failures, is described and analysed. Several administrative distortions are also discussed, including failure to define the target group appropriately, failure to establish well-defined property rights, and the use of complicated procedures for incorporating source location. Finally, the use of a comparative method and the rationale for transferring US experience to European ground is justified before compressing the analysis from Chapters 2 and 3 into an evaluation model, so as to investigate whether it is possible to set up a well-defined market for property rights to pollute in practice. This model is used in evaluating the US experience with permit markets and the political setting in which these markets arose (Chapters 4 and 5). Chapter 6 provides an analysis of $CO_2$ taxation in Denmark and the failed attempt to introduce a common $CO_2$ tax in the EU. Next, the evaluation model is used again, this time as the basis for discussing a potential $CO_2$ market in Denmark, the EU, and the US for organized interests. Finally, perspectives on a global $CO_2$ market are presented.

# 2   Public Choice and Lobbyism

## 2.1   OVERVIEW

A critical problem in market systems is the intrusion of political interests, which may distort the economic outcome. How is it possible to minimize costs following this political distortion in practice? To answer this question, and to design environmental regulation in an appropriate way, it is necessary to understand the logic that drives the behaviour of the main actors in environmental politics and the process of political decision-making. The purpose of this section is to develop hypotheses concerning the behaviour of organized interest groups that operate in the political arena. If it is possible to predict the behaviour of these groups, the design of environmental policies can be adjusted to their patterns of behaviour so as to achieve both political acceptability and economic cost-effectiveness.

First, the public choice approach is analysed in detail by comparing the disciplines of political science and economics. In Section 2.2, three distinctive characteristics are defined and discussed. Section 2.3 focuses on the notion of 'collective goods', such as environmental goods, and the optimal cost-effective provision of those goods. The Coase theorem and the importance of transaction costs are also discussed.

Section 2.4 focuses on Mancur Olson's logic of collective action. Large rational groups will not organize, if left alone, because of transaction costs and free-rider problems. These problems of organizing may be reduced by using individual rewards or punishments (selective incentives) or by the presence of an entrepreneur. Finally, a distinction is made between groups that are beneficial and harmful to economic growth.

The notion that individual rationality drives behaviour seemingly leads to a paradox: on the surface, there appears to be no justification for the State's provision of collective goods. State intervention is explained in Section 2.5, however, to arise from an interest in maximizing tax revenues. The objective of maximizing tax revenue encourages the protection of property rights and the establishment of a peaceful order. The same logic is used in Section 2.6 to explain why lobbyism is present in modern democracy. Section 2.7 discusses why extensive lobbyism and redistribution takes place and introduces the concept of the rationally ignorant voter.

Section 2.8 addresses the consequences of the free-rider problem for interest group behaviour. Here, an important distinction is made between groups operating in the market place and those operating in the political arena. The effect of concentrated benefits and widely spread costs is then used to elaborate more specifically on the types of environmental regulation interest groups will seek. Finally, hypotheses about the political behaviour of the main interest groups affected by environmental regulation are developed in Section 2.9.

## 2.2 PUBLIC CHOICE THEORY AND ITS CRITICS

The literature on public choice refers to the public choice approach by many names. Mueller (1989) uses the term *public choice*, while Olson (1965) uses the term *collective action*. Green and Shapiro (1994:xi) use the term *rational choice* and offer other names, like *social choice theory, game theory, rational actor models, political economy* and *the economic approach to politics*. The public choice approach is interdisciplinary and dates back to 1948. It uses economic methodology, applying to the political (or nonmarket) arena the behavioural assumptions that economists typically apply to the market arena.[6] As such, public choice can be defined as 'the economic study of non-market decision making, or simply the application of economics to political science'.[7]

Public choice theory concerns political economy. That is to say, it brings economic man into the political arena and analyses economically rational group action. In the abstract, it postulates that the study of a market and the study of political decision-making may be based on the utility-maximizing behavioural assumptions of economics. The approach is forcefully parsimonious.

*Table 2.1: Behaviour, arena and method by discipline*

| DISCIPLINE | BEHAVIOUR | ARENA | METHOD |
|---|---|---|---|
| **Politics** | Common interest | *Political* | Inductive |
| **Economics** | *Self interest* | Market | *Deductive* |
| **Public choice** | Self interest | Political | Deductive |

Table 2.1 indicates how the disciplines of political science and economics are combined in the public choice approach. As shown in Table 2.1, public choice is distinguished on three dimensions: the behavioural assumption, the arena and the method.

---

6.  Adam Smith founded the supply side of economics in the 18th century on the observation of man as a grocer: 'it is not from the benevolence of the butcher, the brewer, or the baker that we expect our dinner, but from their regard to their own interest' (Smith [1776] 1991:13). Man is a rational utility maximizer and pursues private interests in contrast to common interests. See Mueller (1989:2) for further references on this point. Aristotle founded political science in the 4th century BC when in Greece he observed man as a political animal. Man's behaviour was socially oriented in the Greek 'polis'.

7.  Mueller (1989:1).

## 2.2.1 Behavioural Assumption

The first dimension concerns behavioural assumption. The basic difference between economics and political science stems from the behavioural assumptions employed in each discipline.

In economics, man is assumed to selfishly pursue private interests, not public or common interests. The assumption about human behaviour is, as such, harsh and simple: only self-interest matters. Each agent will try to maximize his utility.

Political scientists have questioned this idea. Is the behavioural assumption of economics, which is also used in public choice theory, applicable in practice? What if preferences are so unstable that one should rather focus on structure and values within an institutional setting?[8]

Institutions may create norms and values, which strongly influence the actions of individuals. It is simply assumed that those with common interests or values join together spontaneously to pursue common goals. A typical example is Karl Marx' class theory, in which people of a particular class, voluntarily organize to act in their own common interests. The view that individuals with common values will organize has been widely promoted.[9]

In this way political scientists seek to incorporate the perceived values of groups and the efforts made to change preferences. 'What people want – or believe they want – is the essence of politics'. Much of what is considered politics consists of efforts to change wants by arguments, persuasion, threats, bluffs, and education. Political science can thus be described as the study of non-market methods of managing conflict among preferences, and as a discipline, it will be 'as inelegant, disorderly, and changeable as its subject matter'.[10] In this way, political science tests the assumption of fixed preferences in economics and seeks to investigate structure and values in detail.

An extreme example is that of neo-institutionalism, given by March and Olsen (1989). Here, the individual is an object in an organization. The individual adapts already existing norms and values. Coase (1960) represents the other extreme by ignoring all institutional distortions. A more moderate paradigm is offered by North (1991). Here, the individual has some freedom of action and may create new values and norms within a given, institutional framework. Olson (1965) also incorporates institutional distortions by considering interest groups' distortion of productivity in society following extensive

8. This structural approach has characterized political science through most of its history (Green and Shapiro, 1994:24). The structural focus also explains the use of inductive methods, see Section 2.2.3.

9. This view has mainly been promoted by early writers like Mosca, Simmel, and Bentley. They claimed that the 'instinct' to form groups exists and is fundamental. Other writers, like Parsons and MacIver, claimed the group to be an aspect of evolution from 'primitive' societies. See Olson (1965:17).

10. Wilson (1980:363). The notion of the rationally ignorant voter is treated in Section 2.7.

redistribution.

In this book, it is argued that even though interest groups initially fail to recognize their true preferences and interests, they will find them in due course through learning. The perception of a given opportunity is subjective, but learning from actual events will encourage actors to pursue their interests more efficiently over time.

Because the issue is one of institutions and impersonal mechanisms, 'interests' are viewed as being promoted in an anonymous way such as negotiations among interest groups or between a politician and political supporters with whom he is not personally acquainted.[11] The incentive to act derives from the net benefits for a specific group, not the benefits for society as a whole. The representatives of the group are under pressure from the members who employ them to promote their interests.

Investments in activities such as lobbyism are undertaken to increase future income. In principle then, the tenets of political science do not differ from the tenets of economics when actors are assumed to behave rationally and to be capable of learning by their mistakes. The State itself can be expected to learn over time how to maximize its tax revenue.

When people interact in smaller groups with face-to-face contact, norms and altruistic values, such as love, friendship and esprit de corps, count much more.[12] So, even though individual utility includes a vast variety of preferences, the focus here will be on redistribution and the maximization of income only. No moral principles are involved, and the self-interest assumption presumes that groups will unscrupulously seek to maximize their own economic net benefits.[13]

### 2.2.2 The Arena

The second dimension distinguishing economics and political science is the arena. The arena for research in public choice is the political (non-market) arena of political science, not the market as in economics. The question is whether the market and the political arena are comparable when the political arena is concerned with public issues, like the behaviour of interest groups, bureaucracies, political parties, and voters.

A main objection against this comparison is that political science often concerns issues that do not have a common, monetary yardstick. Unlike the market arena and the rational maximization of net benefits, the political arena involves non-market relationships and a non-quantifiable setting. A legislator

11. This behavioural assumption is further justified later on in this chapter by the notion of stationary banditry and an explanation of how economic rationality creates order rather than anarchy.

12. In many face-to-face situations, the behavioural assumption of economic man does not hold. An important exception is found for altruistically based organizations, such as the US Sierra Club. This point is further discussed in Section 2.8.2.

13. Ideology and morality play no role. As Deng Xiaoping once put it: it does not matter what colour the cat is if it can catch the mice.

or organization may wish to regulate the environment, provide more jobs, reduce the foreign trade deficit, or curb inflation. This setting involves situations where each participant wants a different thing, and sometimes several different things simultaneously, and each assigns a different, non-quantifiable value to each goal. Political action requires decisions that bind everyone; individuals have no individual choice. Because of this, not only is a known product consumed (such as the candidate who is voted for), but a large number of unknown products are also consumed (all the policies the winning candidate will help enact).[14]

The result is that political arguments are designed such that a wide coalition can be mobilized. This notion has few parallels in the market place, which commits only the individual making the purchase. In the market place, the decision is private and the individual can consume as much or as little of a given product as he wishes.

However, the focus in this book is on a single and visible preference: redistribution to an organized group. Therefore, one may argue that candidates who do not keep their promises concerning redistribution, will be punished by the dominant interest groups at the next election.[15] This sanction mechanism is assumed to discipline any candidate and make him responsive to lobbyism. As such, the political arena is comparable to the market with respect to the single preference of redistribution.

### 2.2.3  Method

The third dimension differentiating economics and political science is methodology. The methodology used in public choice is that of economics. The behaviour of interest groups in the political arena is treated in the same way as the behaviour of the individual in the market place. A formal, mathematical exposition helps to develop a coherent, parsimonious, and deductive theory.[16] Deduction means that theoretical statements are tested against reality; the researcher moves from theory to empirical evidence and hereby tests his theory.[17]

14. Wilson (1980:363). For example, Wilson mentions that Lyndon Johnson received many votes when promising not to send troops to fight in Southeast Asia, but he did send troops to fight there anyway. In the same way, Richard Nixon promised to fight communism, but then recognized the People's Republic of China.

15. Note that this argument is valid in relation to interest groups and not in relation to the single voter who, in most cases, is rationally ignorant and heavily influenced by propaganda. See Section 2.7.

16. Green and Shapiro (1994:10) and Ordeshook (1993:72).

17. Hellevik (1980:68). Purely deductive methods in economics have been criticized since the 1960s as 'blackboard economics'. Some economists – isolated from reality – have deductively developed highly sophisticated 'Nirvana models' without much relevance for reality. See also Chalmers (1990) for a discussion on inductive and deductive methods.

Conversely, political science has typically described and analysed history using an inductive methodological orientation and weak behavioural assumptions. Induction attempts to discover theories in a bottom-up process. Theoretical statements are based upon single empirical observations. For example, much of structural (institutional) theory attempts to explain cases observed in reality. Typically, the inductive phase is followed by a deductive theory test, but public choice theorists remain sceptical that universal theories of politics can be developed through such a process.[18]

Public choice theory – with its behavioural assumption of rational self-interest – now makes it possible to predict future events and, as such, makes a qualified attempt to write history in advance. Public choice theorists have universalist aspirations. Proponents of the theory seek consistency and universality. Scientific advance is thought to occur when generalizable results can be shown to follow deductively, that is from analytic propositions derived from axioms. Such deductive propositions can consequently interconnect with one and another.[19]

## 2.3 COLLECTIVE GOODS

Decisions made in the political arena are decisions made for the collective provision of 'public' goods. Special interest groups lobby for special governmental favours: decisions that create common benefits for their members by redistributing national income to them. A more detailed look at the notion of public or collective goods is called for in order to explore further the behaviour of these interest groups.

Basically, there are two types of goods in society: public and private goods. A pure public good is traditionally defined by two conditions: first, non-excludability, which means that exclusion is not feasible; second, jointness of supply, which means that a good available to one individual is available to others as well. There is no crowding effect.[20] In contrast, a private good is characterized by both excludability and individual supply.

The abatement of global warming is a rare example of a pure public good because it fulfills both conditions. It is not possible to exclude anyone from enjoying the benefits of avoiding the greenhouse effect, and this abatement is independent of the number of people benefiting from it. No matter how large the world population is, everybody will benefit from avoiding a global catastrophe.

It is not easy to think of other pure public goods for two reasons. First, exclusion is usually possible in some way. For example, people may be

---

18. Hellevik (1980:68).

19. Green and Shapiro (1994:23–24).

20. This definition is consistent with Samuelson's pure collective good, which is a good such that additional consumption of it by one individual does not diminish the amount available to others (Samuelson 1954:387). See also Sandler (1992), Mueller (1989) and Hardin (1982).

excluded from living in an area with less acid rain or from using a highway.[21] Second, if people consume a good, what is left is usually altered. For example, 'free land' in the Wild West, police and court systems and swimming-pools may all become crowded and are therefore not pure public goods.

Imagine the ancient case of a castle wall, inside which nobody can be excluded from the collective good of protection against roving banditry. There is room for only a certain number of people inside the walls, but this type of exclusion does not negate common goals. Such a good can be treated similarly to a pure public good as long as such 'impurities' are within a limited range. Goods that are not pure public goods but approximate them are addressed in the literature as common, public or collective goods.

This book addresses the concept of 'collective goods'. These are goods for which jointness is not a necessary attribute. Collective goods are simply those that yield non-excludable benefits. They therefore meet only the first condition of a pure public good.[22] By using the term 'collective good', the term 'public' is avoided and so is any suggestion that only the state can provide the good.

A collective good can also be provided through collective action. Collective action is action involving two or more individuals that serves individual interests better than individual action can. Collective action provides an inseparable benefit for the members of the group.[23] So, in its most abstract sense, collective action is to be found whenever two or more individuals combine efforts to provide a collective good.[24]

### 2.3.1  Effective Provision

David Hume was the first to treat the collective (public) choice problem in an academic way. In his *A Treatise of Human Nature* of 1739, he wrote that when men protect themselves against one another's weaknesses and passions, by the

21. For a detailed typology of different kinds of goods, see Sandler (1992:5–7).

22. This definition is consistent with Olson (1965:14f).

23. It is not necessary that exclusion be technically impossible, only that it is uneconomic.

24. There are numerous examples of collective action for provision of collective goods. Not only services traditionally provided by governments (for example pollution abatement, flood control, law and order, defence) but also services from any non-governmental or private groups can be listed. After all, private goods are often provided collectively for non-economic reasons. Well-known cases are those of health services, library services, bus services, electricity provision, telecommunication services and railway services. Such non-collective goods can always be provided by private enterprise. Neighbours seeking to beautify their area, a trade association lobbying for a tariff to increase profits of the firms in its industry, a collusive alliance seeking higher prices or wages by restricting supply, and a group of countries lobbying for defence or transnational pollution action (Olson 1992:viii). Other examples could be road signs, dishwashing, parades, disease control, security, expansion of world population, destruction of tropical rain forests, flooding in lowland areas, the overuse of common lands and waters, charity for alleviating the poverty in a community and a common set of weights and measures. A classical example is that of a lighthouse. See, in this respect, Coase's remarks on how lighthouse services have been provided by private enterprise. Charges can be collected at the ports by agents for the lighthouses (Coase 1974).

execution and decision of justice, they 'begin to taste at ease the sweets of society and mutual assistance'.[25] He demonstrated the case where an optimal outcome requires co-operation by providing an example where two farmers both stand to benefit from draining a swamp they own in common.

Let us take a close look at this example. Assume that the farmers have full information and therefore cannot behave strategically, and assume, initially, that only Farmer 1 is active. If Farmer 1 has marginal benefits $MB_1$ from digging the drain and constant marginal costs $Mc_a$, then he or she will drain an amount corresponding to $q_1$, as shown in Figure 2.1.

*Figure 2.1: Two farmers draining a swamp*

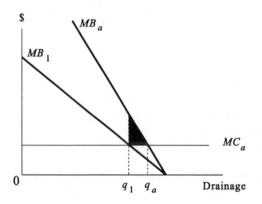

Now assume that both farmers are active, with identical aspirations, and that they share drainage costs equally. Then the vertically-aggregated marginal benefit curve is $Mb_a$ and the aggregated marginal cost curve is $Mc_a$. In this case, the farmers will choose drainage level $q_a$. At this point, aggregated marginal benefits correspond to marginal costs of providing the collective good, so this is the optimal amount of drainage. As shown in Figure 2.1, cooperation leaves each farmer better off. The shaded triangle shows the mutual gain from cooperation.[26]

---

25. Hume ([1739] 1984:589). In illustrating the importance of enforcing property rights and the propensity of human nature to truck, barter, and exchange one thing for another, Adam Smith contrasted human beings with animals by using the image of two greyhounds fighting while running down the same hare. The two dogs fight and do not co-operate because they do not have a contract which defines the property right and guides the sharing of the prey. An animal can only obtain favours from man by attracting his good will. In contrast, man co-operates by offering bargains, Smith ([1776] 1991:12–13).

26. It may be that individual benefits from drainage are so very small that the individual *marginal benefit* curves lie below and never cross $MC_a$. In this case, no mutual trade will occur. In the extreme, no benefits accrue to one of the farmers so that his *marginal cost* curve actually lies above his *marginal benefit* curve. Only when they share costs is drainage beneficial to both parties (that is, if $MB_a$ crosses $MC_a$).

This equilibrium corresponds to the so-called 'Lindahl equilibrium' which is valid also when the two farmers are not identical, that is when they value the benefits from a given collective good differently. If it is possible to make honest preference evaluations, the farmers, in this case, would pay costs proportional to the individual benefits from draining. An optimal provision of the public good follows.[27]

### 2.3.2 Cost-effectiveness

In a realistic model, however, three serious barriers to the optimal provision of a collective good must be considered: difficulties ascertaining citizens' true preferences, transaction costs, and free-rider problems. If these barriers are considered in turn, a realistic model for pollution abatement can be created.

Surveys designed to ascertain preferences are often flawed because, when asked about their preferences in monetary terms, people will often give incorrect values of their willingness-to-pay because costs are only hypothetical; they are not actually paying for anything. Because of imprecise answers, no direct link can be established between Lindahl taxation and the provision of a collective good.[28] This conclusion has important implications for the criteria applied in environmental regulation, and subsequently for the choice of instruments.

The concept of efficiency is the normative yardstick traditionally applied in theoretical microeconomics and by which competing policy alternatives are often judged. An efficient policy is one that maximizes net benefits and corresponds to the optimal provision of a given collective good. This can be illustrated with an example similar to that of the drainage of a swamp: that of pollution abatement.

Assume that as pollution is reduced, aggregated marginal benefits (*MB*) from pollution reduction decline while aggregated marginal costs (*MC*) rise. The efficient level of pollution reduction can then be identified as the point (*P,Q*) in Figure 2.2.

Any increase in pollution control from point (*P,Q*) means that *MC* exceeds *MB* and net benefits are reduced, whereas any decrease in pollution control means that *MB* exceeds *MC*, making an increase in pollution control profitable until *MC* and *MB* are equal once more.

The problem is, however, that the marginal benefits of pollution control are unknown, just as the preferences of the farmers for draining the swamp were unknown. For the case of $CO_2$ emissions, this means that the optimal abatement of global warming will be impossible to quantify due to the lack of information. It will be difficult to quantify the size of the marginal benefits from controlling

27. Erik Lindahl (1919). Each tax share is a personalized price or a 'Lindahl price'. An equilibrium is a set of Lindahl prices so that at those prices everyone demands the same level of each collective good (Atkinson and Stiglitz 1980:509).

28. For detailed discussions and overviews on the 'marginal willingness to pay' and the 'marginal willingness to accept' criteria, see for example Freeman (1994) and Christensen (1995).

one extra unit of $CO_2$, or the value of climate change. Any curves derived from probabilities about occurrences will themselves be imprecise. It is, therefore, impossible to determine the exact location of the intersection $(P,Q)$.

*Figure 2.2: Efficient pollution control*

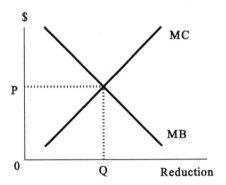

It is possible, however, to quantify the marginal costs of pollution control reasonably accurately – that is only a technical matter. In reducing $CO_2$ emissions, for example, the costs of substituting coal with wind or solar energy, or the costs of installing chemical $CO_2$ scrubbers, can be calculated. The information required exists in the records of the individual firms making the reductions and equating their marginal costs with price.

It is not possible for regulatory authorities to collect all the relevant information from individual firms, but it is nonetheless possible to make usable guesses regarding the position of the marginal cost curve. As such, an appropriate tax in relation to a given target level of $CO_2$ reduction can be determined from estimated reduction costs and can be used to reduce $CO_2$ emissions.

The absence of a marginal benefit curve forces the use of another yardstick in environmental regulation, namely cost-effectiveness. Cost-effectiveness is achieved when an arbitrary reduction target is realized at least cost.

As Figure 2.3 illustrates, a reduction target $Q^*$ set by politicians can be brought about cost-effectively by a tax of $P^*$ per unit of pollution emitted.

The tax leads to an equilibrium, at which firms choose their pollution levels such that the individual marginal costs of pollution control equal the level of the tax. A similar argument is valid for a system of tradable permits if $Q^*$ permits are issued. Then the permit price will correspond to $P^*$.

*Figure 2.3: Cost-effective pollution control*

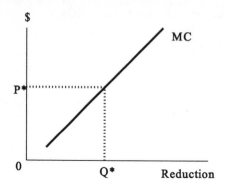

### 2.3.3  Transaction Costs

Let us focus now on the second barrier to the optimal provision of a collective good, namely that of transaction costs.

In the classic example of draining a swamp, Hume touches on these two barriers. He says that it is indeed impossible that a thousand persons should agree on any such action, 'it being difficult for them to concert so complicated a design, and still more difficult for them to execute it; while each seeks a pretext to free himself of the trouble and expense, and would lay the whole burden on others'.[29]

First the difficulty of concerting a complicated design refers to transaction costs, that is the costs of 'making market transactions', for example bargaining costs. Second, the fact that each seeks a pretext to free himself of the trouble and expense refers to the free-rider problem. These two points have been further developed by Coase (1960) and Olson (1965), respectively.

Coase (1960) argues that, in the absence of transaction costs, it is sufficient to define and enforce property rights. A socially efficient outcome will occur, independent of the way rights are distributed. That is, in the relationship between a farmer and a rancher, the one who is liable will build the fence; or in the relationship between a polluter and a victim, the one who is liable will pay the abatement costs.

Typically when only two persons are involved and property rights are

29. However, political society (as an institution) can ameliorate both inconveniencies. 'Magistrates find an immediate interest in the interest of any considerable part of their subjects. Thus bridges are built, harbours opened, ramparts raised, canals formed, fleets equipped and armies disciplined, everywhere, by the care of government, which, though composed of men subject to all human infirmities, becomes, by one of the finest and most subtle inventions imaginable, a composition which is in some measure exempted from all these infirmities'. (Hume [1739] 1984, 590).

defined, transaction costs are low. If the number of people involved is raised to, for example, one thousand farmers, as in Hume's example, transaction costs will be high and an optimal outcome may not occur. It is then difficult for the involved parties to reach an agreement.

### 2.3.4 Free-riding

Let us finally turn to the third barrier and free-rider incentives. While Coase's argument is valuable for analysing transaction costs in many settings, it is not applicable to large groups where the free-rider problem dominates. Suppose, for example, that an outside institution, such as a foundation or a government, pays all transaction costs so that bargaining parties face none whatsoever. According to Olson's 'logic of collective action', if the number of involved parties is high, there may still not be a solution because of free-riding.

In the case of the one thousand farmers, the single farmer will (without organization) avoid paying and then try to benefit from the others draining the swamp or providing any other collective good such as reducing pollution. As Olson states it, 'rational, self-interested individuals will not act to achieve their common or group interests. Those who do not pay for a collective good cannot be excluded (from consuming it)'.[30]

Even when there is perfect consensus about both the desire for a collective good and the most efficient means of acquiring it, the free-rider problem will occur. This point is further developed in the next section.

## 2.4   LOGIC OF COLLECTIVE ACTION

### 2.4.1   Collective Rationality

Olson (1965) concludes in his *Logic of Collective Action* that outcomes are determined by more than the level of transaction costs; they are also determined by the presence of free-riding. That is, all citizens in a given area may benefit from less pollution whether they contributed to the abatement costs or not. In this way, the 'invisible hand' fails for larger groups.[31]

This point called into question the traditional theory of the group, which held that an individual would voluntarily act in support of common group interests and values as a logical consequence of the widely accepted premise of rational self-interest.[32] Groups were simply viewed as voluntary organizations furthering

---

30. Olson (1965:2).

31. The benefits from group action are not priced – they are so-called 'externalities'. As such, the market fails – left alone – in environmental control. The costs of pollution are not internalized in the market price so too much pollution results. The costs of pollution are an externality that the market does not incorporate. Correction of this market failure requires State intervention.

32. Exceptions to this rule can occur when the leadership ignores the group interests and serves other ends. See Olson (1965:5).

their common interests. Olson maintains that this is not so.

Even when the aggregate gains to a group from attaining a collective good greatly exceed the total costs of that action, it does not follow that the action will occur: individual rationality does not necessarily lead to collective rationality. Why is it so? Let us take a closer look at the number of members in a group.

### 2.4.2  Large and Small Groups

If free-riding is an important barrier to the provision of collective goods, why then are numerous collective goods like security and pollution abatement provided? Why does collective action takes place in the political (or non-market) arena? In answering this paradox, Olson uses an analogy to the market. He explains that the incentive for collective action is parallel to that of market structure. His topology of non-market groups builds on reasoning from three types of market structures, as classified in Table 2.2:

*Table 2.2: Market and non-market groups*

| MARKET | NON-MARKET |
|---|---|
| Monopolistic | Privileged |
| Oligopolistic | Intermediate |
| Atomistic | Latent |

*Source:*  Olson (1965:49–52).

In the market, the benefit accruing to the supplier of a collective good is the achievement of higher profit. The monopolistic firm – with no competitors – maximizes its profits by charging a higher price and producing a lower quantity than would a firm operating in a competitive (or atomistic) market. All the gains from the higher price and lower quantity accrue to the monopolist.

Likewise, if a member of a small or 'privileged' group in the political (or non-market) arena were to gain a sufficient net benefit from a collective good, he would be willing to pay all the costs for provision himself. So, in this case, the collective good will be provided even without organization.

The oligopolistic firm – with a countable number of competitors – will not raise the price on its own because it does not get a sufficient net benefit to reduce output. Similarly, no single member in the mid-sized or 'intermediate' group gets a large enough share of the benefit of a collective good to motivate him to provide it himself. In this case, organization is necessary.

Finally, the atomistic firm – with an uncountable number of competitors – stands to gain nothing from lowering its price. As a small producer, it cannot influence market price at all and its market share will be taken over by the other firms which stay at market price. Correspondingly, any individual in the small or 'latent' group acting as an individual would have to bear the cost of providing the collective good, but would have to share the benefit with all group members. He has no incentive to operate outside forced cooperation.

Put another way, the net benefit or advantage, $A_i$, that any individual $i$ would get from a collective good for which he or she pays in full would be the benefit or 'value' , $V_i$, to the individual minus the total cost of providing the good, $C$:[33]

$$A_i = V_i - C$$

If $A_i$ is clearly positive, individual $i$ is part of a small group and the collective good will be provided; if $A_i$ is approximately zero, individual $i$ is part of an intermediate group and the good will not be provided; and if $A_i$ is clearly negative, individual $i$ is part of a large group, and again the good will not be provided. Let us give an example of Olson's theory.

Consider first a group consisting of 1 million members, where the total value of a collective good to the group is $1 billion and the total cost of providing it is $100 million. Further assume that the value of the good, if provided, would be shared equally among all the members, so each would receive a benefit valued at $1,000. Although the group as a whole would stand to reap benefits worth ten times the amount of money invested in providing the good, the net benefit to any individual member who chooses to provide the good on his or her own is clearly negative. In the absence of organization, the good will therefore not be provided. This group would thus be classified as 'large'.

Now suppose the group has only five members. Now if the good is provided, each member will experience a benefit valued at $200 million. Since each individual member's net benefit from providing the good is positive in this case, the good will now be provided even in the absence of organization. This group would thus be classified as 'small'.[34]

As such, the link between individual rationality and group rationality depends on the individual net benefit from contributing to the collective good.[35] The

33. Olson (1965:23).

34. See Olson (1982:32–34) for more examples. The two extreme cases of 'small' and 'large' groups are to be found, respectively, in Hume's example of two and many farmers draining a swamp (Sections 2.3.1 and 2.3.3). This logic is applicable in the arena of environmental regulation (Chapter 6), where it is argued that the small group of large and capital-intensive firms holds a stronger position than the large group of small and less energy-intensive firms.

35. The greater effectiveness of small groups (privileged/intermediate) is evident from experience and theory. Take, for example, a meeting involving too many people. The decisions of the meeting are thus public goods to the participants (and perhaps others) and the contribution each can make becomes smaller as the meeting becomes larger. Therefore, committees are normally created. Also, the earnings of a partnership, in which each partner gets a prearranged percentage of the return, are a collective good to the partners, and when the number of partners increases, the incentive for each partner to work for the welfare of the enterprise lessens. Another example is the income of a corporation as a collective good to the stockholders. The stockholder who holds only a minute percentage of the total stock, like any member of a large group, has no incentive to work in the group

more negative $A_i$ is, the more likely the group will fail. Therefore, the small group is more likely to lobby and win the economic struggle in the political arena. Table 2.3 resummarizes this economic logic.

*Table 2.3: Provision of collective good: large and small group*

|  | **Large Group** | **Small Group** |
| --- | --- | --- |
| **Number of members** | 1 million | 5 |
| **Total gain** | $1 billion | $1 billion |
| Individual gain $(V_i)$ | $1,000 | $200 million |
| **Total cost $(C)$** | $100 million | $100 million |
| **Individual net gain** $(A_i = V_i - C)$ | Negative | $100 million |

### 2.4.3  Social Incentives

Another factor that makes small groups more likely to organize is social pressure. Social incentives are only important in small groups. Small and intermediate groups are thus twice blessed in that they have not only economic incentives, but also perhaps social incentives to realize collective goods.

In a small group, social loss may outweigh the economic gain associated with non-participation in the provision of the good. In general, social pressure and social incentives operate only in small groups where members have face-to-face contact with one another.

Large groups contain more people than could possibly know one another, and social pressures will therefore not develop.[36]

### 2.4.4  Selective Incentives

Accordingly, the larger the group is, the less likely the group will pursue its common interests. Therefore, only coercion or a 'selective incentive' will stimulate a rational individual in a larger (latent) group to act in a group-oriented way.[37] 'Just as governments need compulsory taxation to finance public

interest (Olson 1965:53–55).

36. The individual who succeeds in increasing sales and output in a perfectly competitive industry is usually admired, for example in the farming community, because individual actions do not matter in relation to total outcome (Olson 1965:62). See also Weck-Hannemann and Frey (1995).

37. Coercion is used in the sense of a punishment that leaves an individual on a *lower* indifference curve than he would have been on had he borne his allocated share of the cost of the collective good

goods, non-governmental organizations need special arrangements or "selective incentives" to support themselves'.[38]

Group action can be obtained 'through an incentive that operates, not indiscriminately, like the collective good, upon the group as a whole, but rather *selectively* toward the individuals in the group. The incentive must be "selective" so that those who do not join the organization working for the group's interest, or in other ways contribute to the attainment of the group's interest, can be treated differently from those who do'. [39]

A selective incentive can be either negative or positive. A negative incentive is a loss or punishment imposed on those who do not help provide the collective good. For example, tax payments are collected with the help of penalties for non-payment. A positive selective incentive is an individual reward. Examples include tax deductions, subscriptions to journals, opportunities to rent inexpensive holiday accommodation, and favourable insurance terms. Olson (1965) observes that both positive and negative selective incentives have been used in the US to organize large, latent groups.

The mobilization of large groups – and overcoming the free-rider problem – is difficult and takes time. Only when the right leadership and the right circumstances are present may a group become organized.

Olson gives an example of the young US union entrepreneur, Jimmy Hoffa. Hoffa was one of the workers in a non-unionized warehouse in Detroit. One hot summer's day, a large shipment of strawberries – in danger of spoiling – arrived. Hoffa persuaded his co-workers to strike. The employer found it better to accept Hoffa's demands than to lose his perishable cargo.[40]

### 2.4.5  Beneficial and Harmful Groups

Groups that succeed in organizing may be either beneficial or harmful to economic growth in society. Whenever an individual or a group internalizes an externality, for example the costs of pollution or the costs of crime, an economic distortion is removed and economic growth is enhanced.

When groups organize to lobby for the redistribution of income or other benefits in their favour, however, economic growth often suffers. Because such organizations tend to persist, older democracies typically have large numbers of such groups and thus to be characterized by a large amount of redistribution.

The oldest democracy, Great Britain, experienced economic stagnation after World War II because of the burden of organized groups, in stark contrast to the

---

and not been coerced (Olson 1965:48). Conversely, a selective incentive is the transfer of a private good which leaves an individual on a *higher* indifference curve (compared to the situation in which he only benefits from the collective good).

38.  Olson (1992:ix).

39.  Olson (1965:51).

40.  Olson (1982:38).

rapid economic growth in Germany and Japan, where such groups were absent.[41] When a totalitarian government, a revolution, or a defeat in war destroys the institutional fabric of a society, that society is likely to grow rapidly once a stable legal order is established.

The possibility for groups to have either beneficial or harmful effects on society is investigated further in the rest of this chapter. Two polar cases of autocracy and democracy are explained (Sections 2.5 and 2.6). It is shown how the State itself has come into existence and that it provides collective goods for reasons beneficial to society. However, as new organizations develop alongside the State, they may seek harmful policies as well. Then the notion of 'rational ignorance' is discussed (Section 2.7) before lobbyism in environmental regulation (Section 2.8). Finally, hypotheses concerning rational State and rational interest group behaviour in modern environmental regulation conclude the chapter (Section 2.9).

## 2.5  AUTOCRACY: STATIONARY BANDITRY

It is helpful to go back to the very origins of group organization and the provision of collective goods to trace the development of the role of the State in providing collective goods and its rational interest in providing present environmental regulation. This investigation may be done by using the notion of the stationary bandit.[42]

At the dawn of history, people voluntarily organized into small tribes or bands for the purpose of gathering food and hunting. Each band (50–100 individuals) spontaneously maintained peaceful order. These groups were small with strong social ties. Every family received sufficient benefits from this peaceful order and predictable behaviour to ensure that it voluntarily contributed to maintaining peace and security.[43]

Then, about 10,000 years ago, people began to farm. Newly discovered techniques for agriculture led to enormous increases in production and population. Now there was something to steal. Soon, roving bandits started to plunder farms and villages with the threat, or use, of violence.

Anarchy followed, and this constant plundering discouraged farmers from investing and producing. The farmers were motivated to work with things or

---

41.  Even choral societies were forbidden in Germany. Olson's *The Rise and Decline of Nations* (1982), shows how interest groups eventually succeed in long and stable societies.

42.  Olson (1993a).

43.  This was economically rational for the individual as shown in Section 2.4 with the cases of large and small groups. The social 'tit-for-tat' mechanism for disciplining negotiations meant that it was possible to make collective decisions under full consensus. Many primitive tribes from pre-agricultural periods did not even have chiefs, and if a group grew too big, it would split up. Another interesting feature is that a tribe in the hunting-and-gathering stage would have little or no incentive to subjugate another tribe or to keep slaves, since captives could not generate enough surplus above subsistence level to justify the costs of guarding them (Olson 1993a:567).

goods not easily appropriated by bandits. For example, they avoided storing large quantities of seed corn and instead acted for the short-term by eating what they had produced on the spot, or by immediately exchanging their produce for gold, which could be hidden. In the absence of a peaceful order, production was greatly reduced.

Peaceful order could not be established on a voluntary basis in these larger, agrarian societies. The groups were large because each individual bore the full costs or risks of anything he or she did to help establish a peaceful order (or to provide other collective goods). In contrast to the situation of the small group, for example, a primitive tribe, the farmers now received only a small share of the benefits.

As shown in Section 2.4, a typical individual in a society with, say, one million people, will get only about one-millionth of the gain from a collective good, but will bear the whole cost of any contribution. Therefore, the individual has no incentive to participate and to establish, for example, law and order. As such, large groups are not able to achieve the benefits of voluntary collective action.[44]

The roving bandits are examples of small or intermediate groups. At the expense of society, they received large, individual benefits from plundering. A roving bandit bore only a small share of the reduction in national income associated with his or her actions but received the full benefits of those actions. In a world without morals and where the risk of detection and punishment is low, it is individually rational to use violence and plunder in this way. As such, the logic of large groups and the concentrated benefits for special interest groups leads to anarchy.

Olson's theory predicts anarchy in larger societies. But this has not been the case. Today law and order exists in most countries. Why is this so? What initiated the organization of larger societies and allowed them to move from chaos to order?

Olson found an answer to this question in his readings about the war history of medieval China.[45] In medieval China, local people preferred that a stationary bandit, Feng, settled down in their area even though he robbed them through heavy taxation. Why? Because this bandit could then protect them against roving banditry, in particular against a fearful character called White Wolf.[46] Feng defined property rights, prohibited arbitrary confiscation of property, and monopolized violence, making it possible to keep up production. A vibrant and well-defined market emerged, yielding gains to the local people that were gigantic compared to those achieved before the collective goods of 'security'

44. As Olson laconically states: 'no large society has yet obtained a peaceful order or other public goods through voluntary agreement' (Olson 1993a:568). See also Hardin (1968).

45. Olson (1993a:568).

46. Peaceful order and the removal of roving banditry are collective goods. The bandit tackles a negative externality by reducing the risk of arbitrary violence and confiscation of property rights (which affect production negatively).

and enforcement of property rights were provided. General interaction became predictable, production increased dramatically and the local people prospered, as did the bandit, who was able to collect increased tax revenues.

A similar situation was found in England about a thousand years ago. England was conquered by Danish Vikings in 1013, led by Svein Forkbeard. Forkbeard became king of England, and when he died suddenly in 1014, the people elected his 18-year-old son, Canute the Great, as their new king in spite of Forkbeard's heavy taxation (the Danelaw). These Viking kings were welcomed by most of the local people because they were needed for the collective good of security. Only the Vikings were strong and brutal enough to monopolize violence and to provide protection against roving bandits.[47]

In this way, as though they were led by an invisible hand, conquerors who had learned that they gained more from settling down and becoming stationary bandits than by continuing as roving bandits provided peaceful order. Naturally, these conquerors did not call themselves bandits but, on the contrary, made themselves crowns and called themselves kings.[48] Note that governments of larger groups do not arise because of voluntary social contracts, but because of rational self-interest among those who can impose organization. Only now, the stationary bandit is enabled to steal by taxation.

Citizens do not act collectively because of their common 'class' interest; they act according to terms set by the stationary bandit. They prefer order to anarchy because of increased security and economic gain.[49] The economic growth that follows the monopolization of violence reinforces the incentive of the stationary bandit to tax rationally (Section 2.5.1) and to provide collective goods other than security, for example environmental improvement (Section 2.5.2).

### 2.5.1  Taxation

When a stationary bandit holds autocratic control over a country, he will – as the 'owner' of all wealth – establish a peaceful order, impose a tax and then provide a number of collective goods in addition to a peaceful order.[50] These steps increase national income and maximize tax revenue for the ruler. Let us see how.

The stationary bandit can be expected to try to maximize tax revenue by

---

47. See Jones (1984:354–86). Similar events took place in other Viking settlements. An example is the formal treaty made in Claire Sur Epte, Normandy, between Viking chieftain Rollo and French leader Karl the Single-minded in 911.

48. Olson (1993a:568).

49. There must always exist a better outcome without the use of arbitrary violence because the parties at least can share the saved costs from not using violence.

50. Taxation and the purchase of collective goods can be divided into two separate steps (McGuire and Olson, 1996). Even though tax revenue at a given tax rate depends on the collective goods provided, the revenue-maximizing tax rate is independent of this relationship because it directly expresses the share that the tax collector gets from any increase in national income.

reaching the top point on the Laffer curve, where the product of the tax rate and national income is maximized. What is the optimal amount of stealing for the stationary bandit who rules in an autocracy? Taxation – or theft rates – can vary between 0% and 100%, as the Laffer curve shows in Figure 2.4.

*Figure 2.4: The optimal amount of stealing*

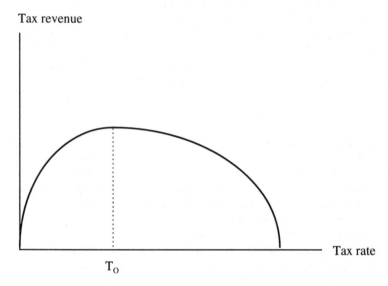

Tax revenue

$T_0$

Tax rate

The stationary bandit will increase the tax rate as long as more revenue is created.[51] At the optimal tax rate, $T_0$, marginal tax revenue will equal the marginal tax payment after which personal income will decrease due to the higher tax rate.[52]

The method of stealing, taxation or confiscation depends on the time horizon. How long does the stationary bandit expect to be around? Consider these extreme cases.

If the bandit expects to stay in control indefinitely, then it will be optimal for him to tax rather than confiscate. Assume, for example, that the optimal tax rate, $T_o$, is *one-third*. At this point, the $1 stolen means a $3 loss in national income.

51. The king may not get all tax revenue in practice. A severe problem to be considered by the autocrat when collecting money is the possibility that his subordinate tax collectors may steal from him. This is an old problem. For example, the Roman tax collectors were reputed for going out to the colonies as poor men, but coming home to Rome as rich men. Eventually, these right to collect taxes and become governor in a distant province was auctioned off.

52. There are many ways for a conqueror to steal through taxation. Taxes on income, products, and services are well known examples. But other methods are also available. An alternative method is to use the money roll. If income has increased 10% one year, then the conqueror can print 10% extra money and keep it. If he prints 20%, then inflation will be 10%. Inflation is a tax on the real value of money.

If the tax rate were any higher, then the loss in national income would be larger and result in a reduction in the bandit's tax income. So, with an infinite time horizon, there is a limit to the amount that can be taken by the bandit.[53]

Now, if the bandit expects a short tenure, because a bigger bandit may come along, then he may consider confiscation of property. When a stationary bandit has no reason to consider the future output of society at all, his incentives become those of a roving bandit and that is what he becomes.

The promises of an autocrat are never completely credible, however, because they are not enforceable. So, whenever the total tax payments over time fall short of the value of the assets belonging to citizens, it will pay the stationary bandit to confiscate. This incentive to seize and confiscate property has often occurred in history and has slowed economic growth.[54]

### 2.5.2 Provision of Collective Goods

After setting a tax rate, how much of a collective good will then be provided in an autocracy? The process of determining the optimal provision of collective goods is analogous to the process described above for setting the optimal tax rate. In general, any ruler will provide collective goods up to the point where the last dollar generates a dollar's increase in the ruler's share of the national income (the gain to society being the reciprocal of the ruler's share).

If the stationary bandit, for example, were to reduce smog so that public health could be improved, he would invest up to the point where $1 spent would result in a $3 rise in income so that he could get back again the $1 spent. The bandit will stop at this point. If he continued up to the point where $1 spent would result in a $2 rise in national income, then the net loss would be $1/3 (the bandit receives only $1/3 tax on each of the $2 which totals $2/3).

Even the stationary bandit will therefore provide collective goods. For example, he may build bridges to lower transportation costs or reduce pollution to secure the health and productivity of his citizens.[55]

The first known policy for reducing air pollution was instituted in London in 1308, at which time the English king banned the use of coal under the threat of capital punishment. Urban settlement and the use of coal as fuel had created serious 'smog' problems in London.[56]

Though the amount collected at any tax rate will vary with the level of collective good provision, the revenue-maximizing tax rate should not. The tax rate determines exactly how encompassing the interest of the autocrat is in society, that is his share of any increase in the national income. The more

---

53. Olson (1993a:569).

54. See Bradford and Shleifer (1993) for historical accounts on this issue.

55. Olson (1993a:568).

56. It is known that a Londoner was caught burning coal and executed (Raufer and Feldman 1987:9). See also Brimblecombe (1976) for historical accounts.

encompassing an interest he has, the greater the social losses from his redistributions to himself. Conversely, the narrower his interest, the less he will take account of the social costs of redistribution to himself.[57]

Note that the stationary bandit will not redistribute to himself solely for his private needs for luxury. His main ambitions will be to acquire military power and larger domains. A stationary bandit must keep an eye on his neighbours, for they cannot be trusted. He therefore pours money into the military, not just to protect his territory but also to expand it. If he expands his territory, he can expand his tax base and grow economically stronger.[58]

Through the actions of the stationary bandit, citizens benefit from both an increase in national income and the provision of collective goods. According to Olson (1982), this new prosperity, interrupted only occasionally by roving banditry (for example the Thirty Years' War), leads to our civilization and the start of majority-rule. Given time, different groups overcome the problems of organizing, even in the presence of a stationary bandit. A balance of power evolves where it is in the interest of dominant groups to exclude dictatorships and to introduce democracy – some redistributive power is better than none.

## 2.6 DEMOCRACY: MAJORITY BANDITRY

In contrast to dictatorships, democracies with lasting institutions mean that no individual has the capacity (unilaterally) to seize property or to use taxation to further his or her own ends. What is the logic behind taxation and the provision of collective goods in democracies?

### 2.6.1 Taxation

The logic regarding taxation is basically the same as that for the autocrat. A presidential candidate needs only a majority to win. He will therefore 'buy' the majority by redistributing to this group from the population as a whole. The necessary taxation distorts incentives in the market and reduces production in society. However, the tax rate will be lower than that chosen by the autocrat.

Consider the democratic candidate who 'buys' a victory by promising a majority redistribution. Assume again that the revenue-maximizing tax rate is one-third and that the winner represents a majority that earns one-third of the national income. Recall that with a tax rate of one-third, an autocrat will find the point where the last $1 he collects in taxes reduces the national income by $3.

---

57. See Olson (1993a:570–71) and McGuire and Olson (1996).

58. The implication of this argument is the desire for world government by any stationary bandit. For example, the Romans conquered what they could. So did the Chinese, dominating a part of the world bordered by Siberia, the jungles of Indonesia, Himalaya, and the sea. In such cases, each group took 'its' part of the world as defined by natural borders and the existence of then-current technology. In our century, two notorious examples would be those of Hitler and Stalin. Both may be viewed as conquerors trying to expand their territories as much as possible, see Olson (1993b).

However, if the majority chooses the same tax rate as the autocrat, it will lose $2: the same $1 lost by the autocrat in the form of reduced tax revenue, and an additional $1 because it itself earns one-third of the national income.

In other words, the majority will benefit from reducing the tax rate until the last $1 collected equals the sum of reduced tax revenue and the reduction in the majority's share of the national income. Thus, a majority would maximize its total income with a lower tax rate and a smaller redistribution to itself than would be chosen by an autocrat. The fundamental difference stems from the fact that a democracy will redistribute as much as possible to the majority, whereas an autocrat will redistribute as much as possible to himself.[59]

### 2.6.2  Provision of Collective Goods

A democracy will provide more collective goods than will an autocracy because the majority owns a share of national income. After winning an election – and the right to control public revenue and expenses – the majority will consider whether it is worth investing part of the tax revenue in collective goods. Raised national income brought about by the availability of collective goods may create a net profit for the majority in the form of tax revenue.

Assume that the majority earns one-third of the national income. If, like the autocrat in the previous example, a democratic candidate provides collective goods up to the point where the last $1 spent results in a $3 increase in national income, he will provide even more collective goods than would the autocrat; the majority will get $2 ($1 in the form of increased tax revenues and $1 in the form of increased income). Therefore, it pays to buy even more of the collective good, for example to invest in more pollution abatement, until the $1 invested is exactly returned as increased tax revenue and ordinary income.[60]

In this way, the majority will try to maximize its slice of the national income pie by setting the tax rate lower than where the autocrat set it, and by providing more collective goods. The optimal tax rate and the amount of collective goods provided will vary because the encompassing interest of an officeholder, political party, interest group or monarch varies with the size of the stake in society. The larger the stake, the greater the incentive to provide collective goods.[61]

In practice, however, the tax rate in democracies can be very high too. This

---

59. Olson (1993a:570). Note, that in contrast to the stationary bandit, a democracy has no incentive to expand its territory. It does not pay democracies to conquer. A conquest means only a larger majority to tax a larger minority. There is no per capita gain unless an area is taken over without allowing the conquered people to vote.

60. Olson (1993a:569).

61. In some parliaments, like that of Denmark, the electoral system of proportional representation gives room for many small parties. Because the small parties each encompass only a tiny percentage of society, they may consider only the interests of their narrow constituencies (not those of society as a whole). The final voting results, if determined on balance by only a few of these small parties, may therefore not be of encompassing nature.

is caused by extensive redistribution following lobbyism and can be exemplified once more using the metaphor of the criminal.

Insignificant bandits in a democracy can ignore their diminishing effect on the national income. For example, a person who litters the pavement will enjoy all the convenience of having littered but only has to pay a very small share of the clean-up costs. As in the case of roving banditry, crime can be rational for the individual who (inclusive of the risk of detection and punishment) can earn more as a criminal than, for example, as a street sweeper. Although the individual criminal benefits from crime, production in society suffers because of the costs placed on the others.

Leaders of the organized mafia in Italy and Russia, who sell protection against themselves and others, are examples of modern stationary bandits in societies where the central government is not strong enough to monopolize violence and enforce property rights. The Russian mafia has grown so large and tough that it has monopolized crime in some areas to the extent that no other thieves exist there.

Pollution exists for the same reasons. A firm that does not have to pay for the costs it imposes on society for its noxious emissions will get all the benefits itself because it can dump at zero costs. When the property rights to nature are not defined, the polluter receives all the convenience of polluting, but must pay only his minute share of the costs to the community.

The collective good for polluters of avoiding pollution abatement costs is a cost to society as a whole. Like all other redistributional phenomena, the provision of this good can be traced back to the gains for special interest groups.[62] Experience shows these groups how to increase their slice of the national income pie. It is even possible that single firms with privileged interests will organize to influence decision-makers in a direction that is desirable for them. Given this process, resources are channelled to less productive places in society.

When a society subsidizes and favours specific groups, production is steered in the wrong direction. The most talented and best skilled individuals in society are encouraged to cultivate the subsidized areas. For example, a complicated tax legislation results in high wages for tax experts so that substantial parts of the productive capacity inevitably will move into tax-favoured areas.

Why do taxpayers accept lobbyism and these substantial redistributions, also those following environmental policies, to special interest groups? A plausible answer stems from the rather sad notion of the 'rationally ignorant voter', which also fits the logic of collective action.

---

62. In Section 2.8, the link between State interest, lobbyism and redistribution is further developed and exemplified in relation to market and non-market groups.

## 2.7   THE RATIONALLY IGNORANT VOTER

All taxpayers would be better off if each citizen critically investigated all public affairs. Such action would result in decisions that would better serve the taxpayers' common interests and stop the redistribution to special interest groups. However, reality differs. Why? The answer follows from the same logic as that presented in Section 2.4. On an individual basis, this action does not pay. The typical citizen receives only a small share of the gain from more rational politics. Because other citizens get almost all the gains, the individual citizen has little incentive to devote time to thinking about the welfare of the country. The group of citizens is large and will not organize.[63]

Consider, for example, a national election. The probability that the individual vote will change the outcome of the election is extremely low. Therefore, the voters are rationally ignorant. But because some people vote and participate in public affairs, two exceptions may be linked to the main rule.[64] First, participation may have entertainment value, which turns participation into a private good for the individual. Second, certain individuals may have a professional interest in participating and will be rewarded with private goods, such as money, prestige or power. Politicians, lobbyists, journalists and social scientists, for example, can receive individual benefits from following the development of public affairs.[65] Still, for the vast majority, it is rational to stay ignorant.

This ignorance creates fertile soil for ideologies. Ideologies are, in part, substitutes for detailed research and critical reflection about public affairs. Simple ideologies and political slogans give guidance about how to vote and can be acquired at little or no cost. These are the dominating features of political life in spite of the fact that both 'left' and 'right' are often unfaithful to their 'ideologies'. Therefore, many of the average citizen's ideas about what is in the national interest are derived indirectly from the propaganda of organized interests.[66] The old Danish saying: 'the wise trick the less wise' comes true, ironically due to the economically rational choice of both parties.

## 2.8   LOBBYISM

What will be the role of the State and the main interest groups in environmental regulation? First, it is important to distinguish between organizations inside and outside the market (Section 2.8.1). Second, it is important to know what kind

---

63. See also Olson (1991:130).

64. Downs (1957). The gain from voting is the difference in the value to the individual of the 'right' election outcome multiplied by the probability that a change in the individual's vote will alter the outcome.

65. Schumpeter lists some important private interests for intellectuals in dealing with public affairs. (Schumpeter [1943] 1994:151–53).

66. Olson (1991:134f) and Downs (1957:96f).

of regulation will lead to a politically acceptable equilibrium between the State as tax collector and the main organized interests (Section 2.8.2).[67]

### 2.8.1 The State, the Market and the Political Arena

The main organized actors in environmental regulation are the democratic state (regulator), the polluting industry, and the environmental groups.[68] Following the economic logic described in the previous sections, the State's objective is to maximize tax revenues.

An autocrat can be expected to redistribute a larger proportion of national income than will a democratic government, and an autocrat will redistribute to himself whereas a democratic government will redistribute toward its constituency, the majority. One must assume that this fiscal incentive is present in environmental regulation too. The use of 'green taxes' is an innovation in tax collection because it results both in the provision of a collective good (environmental improvement) and in the collection of state revenue. If a small country like Denmark were to introduce green taxation on global pollutants, such as $CO_2$, State revenue could then be used for lowering other distortive taxes, for example income taxes on labour. Lowering distortive taxes on labour could bring about higher employment and increased national income (higher tax revenue) over time.

In a democracy, the State is counteracted by interest groups. A balance of power exists.[69] Lobbying by interest groups in the political arena affects the final design of a given policy and thereby determines the resulting economic outcome. The democratic State cannot just pursue the economic interests of the majority. In order to achieve political acceptability, reduce conflict and consequently implement rules of legislation, it must also mediate among the main organized interests.[70]

Let us look closely at the difference between industrial and environmental groups organized in the market and the political arena, respectively, to understand past behaviour and predict future behaviour. How will the main actors

67. This subsection draws heavily on Svendsen (1998d).

68. See Hahn (1990), Tietenberg (1985), Raufer and Feldman (1987), Frey (1994), Ursprung (1991), Grossman and Helpman (1994), Hillman and Ursprung (1992), Aidt (1997), and Frederiksson (1997).

69. This balance of power formed the transition to democracy from autocracy. See Sections 2.5 and 2.6 above.

70. Adam Smith was the first to observe merchants lobbying for the establishment of harsh cartel rules: 'our woollen manufacturers have been more successful than any other class of workmen in persuading the legislature that the prosperity of the nation depended upon the success and extension of their particular business. They have not only obtained a monopoly against the consumers by an absolute prohibition of importing woollen cloths from any foreign country, but they have likewise obtained another monopoly against the sheep farmers and growers of wool by a similar prohibition of the exportation of live sheep and wool'. Draconian penalties were imposed for violations of the cartel (Smith [1776] 1991:582).

lobby? What are their interests? In what way can they be expected to affect environmental regulation?[71]

Organization takes place both in the market (market groups) and outside the market (non-market groups). This distinction is important because the attitude of a group member toward the size of the group differs. In the market, a firm strives for monopoly. It seeks to create barriers to entry – to keep new firms from coming in and sharing the market – and it tries to get as many rivals as possible to leave the industry. In contrast, a non-market group member seeks to maximize group membership. Rather than bringing about more competition, larger membership means lower costs for the individuals already in the group. Again the free-rider problem occurs, just as in the market place: it is not rational for the individual agent or firm to sacrifice time and money to support a lobby organization to obtain government assistance for the industry. For this reason, non-market groups often choose to make membership compulsory.[72]

This difference in the desires of the two groups is caused by the type of collective good and its benefits. In the market, the collective good is that of higher profits. All firms in an industry have a common interest in higher profits. Higher prices can be charged, however, only if fewer units of output are supplied.[73]

Therefore, organizations may operate in *both* the market (to raise prices by restricting output) and in the political arena (to further other common interests). Along with the incentive to exclude competitors, there is, paradoxically, an incentive to include competitors as well, because the larger the group, the more likely it is to influence government policy. Market action encourages exclusion of both existing and potential competitors, whereas political action encourages the inclusion of other firms: 'whether a group behaves exclusively or inclusively depends upon the nature of the objective the group seeks' (Olson 1965:39). Once a group becomes large enough to succeed politically, it will typically become exclusive. At this point, it is in the interest of the existing members to exclude new entrants.[74]

---

71. Lobbyism and campaigning may take forms such as hiring public relations experts to influence the media, advertising, bribing, hiring professional organizers of public meetings and the writing of letters to members of congress or parliament.

72. Olson (1965:37).

73. In Olson's terminology, higher profits in an industry constitute an exclusive collective good. The firms in an industry thus have an incentive to form cooperative agreements to restrict output. An interesting feature linked to a cartel is that a single holdout gets extraordinary bargaining power. When bargaining power is reduced, group-oriented action becomes more likely (Olson 1965:41). The success and failure of the OPEC cartel may illustrate this point. It shows how a non-participating member, like Libya, can deprive the collusive of benefits from an exclusive collective good by continually expanding its output and taking advantage of the higher price brought about by the colluding firms. This imparts an all-or-none quality to collusive groups (100% collusion is needed for success).

74. Olson (1982:66–69) describes the optimal size of a group as a 'minimum winning coalition'. Numbers are kept down but high enough to win. It is advantageous for the group to be small in

Following the logic presented in Section 2.6.1, a majority will stop redistributing to itself when the last dollar collected equals the sum of reduced revenues and the reduction in that group's share of national income. An interest group will behave in the same way as a group of voters. When an interest group has accomplished the task of organizing for collective action, it will try to steal as much money as possible from, for example, the treasury and redistribute as much as possible from the taxpayers to itself.

A typical lobbying group in the US, for example, represents 1% of the national income. It follows that the group will only stop redistributing to its clients when the reduction in its share of national income is 100 times as great as the amount it wins in the redistributional struggle. In contrast, if the interest group tries to influence policy in the interest of society as a whole, the group will receive only 1% of the benefits, but will bear all the costs.[75]

If the lobbying group is bigger in size, it will stop the redistribution at an earlier point. For example, a group that represents 50% of the national income will stop redistributing to itself when its share of the national income is reduced by twice the gain. Similarly, the group will get half of the benefits from better policies, so that it pays to promote policies that increase the group's share of the national income by more than twice of its costs of undertaking this action. In this way, less redistribution will take place than in the case of the group that represents only 1% of national income. If the smaller group is strong enough to win its desired favours in the political arena, its individual members stand to gain much more from the redistribution.

Concerning the dynamics within groups, this theory leads to the tendency for the small to 'exploit' the large. Once a smaller fraction (in a small group) has the amount of the collective good it gets free from the largest member, it has more than it would have purchased for itself, and has no incentive to obtain any of the collective good at its own expense. The collective good may, therefore, be provided by the voluntary, self-interested action of other members of the group, in particular, when small groups have members with unequal interest in the collective goal.[76] That the small will exploit the great is exemplified by: the buffer role of Saudi Arabia in the OPEC cartel; large countries that bear disproportionate shares in multinational organizations like NATO and the UN; and large countries that threaten military reprisal allowing smaller countries to remain neutral. Big countries like the US have contributed the most to post-war

relation to society. See also Becker (1983).

75. Olson (1993a:571, 1991:140). Most redistributions are from unorganized groups to organized groups. When nations subsidize the non-poor, they channel the time and energies of some of their most productive people and assets into less productive pursuits and thereby reduce social efficiency. Cartels like those ruling law and medicine are costly to society because the time of some of the most highly educated and energetic people in the society is being misdirected. Tax loopholes are another example of redistribution. They induce much of the productive capacity of the society, such as accountants, to move into tax-favoured activities (Olson 1991:146).

76. Olson (1965:34–36).

security policy and, for example, the protection of Europe, leaving small countries like Denmark and Sweden to follow pacifist tendencies. The fact that Denmark is taking a leading role with respect to $CO_2$ reduction seems irrational at first sight. According to the theory, Denmark should – as a small country – behave in the same way as countries do with respect to security policy; it should wait for the larger countries to act.[77] However, it may still be rational in a fiscal sense because Denmark uses $CO_2$ taxation. Such 'green taxation' may fit State interest as a new way of collecting revenue.[78]

In contrast, in non-market situations, the benefit from a collective good is not fixed in supply. The collective good is inclusive. Assume that an environmental organization achieves the common goal of better environmental quality. Then everybody will benefit, no matter how many members there are in the group. Members have no incentive to exclude each other. Therefore, bargaining or strategic interaction is much less important in inclusive groups. An individual in a non-market group that prospers may even have an incentive to pay a larger share of the cost of the collective good. Also, in an inclusive group, it is not essential that every individual participates, because lack of participation does not take away benefits from those who do.[79]

The incentives facing industry and environmental groups are summarized in Table 2.4.

*Table 2.4: Industry and environmental groups*

|                        | Common Goal           | Market (Exclusive) | Non-Market (Inclusive) |
|------------------------|-----------------------|--------------------|------------------------|
| **Industry**           | Higher price          | Monopoly           | Lobbyism               |
| **Environmental Groups** | Improved environment | n.a.               | Maximize membership    |

### 2.8.2  Attitudes toward Environmental Regulation

When considering what kind of environmental regulation each of the main organized actors – the State, industry, and environmental groups – would choose, three options are considered relevant: first, traditional command-and-control (CAC) regulation, where proportional roll-backs for individual sources are defined; second, an emission tax on all emitted units; and third, a

77.  Olson and Zeckhauser (1967). Protection against Stalin corresponds to protection against global warming.

78.  We will return to the case of Denmark in Section 6.2.

79.  Olson (1965:37, 40 and 42).

grandfathered permit market, in which polluters are given their initial distribution of permits free of charge, typically according to historical emissions.[80]

One can presume that the State would choose environmental taxes in an effort to maximize state revenue. What kind of regulation would industry and environmental groups elect?

As seen at the beginning of this chapter, the distribution of benefits and costs from regulation can either be concentrated in a small, narrowly defined part of society (small groups) or spread out over a large and more general sector (large groups). This distribution of costs and benefits from regulation determines the incentive for political actors to organize.[81]

Economists typically assume that firms strive for profit maximization and monopoly power. Having achieved monopoly positions, publicly regulated firms like public electric utilities can be expected to aim to retain these positions. Their efforts along these lines have led to complicated state regulation. Utilities have entwined the State, the regulator, in a rigid web of regulation and centrally-planned resource-allocation systems.[82] These efforts basically serve one purpose: to keep out potential competitors. The successful fulfilment of this purpose has made the electricity industry perhaps the most regulated industry of all. The electric utilities have accomplished the goal of becoming a part of State monopoly.[83]

In return for State protection against competition, electric utilities can be expected to promote state regulation in other fields, such as environmental regulation. For example, they can be expected to support traditional CAC regulation or innovative green taxation in the interest of the State.

Contrast this scenario with the one for private industry in a competitive setting. Here, there is a strong incentive to promote permit markets because the trading of permits can lead to lower pollution-reduction costs and more flexibility in responding to consumer demand than is possible with traditional CAC regulation or emission taxes. Also, industry can be expected to demand the type of regulation that creates the collective good of barriers to entry against potentially competing producers.[84] This is the effect of grandfathering; existing

---

80. For a thorough treatment of these three options, see Baumol and Oates (1988).

81. Wilson (1980) follows this line in linking cost distribution and political decision-making. He labels the two decision-making categories in environmental regulation *entrepreneurial politics* (general benefits and concentrated costs) and *client politics* (concentrated benefits and general costs). Both are asymmetric, and disequilibrium occurs. The lack of balance between benefits and costs encourages the affected actors to organize for the purpose of influencing policy outcomes. See also Svendsen (1993a) and Nentjes and Dijkstra (1994).

82. The regulator is 'captured' by the regulated party to create certain outputs (regulation runs the opposite way, that is, it is 'reversed'). The regulated party, typically a 'natural' monopoly, has in fact turned into an element of State planning. See Mitnick (1980:14pp) who also lists four interesting theories on the development of public utilities.

83. See Mueller (1989: 229pp) concerning State monopoly.

84. Buchanan and Tullock (1975) show that existing firms will prefer CAC measures to taxes because CAC measures create a barrier to entry and are more open to negotiations and lobbyism.

sources are given permits free of charge whereas new sources are forced to buy their way into the market.

Under a tax solution, the polluter must pay for all emitted units. In this way, the tax solution may involve enormous increases in costs to polluters, and this lowers the political acceptability of the tax. The tax represents a transfer payment from the viewpoint of society, but it is an operating cost for the firm.

Why, then, is the tax met with political opposition in practice? Why cannot the tax revenue be refunded in a politically acceptable way? The problem is that the refund must be independent of the pollution. Otherwise, the incentive to reduce pollution would be removed; that is, it would not matter to the polluter how much he discharged or emitted, because all the money paid in taxes would be refunded. If, for example, a source is given back its $CO_2$ tax payments, then it will have no incentive to reduce $CO_2$ emissions at all.

Still, one could argue that increased production costs under the tax solution could be avoided by constructing other types of general refund systems not linked to emission. A general refund could, in theory, create a symmetrical situation where losers (capital-intensive firms) would be balanced by winners (labour-intensive firms). Such a political equilibrium would allow the State to establish the tax, but three arguments suggest that this situation is highly unlikely in pollution and $CO_2$ regulation.[85]

First, if the State is to use taxation, then it should clearly identify winners first and mobilize their support by refunding revenue as financial transfers and not as complicated subsidies. However, the actual design might not have a clear-cut and simple refund system. As such, losses for losers might be evident and transparent, whereas potential winners might not be so easily identifiable; for example, potential winners first have to apply for earmarked subsidies.

Second, potential losing firms in an arguably competitive industry may claim that they are in normal profit equilibrium and that further taxation will have damaging effects. Because they cannot pass on the costs of $CO_2$ reduction to consumers by raising product prices, taxation will lead to lost jobs. Even if both winners and losers have the starting point of normal return or zero profit, and even if winners can offset the loss in jobs by creating new jobs, winners are in a less critical situation. In contrast to the losers, the winners are not forced out of business and will therefore have lesser gains in utility terms.[86]

---

Permit markets provide an even stronger barrier to entry, however, because existing sources here have grandfathered their initial rights free of charge. See also Buchanan and Tullock (1976) and Lohmann (1994).

85. I am grateful to Professor Mancur Olson, Department of Economics, University of Maryland, for suggesting these three arguments. See also Raufer and Feldman (1987:16–17), Raufer and Hill and Samsa (1981), and Stavins and Whitehead (1992). For a discussion of revenue-neutral tax reforms, creation of trust funds and potential pitfalls and distortions following green tax reforms, see Oates (1995a).

86. Also, the State has the opportunity to reduce or remove the financial refunds in the future. Firms are often suspicious of state taxation.

Third, and most important, capital-intensive firms are usually bigger and more likely to have a small-number advantage when organizing and lobbying in the political arena. This argument follows the logic introduced in this chapter. As such, a major firm can have a privileged interest and become a collective actor against $CO_2$ taxation all by itself.

These three arguments are critical objections against any general refund system for $CO_2$-emitters and lead to the hypothesis that the demand for $CO_2$ taxation will be asymmetrical among the individual $CO_2$-emitters. Capital-intensive polluters will, as potential losers in a small group, more aggressively oppose taxation with the argument that their competitiveness will weaken; labour-intensive polluters may, as potential winners in a large group, fail to seek a taxation and refund system because they may not organize. Therefore, the refund system can hardly be modelled such that it would satisfy the small group of potential losers.

In summary, industry would be expected to oppose a tax because a tax raises production costs for capital-intensive firms and does not create barriers to entry. Existing and future producers will be charged the same amount per unit of taxed emissions. Private industry will, therefore, prefer a grandfathered permit market because it imparts no initial costs and works as a barrier to entry. Newcomers must buy their way into the market, while existing firms get their permits for free. Likewise, if some permits were to be withdrawn from sources for an auction, the auction should expectedly be made revenue-neutral so that all revenue would be refunded to the existing sources in proportion to their contribution. Again, as in grandfathering, no further costs will be imposed on existing firms; payments from new firms at a revenue-neutral auction will be redistributed to the existing firms from which the permits were taken.

The third organized actor, the environmental group, is a large group because benefits and costs are general and so free-riding is rational. Entrepreneurship and favourable conditions are needed to mobilize support for environmental issues and overcome the lack of incentive to organize. As shown above, environmental groups try to maximize membership for achieving the collective good of environmental improvement. Given that these groups eventually become institutionalized and hire a professional staff, it may be argued that the interests of the leaders may best be served by instigating political conflict. Conflict encourages collective action, raises the number of members, and thus raises the organization's revenue potential.[87]

The environmental policy traditionally preferred by environmental groups has been CAC regulation. One seemingly plausible explanation for this is that CAC regulation offers plenty of potential conflicts: cases can be considered individually and can be criticized at both the state and federal levels. Leaders of environmental groups would then be motivated to strive for increasingly

---

87. Dowie (1995) and Bonner (1993) criticize the environmental movement for letting fund-raising objectives drive their policy positions. See also Snow (1992), Nelson (1995), and Goodin (1994).

stringent technology-based standards against the protests of affected industries, which, as discussed above, would prefer permit markets.

In the cases in which a tax is set or a permit market is initiated, the decisions of how much to pollute are left to the sources. In principle, no individual cases have to be considered. Rather than being constrained by State-determined standards, polluters are free to choose their level of emissions as long as they pay the corresponding tax or hold the corresponding quantity of tradable pollution rights. Adopting an emission tax or a permit market rather than CAC regulation would tend to leave environmental groups in a less significant role.

On the other hand, even though institutionalization takes place, the goal of environmental groups is still to pursue improvements in environmental quality. Note that payments are not compulsory in any way; the contributions from members are voluntary, indicating that moral incentives are at work. The experience of the Sierra Club, a US environmentalist group, is illustrative of both institutionalization and the use of moral incentives.

In 1981, about 60% of the members of the Sierra Club were active; 40% did no more than receive the club magazine, *Sierra*, in return for their annual dues (which, at the time, were $25, of which $3 was for the magazine). The total budget was roughly $7 million. $2 million went to 'studying and influencing public policy' whereas $5 million went to 'outdoor activities, publications, and organizational functions'. In this way, redistribution of most of the budget took place from non-active members to active members. Economic self-interest can, therefore, explain the participation of active members, but not the participation of non-active members.[88]

One would expect that instead of joining and paying dues, the non-active members would free-ride on the already existing provision of the collective good. To explain why this membership exists, it is necessary to add moral considerations or extra-rational motivations to the notion of an economically rational agent.

Incentives other than economic ones exist: morality, prestige, respect, friendship, social and psychological objectives, etc. The existence of these social incentives to group-oriented action strengthens this analysis, for social status and acceptance are individual, non-collective goods. Social sanctions and rewards are also 'selective incentives', those which may be used to mobilize a large group and distinguish among individuals: the 'recalcitrant individual can be ostracized, and the cooperative individual can be invited into the centre of the charmed circle'. Even in the case where moral attitudes determine whether or not a person will act in a group-oriented way, the moral reaction serves as a selective incentive. Not everybody will use just any means to reach a desired end. Many people will choose not to engage in certain activities, such as stealing or committing other crimes, when there is no risk of detection. Indeed, such a

88. More data on the Sierra Club are reviewed in Section 5.4.3. The data used in this connection are selected from Hardin (1982:103–108).

moral code is often needed to overcome the problems of organization.[89]

The Sierra Club exemplifies both institutionalization and moral commitment. Some members are in it for the social activities only and would as such accept whatever politics the group's leaders may choose. Other members are morally committed in the sense that they contribute exclusively to support the group's political activities. If the club drastically changed its political focus or cut back its political activities, presumably the latter group would not stay long.

The leaders have to present results to those members whose moral commitment makes them indifferent to the method by which environmental improvements are achieved. As Hardin points out, organizations that depend on moral contributions must pursue relevant goals.[90] Leaders must convince contributors that their leadership is effective or they risk losing contributions. When motivated by moral or political commitment, the organization's position on policy is far more likely to be consistent with positions taken by the organization's contributors. Hence, more generally, organizations whose goals are supported by moral commitments, rather than by mere self-interest, are likely to be more persistent in working toward their goals.[91]

However, these voluntary contributions seem to contradict the logic of collective action. Each member is supposed to free-ride and benefit from the provision of a collective good (improved environmental quality) without paying for it. The moral incentive among non-active members is clearly an exception to the rule. It may be partly explained in three ways. First, each member receives a journal which is a positive selective incentive. Second, the annual due payment is relatively low. Third, the total amount of voluntary and philanthropic contributions in society are negligible compared to those of taxes and compulsory payments.[92] Therefore, it seems reasonable to maintain the chosen theoretical focus of free-riding and economic rationality as a main explanation of collective action to achieve parsimony and catch as much as possible with as little as necessary. Still, moral commitment is an important part of the story concerning voluntary contributions in environmental groups.[93]

Given the moral aspects of the environmental group, CAC regulation does not offer results that are significant enough. The explanation that environmental groups have promoted CAC regulation because they thrive on conflict is therefore not valid. As will be shown in Chapter 5, the main reason for environmental groups' opposition to economic instruments, which allow sources to pay for the right to pollute, has been a symbolic goal of zero pollution. This objective is unrealistic, however: pollution will always exist if only in minute amounts. Still, the pursuit of this goal has historically prevented the use of economic

---

89. Olson (1965:61).

90. Hardin (1982:123).

91. Olson (1965:61).

92. Olson (1965:11–14).

93. See Paldam and Svendsen (1998) for a general discussion of moral and voluntary organizations.

instruments. It will be shown in this book that environmental groups are best served by lobbying for permit markets and by co-operating with their traditional opponent, private industry.

Concerning unorganized interests, such as the transportation sector and tax-paying households, it is reasonable to expect that they will not protest against a grandfathered permit market for industry. This in spite of the fact that taxing industry would be preferable. Tax revenues could then be used, for example, to lower income taxes.

This argument follows the logic developed for large groups in this chapter and the notion of the rationally ignorant voter. The taxpayers are only affected by the tax at the margin and calculated individual benefits, from starting organizing interest group opposition, are expected to be smaller than the costs of doing so. It does not pay the individual taxpayer to follow public affairs and study the consequences of introducing a grandfathered permit market for industry. Following the same logic for large groups, it is furthermore possible to tax the unorganized interests, if these are immobile. Again, it does not pay the individual taxpayer to protest and provide the collective good of avoiding taxation.

## 2.9  HYPOTHESES

The previous discussion, on the public choice approach for predicting interest group behaviour towards environmental regulation, suggests the following five hypotheses:

First, the State will aim to maximize tax revenues by using green taxes because these taxes can provide the collective good of better environmental quality while possibly enabling reduced taxation of labour, which eventually would result in higher production and more tax revenue.

Second, heavily regulated industries, such as electric utilities, will follow the State's interest in environmental regulation in return for their monopoly, that is they will promote green taxation.

Third, private industry will resist a tax because capital-intensive firms will protest against the extra production costs. It will alternatively prefer a grand-fathered permit market because the initial, historical distribution of permits is free for existing sources and because it creates a barrier to entry, since new sources must buy their way into the market.

Fourth, environmental groups operate in the political arena and are inclusive. They can maintain voluntary contributions from their members only if they achieve the best environmental results by co-operating with private industry, that is by lobbying for permit markets.

Fifth, where benefits and costs both are generally distributed, as is the case for tax-paying households and the transportation sector, green taxation can take place because each taxpayer is only affected on the margin, and because the individual benefits from organizing interest-group opposition are smaller than the added costs of doing so.

What is the predictive power of these hypotheses? Is there a demand for a $CO_2$ market in practice, and would it be workable?

Before turning to the empirical evidence in Chapters 4, 5 and 6, it is necessary to portray green taxation and emission trading in more detail so as to make an evaluation model. The model will incorporate political barriers and give a more complete picture of the setting in which costs are to be minimized in practice. Chapter 3 therefore compares tax and permit markets in detail, with regard to their practical applications, the financial consequences for polluters, the design of a grandfathered auction, potential market failures in a permit market, source location, and finally a comparative method that can be used to justify the transfer of the US experience with permit markets to a European setting.

# 3 Tax Systems and Permit Markets

## 3.1 OVERVIEW

The previous chapter focused on political distortion and prediction of behaviour in the political arena. Based on this knowledge, it concluded that a permit market would be politically feasible in relation to well-organized interest groups while a tax system would be politically feasible in relation to poorly organized interest groups. Building on this political factor, Chapter 3 adds two other potential market distortions, namely economic and administrative distortions.

Sections 3.2 and 3.3 compare the systems of taxation and permits. Section 3.4 discusses the financial consequences for sources subject to taxation and permit markets, respectively, and also introduces the concept of a technological price as a worst-case benchmark. Section 3.5 shows how an auction, linked to the market, can be designed in a revenue-neutral way. Section 3.6 considers potential economic market failures in the permit market which may impair performance. Section 3.7 focuses on the administrative way source location can be incorporated into the analysis so that the actual performance of US permit markets can be understood. Section 3.8 explains why it is possible to transfer experiences from one country to another. Section 3.9 summarizes the chapter and Section 3.10 compresses theory into an evaluation model.

## 3.2 SIMILARITIES

### 3.2.1 Dynamic Incentive

An economic incentive to invest in new abatement technology over time is present under both permit markets and taxes. If superfluous permits can be sold – or tax payments avoided – it is economically favourable to invest. Both a tax system and a permit market allow polluters to consider whether they will pay the permit price (tax) or invest in new abatement technology. A firm will invest whenever the expected economic gain exceeds the price of new technology. When the permit price or the tax is known, it is easy for the firm to calculate its economic gain from reducing emissions by multiplying the permit price (or tax) and the corresponding reduction in emissions. Look at the situation in which a firm considers investment in new abatement technology, as in Figure 3.1.

Before the investment, the firm reduces emissions by $q$ units at a marginal abatement cost of $MC$. After the investment, $MC$ is lowered to $MC_1$. How much does the firm earn? If the firm is allowed to sell permits (or save the corresponding tax payments), it earns the area $A + B$. Why? Because $A$ represents the lower costs from using new technology when reducing emissions by $q$ units, and $B$ represents the profit from selling permits (or saving tax payments) when emissions are reduced from $q$ to $q_1$. So, in this way, firms have an economic incentive to invest in new abatement technology.

*Figure 3.1: Investment in new abatement technology*

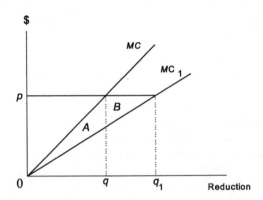

*Source*: Tietenberg (1985:33)

An illustrative counter-example is that of CAC regulation where the firm is required to reduce its emissions by the amount $q$. Here, a firm will only save $A$ from moving to new abatement technology. Nothing is earned from reducing emissions from $q$ to $q_1$, so the source will not voluntarily reduce its emissions further than $q$. The incentive to invest in new abatement technology is thus stronger under a permit market/tax than under traditional CAC regulation.

### 3.2.2  Administration

#### 3.2.2.1  Target group
A single instrument is hardly appropriate for all sources. The choice of target group must be based on both the contribution of emissions by that group and whether control is administratively feasible. As such, the benefits connected with individual control must be weighed against the administrative costs. The administrative costs of, for example, controlling every single car owner or housekeeper are likely to exceed the potential gains to them from an individual control system that lowers emissions reduction costs. The transport and household sectors contain numerous small sources, and for this reason they may be

rejected as a target for individual $CO_2$ emission control systems.[94] Larger stationary sources, such as industry and electric utilities, are of rather more interest. These larger, stationary sources will typically be regulated and controlled already, so that a permit market could build on the existing administrative infrastructure without adding further administrative costs.[95]

However, it may pay to incorporate smaller sources if they collectively contribute significant emissions. This choice of target group for individual emission control must, as such, be considered for each individual case. When a target group has been chosen for the use of a specific economic instrument, the next question is whether the design fits political reality, which may call for a mix of instruments.

### 3.2.2.2   Control system

Control systems rely on precise monitoring and well-functioning sanction mechanisms, typically based on the economic incentive of fines. If these two conditions are not met, sources may find it profitable to cheat. Also, local authorities may have strong free-rider incentives to protect their 'own' firms against strict control, so some kind of central control is needed.[96]

How will an economically rational source consider its option of cheating? What should be the size of the fine per unit? A source may calculate on paying the expected fine, $f$. If it is assumed that this fine is lower than the price $p$ per unit of paying a tax or a permit, then the situation shown in Figure 3.2 arises, where $MC$ represents the marginal cost to the source (or the aggregate industry) of reducing pollution.

If a tax of $p$ is in place and a fine of $f$ is introduced, pollution reduction will drop from $q$ to $q_f$. The lowering of a tax or fine will determine the amount reduced. The same result is valid for a permit market, where the permit price will drop to $f$ from the starting price $p$. Contrast this to the situation where the

94.  Taylor (1992) has suggested the use of permit markets in the transportation sector so that a norm or standard is set for fuel efficiency. This standard could, for example, be defined in relation to $CO_2$ emissions. A car producer is then credited if a new car is more efficient than the standard. If it is less efficient, the car producer must buy credits (permits) from other producers and/or the regulatory authority. See Rubin and King (1993) as well.

95.  Note that because no $CO_2$ abatement technology has been developed for the market yet, it is possible to put the tax on an input, for example, to use a traditional energy tax based on the fuel's $CO_2$ content. However, new technological knowledge about $CO_2$ reduction may change this situation in the future. Two new Dutch reports concerning technical $CO_2$ reduction costs show that it is now possible to reduce $CO_2$ profitably from energy production and industrial processes. If an emitter in this way chooses to remove $CO_2$ chemically, individual emission control becomes a necessity. Presumably, in the near future, there would no longer be a proportional link between fossil fuel consumption and $CO_2$ emission. Chemical $CO_2$ reduction gives an important yardstick for the level of reduction costs and for a cost comparison between actual $CO_2$ regulation and a potential $CO_2$ market. See Sections 3.4.2 and 6.9.

96.  Local firms may be given substantial room for cheating in this kind of system because local authorities may accept violations in the interest of attracting industry (and a larger tax base) to their area. See Oates and Schwab (1988).

fine $f$ is set higher than the tax (or permit price), $p$. Then the reduced amount
will stay at $q$ because the tax (or permit price) now is the binding payment. So,
to establish a well-functioning fine system, the expected fine (including the risk
of detection) must always be set higher than the tax (or the permit price).[97]

*Figure 3.2: The size of a fine*

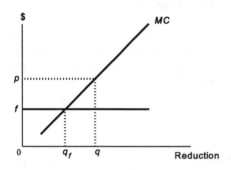

## 3.3   DIFFERENCES

Both the tax and permit systems have the theoretical capacity of achieving a
target level of emissions at least cost. In practice, however, permit markets may
prove to be a better idea for a number of reasons. Baumol and Oates have listed
the following five reasons for preferring tradable permits to a tax system:[98]

   First, a tax cannot ensure the target level of pollution control. Second,
complications arising from price inflation and economic growth occur in the tax
system. Third, tradable permits may be more familiar. Fourth, for pollutants for
which source location matters, it may be easier to incorporate the spatial dimension in a permit market than in a tax system. Fifth, the tax solution may involve
enormous increases in costs to polluters, and this lowers the political acceptability of the tax. These five points and an important assumption – that the permit
market performs well and is not blocked by significant market failures – are
discussed below in turn.

### 3.3.1   Target Level

As noted in Section 2.3.2, the exact position of the marginal cost curve is not
known by administrators. Therefore, the response of polluters to a given tax is

---

97.  See Hahn (1989a:15–16), Segerson and Tietenberg (1992) and Tietenberg (1992) for further
comments on this issue.

98.  Baumol and Oates (1988:178–80).

uncertain. If the administrators set the tax too low or too high, the tax must be adjusted in a 'trial-and-error' process. This means costly readjustments by polluters in the levels of pollution control and associated abatement technology. Repeated administrative changes create regulatory uncertainty. In contrast, tradable permits allow administrators to control the level of pollution from the start.

### 3.3.2  Price Inflation and Economic Growth

Inflation erodes the real value of a tax, and expanded production increases pollution. For these two reasons, a tax must be raised continually, whereas a permit market automatically translates any rise in demand for permits into a higher price with no increase in pollution.

### 3.3.3  Familiarity

In the US, a new tax system is an alternative to traditional CAC regulation for controlling pollution. Because permits already exist, explicitly or implicitly, it may be a less radical step to make these permits marketable than imposing a tax system. In contrast to the US, familiarity with the use of taxes is high in Europe.[99] Still, the traditional way of dealing with pollution in Europe has been that of CAC regulation. Therefore, when introducing permit markets, it is, as in the case of the US, possible to build on already existing administrative infrastructures.

The only difference between CAC permits and tradeable permits is the property right of the permits. Under CAC regulation, sources hold non-transferable permits whereas in a permit market, sources can trade permits freely. The market can be initiated by transferring to sources the property rights of the permits they already hold freely or by auction. The sources will then trade permits whenever they can benefit from doing so.

### 3.3.4  Source Location

It may be easier to incorporate the spatial dimension in a permit market system than in a tax system. The reason is that a tax approach will require individual taxation for each source in relation to its location. Such different tax levels may either be explicitly illegal or politically infeasible. In contrast, tradable permits may be based on different concentration standards at different receptor sites.[100]

$CO_2$ emissions are particularly well suited for individual control because the environmental costs resulting from $CO_2$ emissions are independent of source location, in contrast to those resulting from, for example, $SO_2$ and $NO_x$

---

99.  See, for example, Tietenberg (1990a) and Opschoor (1993).

100.   See Baumol and Oates (1988:181–88), Tietenberg (1985: ch.4).

emissions. This point simplifies the present analysis greatly since cost-effective incorporation of the spatial dimension is extremely difficult.[101]

### 3.3.5 Cost Distribution

The distribution of costs for reducing a given pollutant, can be categorized in two ways. The first category is financial transfers to or from the State. This includes subsidies, auctions and taxes. The second is financial transfers among the polluters themselves, where no financial transfers to the State are involved.

Look at the distribution of payments and reduction costs in the first category, where financial transfers between the State and polluters take place. Either a subsidy, a tax or an auction may ensure the desired reduction of a given pollutant, but the distribution of costs will vary, as shown in Figure 3.3.

*Figure 3.3: Size of total reduction costs*

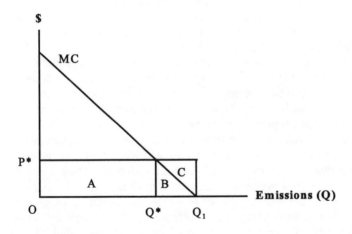

Note that the *MC* curve is downward-sloping since $Q$ is now emissions, not reduction in emissions. Subsidies may be perceived as 'negative' taxes. If the aim is to reduce $Q_1 - Q^*$ units, this may be achieved by giving sources a subsidy of amount $P^*$ per reduced unit. The polluter will then reduce $Q^*$ units, use area $B$ for reduction investments, and receive $B + C$ in the form of a subsidy

101.   Location does not matter for $CO_2$ emissions because the assumed damage caused by $CO_2$ emissions (global warming) is solely dependent on the emitted amount. However, it matters for the pollutants regulated to date in the US by permit markets. For example, $SO_2$ and $NO_x$ lead to acid rain in certain areas, depending on the concentration of the substances, source location and meteorological conditions. In this way, the abatement of localized pollution, like smog or acid rain, would be a collective good for a specified geographical area, whereas the prevention of global warming would be a collective good for everyone. The precautions taken to avoid the occurrence of 'hot spots' are critical for understanding performance, as will be discussed in Section 3.7 and Chapter 4.

payment from the State. Because the polluter receives area $B + C$ and uses area $B$ for reduction, $C$ is the profit.

A subsidy has the same effect on emissions reduction as a tax or auction, but due to the profit, $C$, too many firms are encouraged to enter the industry. Polluters choose processes with large emissions in order to get as many subsidies as possible. Therefore, the use of subsidies should be avoided.

In contrast, taxes or an auction mean that the polluter must pay $P^*$ per unit emitted. In this case, the polluter will pay $A$ in taxes or in an auction and use $B$ for reduction investments.[102]

If the polluters were to choose from these three solutions, they would, of course, choose subsidies and gain the profit represented by area $C$. Both a tax and an auction mean a transfer of areas $A$ and $B$ to the State.

An alternative approach to that of using subsidies is a grandfathered permit market. This approach belongs to the second category, the cases when no transfers between the State and sources are involved. Here, permits are initially distributed for nothing to existing sources. In the case of Figure 3.3, permits allowing $Q^*$ emissions may be grandfathered so that original sources only pay $B$, in contrast to a tax system or an auction where they pay $A + B$. Compared to a subsidy, existing sources only lose the profit $C$.

The distribution of costs in environmental regulation may be viewed as a struggle between polluters and society over the property rights to nature. If property rights are assumed to belong to society, the polluter-pays principle can be applied, for example by taxing the use of natural resources or by auctioning off the rights to pollute. If property rights belong to the polluters, a victim-pays principle takes effect and society has to subsidize sources to reduce pollution.[103] Grandfathering is a combination of these two principles. It is a victim-pays principle concerning the limited stock of permits transferred for free to polluters. However, society retains property rights to the residual permits, for example the polluters have to pay for the pollution reduction (an amount represented by area $B$ in Figure 3.3); in this way, the polluter-pays principle applies. Section 3.4 further develops and exemplifies the grandfathering approach, which is the focus of this book.

### 3.3.6  Market Failure

Note that the performance of a permit market depends critically on the absence of market failures, so that individual marginal abatement costs are equal to the permit price or tax. Here, traditional neo-classical theory can be applied to test the competitiveness of the market. Market failure occurs when the equilibrium

---

102.  See Pigou (1920).

103.  As Coase (1960) argues, the optimal outcome does not depend on whether polluters or victims pay when property rights are well-defined and enforceable and when transaction costs are low. See Section 2.3.3.

in a permit market does not result in a cost-effective allocation.

Market failures can be grouped under five types of distortions: 1 differentiated product, 2 externalities, 3 political interference, 4 complete competition and 5 imperfect knowledge.[104] If significant market failures exist, the associated costs may be critical to the advisability of using a permit market. Therefore, it is important to evaluate the potential costs, entailed with each of the five.

The first distortion is not present here because permits are homogeneous and standardized, that is, they are perfect substitutes. Nor is the permit market linked to externalities, because it is designed to remove the externality of pollution and to provide a collective good.

The third distortion, political interference is, however, quite relevant. Special interest groups may easily create economic distortions following redistributive policies, as hypothesized in Chapter 2. For example, refund systems, like the one used with energy-intensive firms under the Danish $CO_2$ tax, are based on political considerations and distort performance. The more politically attractive options of grandfathered tradable permits and revenue-neutral auctions are addressed in Sections 3.4 and 3.5.

The fourth distortion, complete competition, concerns many small and price-taking agents in an atomized market in which no barriers to entry exist. In the case of a permit market, there must be many agents to prevent any single permit holder from dominating the market. Grandfathering provides a barrier to entry because new entrants have to buy their way into the market. Section 3.6 analyses the notion of complete competition in a permit market setting.

The fifth market failure condition concerns full information about present and future markets for the product, that is a permit. What is the price and what are the transaction costs, including those of administration? Are any brokering services available? Does regulatory uncertainty exist concerning the future value of the permit? Is there, for example, a risk that some permits may be confiscated by authorities? This potential economic market failure is commented on in Section 3.6.

## 3.4 GRANDFATHERING AND COST DISTRIBUTION

What are the costs of environmental regulation to the regulated parties? This question is important because the answer may determine the political feasibility of any proposal, no matter how well-designed it may be. The intention here is to make a cost comparison between a tax and a grandfathered permit market, and to use the case of $CO_2$ taxation in Denmark.[105] The $CO_2$ tax in Denmark has been used to accomplish a politically determined goal of 20% $CO_2$ reduction of

104. See Scherer and Ross (1990:16), Begg, Fischer and Dornbusch (1984:333–34) and Strøjer Madsen, et al. (1986:107).

105. See for example Baumol and Oates (1988), Cropper and Oates (1992), Svendsen (1993a) and Hjorth-Andersen (1989).

the 1988 level by the year 2005. However, the tax has been set much too low to change $CO_2$-emitting behaviour sufficiently. Therefore, the Danish government has recently proposed to increase the size of the present $CO_2$ tax six-fold.[106]

What is the cost relationship between taxation and a grandfathered permit market, that is how much will the regulated parties *save* in a permit market compared to the private costs associated with taxation when a 20% cut in $CO_2$ emissions is mandated? In addressing this question, the possibility of refunding tax revenue to industry will be ignored.[107]

### 3.4.1   Cost Comparison

Nobody knows the exact position and slope of the marginal $CO_2$ emissions reduction curve for Danish industry. Assume that these marginal costs *(MC)* decline linearly as the quantity of $CO_2$ emissions (Q) rises, as illustrated in Figure 3.4 below.[108]

*Figure 3.4: Cost comparison between a tax and a grandfathered market*

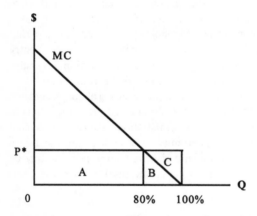

Assume, now, that the correct $CO_2$ tax to accomplish the 20% target reduction level is the price *P\**. What are the aggregated costs under a tax and a

106.   Danish Ministry of Energy (1990). The Danish $CO_2$ tax is discussed in Section 6.2.

107.   It is hard to find a politically acceptable way of doing this. As noted above in Sections 2.8 and 2.9, large and capital-intensive $CO_2$ emitters will seek large refunds. But if they are successful, they will lose the economic incentive to reduce $CO_2$.

108.   This assumption has no implications for the final result. A good guess would be that the MC curve over the first 20% reduction range is relatively flat – the first units are cheap to reduce because a factory may start by reducing its use of fossil fuels by switching off lights or some of its machines at night. See for example Larsen et al. (1993), which shows that there is substantial room for easy savings in Denmark. For a discussion concerning the empirical problems linked to the estimation of marginal reduction costs, see Morthorst (1994), and for a theoretical discussion of this information problem, see Mortensen and Andersen (1990).

grandfathered permit market, respectively?

In Figure 3.4, total costs under a $CO_2$ tax will be the areas $A$ and $B$. Polluters will reduce 20% of their emissions at a cost to them of area $B$ and pay the tax on each of the units they continue to emit for a total tax bill of area $A$.

In contrast, the explicit costs to the polluter in a permit market will be $B$ only.[109] A tax requires the polluter to pay for all units emitted, whereas under the permit market, the polluter receives the right to emit the targeted level of emissions.

Take a closer look at the costs associated with the 20% $CO_2$ reduction. In Figure 3.4, areas $B$ and $C$ will always correspond to one fifth of the total area $(A + B + C)$. Furthermore, when $MC$ is linear, $B$ and $C$ will always be the same size, that is $B$ will always be a mirror image of $C$. But note that $C$ does not represent any reduction costs because this area is situated above the $MC$ curve.[110]

In a permit market, permits will be transferred among polluters. Polluters will reduce or increase their individual $CO_2$ emissions until all firms' marginal reduction costs are equal to the permit price.[111] Consequently, the total reduction costs to industry will be the area $B$ when the permit price is $P*$.[112]

In contrast, the tax payments under a tax regime are the area $A$, which will always be eight times as large as $B$, the level of private reduction costs for the industry. In other words, taxation is nine times more costly than the permit market: the costs to industry under this approach include the tax payment, $A$, plus private reduction costs, $B$.

Another example is the US Acid Rain Program, which aims to reduce $SO_2$ emission by 50%. Historical polluters only have to pay for the reduction because

109. I am grateful to Professor Wallace E. Oates, Department of Economics, University of Maryland, for suggesting this solution to me and for our discussions on the matter. Also, I am grateful to Professor Jesper Jespersen, University of Roskilde, for valuable comments. There is an opportunity cost connected to area $A$ because polluters can sell the permits, or – put in another way – the free transfer of property rights of permits represents implicitly a subsidy.

110. As discussed in Section 3.3.5, a subsidy at the level of $p$ means that polluters would receive the area $C$ as a profit.

111. Hjorth-Andersen (1989). Here, I assume that sources have different MC curves. If all sources have identical MC curves, then a simple, proportional roll-back of 20% would achieve a least-cost allocation as well, that is a traditional CAC approach. But if substantial variation in MC curves exist – which is the typical case – then a proportional roll-back will be very costly because permits cannot be transferred among sources.

112. The tax represents a transfer payment from the viewpoint of society, but it is a cost of operation for the firm. This could mean that even an inefficient and costly CAC program would be more attractive to sources than a tax system without a refund. Baumol and Oates refer to an illustrative US study of how to reduce the emission of certain halocarbons. A CAC program would total about $230 million in abatement costs. A tax system or system of tradable permits that uses an auction without a refund would reduce these costs to $110 million (roughly 50% savings), but the total costs to polluters would then total about $1400 million, that is a six-fold increase in total costs to polluters relative to a program of CAC, Palmer et al. (1980), adapted from Baumol and Oates (1988:178–79).

emission rights were provided to them for free. If the polluters had been taxed, they would also have to pay taxes for all units emitted. In this case, taxation would be three times more costly to the polluters than the grandfathered permit market.[113]

Let us return to the Danish target level. The private reduction costs that follow the 20% $CO_2$ reduction will vary over different industries and different firms. If firm $F_1$ has a low $MC_1$ for the units first reduced, $F_1$ can earn money by trading, as illustrated in Figure 3.5.

Firm $F_1$ will choose to reduce the first 20% itself at the cost of area $B$. However, because $F_1$ can reduce an additional 30% at a cost per unit that falls below the price, $P^*$, it will do so and sell a corresponding number of permits. The firm's revenue from selling these permits corresponds to the area $abcd$, and its profit corresponds to $abcd$ minus the costs from private reduction, $D$. Because the profit is greater than area $B$, firm $F_1$ will earn the difference when a permit market is introduced.

*Figure 3.5: Polluter with low marginal reduction costs*

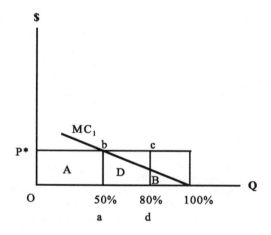

In contrast, if the MC curve for a polluter $F_2$ has a greater slope than the aggregate $MC$ curve, then $F_2$ will choose to buy permits. This situation is depicted in Figure 3.6, where polluter $F_2$ has the high marginal reduction costs of $MC_2$.

As shown in Figure 3.6, $F_2$ will reduce emissions by 10%. Hereafter, it is cheaper not to reduce emissions but rather to buy permits from others at price $P^*$. The costs of buying permits correspond to the area $abcd$. If $F_2$ were prevented from buying these permits under CAC regulation, for example, its costs

---

113.    The reduction target level from the UN conference in Kyoto, Japan (December 1997), is also an illustrative example. Here, the industrialized countries voluntarily agreed on reducing $CO_2$ by 5% from 1990 to 2012. In this case, it can easily be calculated that taxation without refund would be 38 times more costly to polluters than the permit market.

would include area *aecd*. So, in a permit market, $F_2$ must in total pay the areas *B* and *abcd*, but it saves the area *bec* relative to the situation where trading is not allowed.

*Figure 3.6: Polluter with high marginal reduction costs*

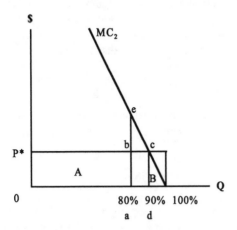

### 3.4.2 Technological Maximum Price

Another cost scenario for a permit market may be based on a technological maximum permit price. Intuitively, an overall maximum price for a $CO_2$ permit cannot exceed the technological reduction costs. $CO_2$-emitters are unwilling to pay more for permits than they would have to pay for the purchase and running of a machine that absorbs atmospheric air and recovers and stores $CO_2$.[114] The application of such a 'free air machine' is not profitable for the time being. It would use so much energy itself that the net result would be $CO_2$ emissions far beyond the $CO_2$ recovered and stored.[115] But modern technology now makes it possible to remove and store $CO_2$ from industrial processes in which $CO_2$ appears in concentrated forms. Two new Dutch reports concerning $CO_2$ scrubbers show that it is possible to reduce $CO_2$ profitably from energy production and industrial processes.[116]

114.  I am grateful to Professor Martin Paldam, Department of Economics, University of Aarhus, for suggesting this approach.

115.  This is due to the fact that atmospheric air only contains a very small $CO_2$ fraction, about 0.03%, and that $CO_2$ is technically very demanding to recover. However, in some production processes, larger $CO_2$ concentrations occur. This is normally the case for closed industrial energy production. Interview, June 16, 1993: Mogens Weel Hansen, consultative engineer, dk-Teknik.

116.  In section 6.9 these pilot projects and chemical $CO_2$ reduction are described in more detail and the resulting technological maximum price for a Danish $CO_2$ market is used in a cost scenario.

The existence of such a technological maximum price makes it possible to describe a worst-case scenario for a permit market where no trade takes place and all emitters have to reduce on their own. Assume that a permit is valid for one year at a time and that the technological maximum price is $50 per ton of $CO_2$. If the permit is to be valid for a longer period the value must be capitalized. That depends on the time horizon and the discount rate. In an extreme case, the permit gives the right to emit one ton $CO_2$ a year forever. Following Kort (1992), the capitalized value of the infinite permit, $p$, can be estimated by the corresponding one year permit price, $\tau$, and the discount rate $r$:

$$p = \tau/r$$

If $\tau$ is $50 in the worst-case grandfathered market, and the discount rate r is 5%, as assumed in the Dutch reports on chemical $CO_2$ reduction, then the capitalized value of an infinite permit is $1,000.

## 3.5 REVENUE-NEUTRAL AUCTION

The notion of a revenue-neutral auction was first suggested by Hahn and Noll in 1982.[117] In such an auction, all revenue is returned to the polluters according to a distribution rule. The distribution rule considered here is grandfathering. Every polluter gets their historical emission rights for free and must offer these rights (or some part of them) for sale in an auction. The political appeal of this system, compared to that of a traditional auction or a tax, is obvious: the revenue is refunded to all polluters participating in the program. All economic transactions take place among the polluters themselves. All interested parties may bid at the auction by specifying the number of permits they desire at each of the different prices. Potential buyers must in this way give the auctioneer their individual demand schedules for permits.

Revenue-neutral auctions can be divided into two types: discriminative and non-discriminative. The basic difference is that in a discriminative auction, there are several prices and the bidder pays what he bids, whereas in a non-discriminative auction, there is a single price, that is, the bidder pays the minimum or clearing price. This difference has an important implication for the size of the revenue. The two types of auctions are depicted graphically in Figure 3.7, which depicts the difference in revenue generated when bidders bid their true value.

Assume that q* of the permits in circulation are auctioned off.

In a non-discriminative auction, the auctioneer will gather all individual bid-schedules and set the minimum price, $p^*$, as the single-price equilibrium where

---

117.   Hahn and Noll (1982a:141). Further literature on revenue neutral auctions includes Tietenberg (1985), Cason (1995;1993), Franciosi et al. (1993), Hausker (1992), Holcombe and Meiners (1981;1980), Oates (1981), Lyon (1986;1982) and Oehmke (1987).

the (revealed) aggregated demand schedule for permits, $D$, meets the inelastic supply schedule, $S$. Because all winning bids pay the equilibrium price, $p^*$, total revenue from the non-discriminative auction is area $A$.[118]

*Figure 3.7: Revenue in non-discriminative and discriminative auctions*

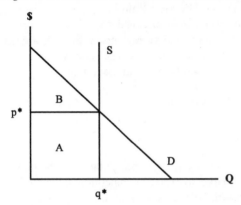

When the auction is revenue-neutral, all payments are refunded to the contributing polluters, so total payments equal exactly the total revenue. If authorities withdraw permits from the market for the auction, then sources will receive the revenue from the sale. Suppose a source offers 100 permits and that the auction price is $100 per permit, that source will then receive $10,000.[119]

In contrast to the non-discriminative auction, a discriminative auction is multi-priced. The bidder pays what he bids, which allows the auctioneer to price-differentiate. If sources do not have any information about the expected equilibrium price, their bids will follow the demand curve, $D$. By this, revenue from the auction is maximized.

As shown in Figure 3.7, the extra revenue is illustrated by the triangle $B$. Revenue will be largest in the discriminative auction ($A + B$). In this case revenue will be returned to sources according to the average price, which is higher than the equilibrium price, $p^*$.

In practice, the situation may differ from the hypothetical cases described above. Because only some of the permits are auctioned off, sources may have

118.   Each bidder pays the auctioneer $p^*q_i$, where $q_i$ is the number of permits demanded by the $i^{th}$ source. The collective payment is a summation of individual payments $\Sigma p^* \, q_i$.

119.   Let $q_{0i}$ represent source $i$'s initial contribution of permits to the auction. Because $q^*$ represents both the total number of permits offered and the total number sold at the auction, it must be so that $\Sigma q_{0i} = q^*$. Revenue is then returned in such a way that each polluter receives a payment equal to the market value of their initial contribution of permits at the auction, $p^* \times q_{0i}$. If $q_i$ represents the number of permits purchased by source $i$ at the auction, each bidder makes a net payment of $(q_i - q_{0i})$ $p^*$ to the auctioneer. If $q_i > q_{0i}$, the polluter is a net purchaser of permits and pays more than he receives. If $q_i < q_{0i}$, the polluter is a net seller and receives more than he pays. In sum, $\Sigma p^*(q_i - q_{0i})$ = 0.

some knowledge from the permit market of what the expected equilibrium price will be. Therefore, they may bid in relation to their expectations rather than in relation to their marginal reduction costs. In both auction types, the bidders would then bid lower and attempt to get the permits cheaper than in the market, where it is always possible to buy.[120]

The actual auction results from the US Acid Rain Program described in Section 4.5.4 are generated by a discriminative auction design. The 'two-price' signal to the market whereby the minimum and average prices differ is argued to be non-desirable because it raises transaction costs. The seller wants to sell at the average price, whereas the buyer wants to buy at the minimum.

## 3.6   ECONOMIC MARKET FAILURE

### 3.6.1   Incomplete Competition

Incomplete competition may stem both from price manipulation in the permit market and from using the permit market to exclude competition in the product market.[121] These two possibilities will be examined in turn.

#### 3.6.1.1   Price manipulation in the permit market

In the permit market, a dominating source (or a coalition of sources) may attempt to manipulate the price as a monopolist or a monopsonist. This market power depends on the firm's size relative to the market in which it is operating. If the dominating source offers too few permits, it can exert monopoly power by raising the price. If the dominating source buys too few permits, it can exert monopsony power by reducing the price. In both cases, the source may achieve a net gain at the expense of cost effective outcome.

A critical factor in this respect will be how the initial distribution rule is defined in practice. The more permits a source (or coalition of sources) initially holds, the more likely it is to become dominant and engage in price manipulation.[122]

#### 3.6.1.2   Excluding competition in the product market

The other form of incomplete competition stems from the incentive to exclude competitors in the product market by keeping them out of the permit market. A source – or a group of sources – may refuse to sell permits to new entrants and thereby create a barrier to entry.[123] Such a 'predatory' source may in this way

---

120.   See also Vickrey (1961).

121.   Tietenberg (1985:125).

122.   See Hahn (1984:754), whose principal result is that the degree of inefficiency observed in the permit market is systematically related to the distribution of permits.

123.   Stigler (1968:67) has defined a barrier to entry as 'a cost of production, which must be borne by a firm which seeks to enter an industry but is not borne by firms already in the industry'.

increase its opportunities for manipulating the price in the product market. However, such behaviour would occur only if the two engaging sources were direct competitors in the same product market and emitted the same pollutant in the same regulated area. This set of conditions may be quite rare in practice.[124]

A contestable product market may in itself force agents to produce at lowest costs including cost-effective permit trading. If a firm can enter and exit a product market easily, the market is contestable even if the conditions for pure competition are not met.[125] For example, the threat of entry and potential under-bidding is sufficient to force a local electricity company to act in a competitive way, even if it is the only local supplier of electricity.

### 3.6.2 Missing Information

If missing information in the permit market creates uncertainty, the best strategy may be to wait and see. Information and stability are necessary preconditions for investments and trade. This is particularly the case for large investments, like those occurring in the electric utility industry where the horizon of planning is extremely long, typically 15–20 years.[126]

As shown in the next section on the incorporation of source location, the trading rules in the permit market may be so complex that they create uncertainty and high transaction costs. Three actions are required, therefore, for the creation of a successful permit market. First, the authorities must guarantee the property right of the permits. No arbitrary confiscation may take place. Second, the incorporation of source location must be simplified, or location must be ignored, if possible. Third, brokerage services should be encouraged. Private dealers, such as banks and brokers, should be allowed to mediate trades. The establishment of an auction may lower transaction costs by providing a price signal.

## 3.7  PERMIT MARKETS AND SOURCE LOCATION

It is necessary to analyse the problem of incorporating source location in the design of environmental policy, because this has been attempted in most of the US permit markets. This spatial consideration is relevant whenever environmental quality depends on pollutant concentration at a receptor and not directly on the size of emissions at the source.

Both tradable permits and taxes could be used as cost-effective instruments

---

124.  Tietenberg (1985:138–46) uses the concept of predatory behaviour.

125.  See Baumol, Panzar and Willig (1982), Scherer and Ross (1990), Mortensen and Olsen (1991) and Svendsen and Steiner (1997).

126.  See Raufer and Feldman (1987:32), who recommend the option of leasing permits in the electric utility industry.

in this respect. However, for two reasons, it may be politically and administratively more feasible to incorporate the spatial dimension in a permit market system than in a tax system. First, a tax approach will require individual taxation for each source in relation to its location. Such different tax levels may not be politically feasible, as discussed in Section 3.4. In contrast, tradable permits may be based on concentration standards at specific receptor sites.[127] Second, such an 'ambient' tax would impose the same information burden on authorities as would a system of tradable permits that incorporated the spatial dimension, but the tax system would furthermore require a determination of the size of the tax that would bring about the target pollution concentration levels in a cost-effective way. Here, the permit market approach requires less information because it generates the appropriate market price itself. [128]

This section will analyse five permit markets. The first permit market system, Emission Permit System (EPS), ignores source location whereas the second permit market, the Ambient Permit System (APS), takes source location fully into account. The last three permit markets discussed – Pollution Offset (PO), Non-degradation Offset (NO) and Modified Pollution Offset (MPO) – are mixed cases, each containing elements of EPS and APS.

### 3.7.1 EPS and APS

The standard in the EPS is defined as an emission level. EPS treats emissions from different locations as having the same effect on all receptors. Sources are then free to trade emission permits on a one-to-one trade ratio within a single market, making the EPS easy to administer. Administrators do not have to approve each trade because the trade ratios is predefined. Hence, EPS is cost-effective for pollutants where source location does not matter, for example, global pollutants such as $CO_2$.

EPS may, however, present substantial costs when applied to pollutants where source location does matter. This loss has been judged for certain cases in the range of two to four times compared to the situation where source location is taken into account.[129]

The emission of a local or regional pollutant results in different concentrations at different receptors depending on the physical position of the emission point. Emission is measured in quantity per time units whereas concentration is measured in cubic content units.[130] Emission must therefore be translated to

127.   See Baumol and Oates (1988:181–88), Tietenberg (1985: ch.4).

128.   See Tietenberg (1996; 341–43).

129.   Tietenberg (1995:100).

130.   In terms of emission, $CO_2$ is measured in tons per year because source location is without any importance for environmental quality. $CO_2$ goes up in the air and disperses itself evenly in the atmosphere. It makes no difference whether a quantity of $CO_2$ is emitted in Denmark or in China. In contrast, when source location and concentration matters, $SO_2$, for example, is measured in $mg/m^3$ (air pollution) and nitrogen in $\mu mol/litre$ (water pollution). For example, more fossil fuel burning

concentration contributions. Otherwise, distant sources, in relation to a receptor, must pay the same price as closer sources for an emission permit. Consequently, the price of an emission permit fails to reflect the costs of reducing pollution at a receptor. Polluters will not have the incentive to locate at a distance from crowded receptors.

In contrast, the standard in the APS is defined as a concentration level and is monitored at numerous receptor sites that cover a given regulated area. A market is created for each of the receptors, and no individual approval of trade is necessary since the trade ratios are predefined. The trade ratios vary with source location.

Therefore, the APS sets out to deal cost-effectively with pollutants when location matters. Permits are distributed (based on a dispersion model) so that the number of emission permits are maximized in terms of concentration at each receptor. This means that the concentration level matches the threshold of each ambient standard.

Let us illustrate how the APS works in the most simple case with two sources and one receptor. Assume that the two sources are identical and that distance determines how much each source affects the receptor in terms of concentration contributions. Figure 3.8 shows how *source 2* ($S_2$) compared with *source 1* ( $S_1$), is located twice as far away from receptor $R$. This means that $S_2$ affects $R$ half as much as $S_1$ in terms of concentration units when both sources emit the same amount.

*Figure 3.8: The case of two sources and one receptor*

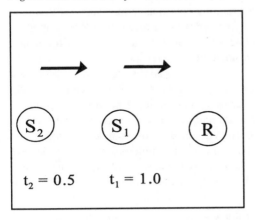

Emission units (E) can in this way be 'translated' into concentration units (K) by the use of a transfer or dispersion coefficient, labelled $t_i$.[131] In this case, $S_2$ is

in Great Britain would mean more acid rain in Scandinavia.

131. This transfer coefficient represents source *i's* concentration contribution, as determined in

given the transfer coefficient, $t_2 = 0.5$. $S_1$ is twice as close so $t_1 = 1.0$.

This means that the two sources must trade at the emission trade ratio 2:1. If $S_1$ wants to sell the right to contribute 1K, it can sell 2E to $S_2$ because at the location of $S_2$ 2E corresponds to 1K at receptor. So, 1E reduced at $S_1$ gives the right to increase emission by 2E at $S_2$. If trade moves the opposite way so that $S_2$ wants to sell 1K to $S_1$, then it must reduce 2E.

APS is cost-effective because each source will equate its marginal costs of reducing 1K to the market price. Because $S_2$ affects receptor $R$ only half as much as $S_1$ does, it is twice as expensive to reduce 1K at $R$ at this distance. The individual source's marginal cost of reducing 1K, $MC(K_{red}^i)$, is therefore linked by the transfer coefficient, $t^i$, to the marginal cost of reducing 1E, $MC(E_{red}^i)$:

$$MC(K_{red}^i) = MC(E_{red}^i) / t^i$$

Each polluter in the market for concentration permits will be induced to reduce or increase its emissions until its $MC(K_{red}^i)$ corresponds to the permit price. If the $MC(E_{red}^i) / t^i$ is higher (lower) than the market price, the source will buy (sell). When the two sources have adjusted their $MC(K_{red}^i)$ to the market price, the distribution of concentration permits will be cost-effective in relation to the ambient standard at receptor $R$.[132]

Because the number of concentration permits necessary for a source to establish itself decreases when $t^i$ decreases, the sources get an economic incentive to locate themselves as far away as possible from receptor and potential 'hot spot' areas.[133] Therefore, the trade ratio for emission permits varies with source location. If one source is located four times as far away from $R$ as is another, then the emission trade ratio will be 4:1. Some areas need extra environmental protection, and the concentration standard at the receptor can then be adjusted to the desired level of environmental quality. The APS system has not been used in practice yet, and the potential transaction costs are so high that it is not likely to be used in the future for two reasons. First, even if it is possible to register all sources and affected receptors in a regulated area, authorities must create a separate market for each receptor. High transaction costs can be expected for the individual polluter who must buy and sell in numerous permit markets at varying market prices. Second, there is a risk that some of these markets may only engage a few polluters and, as such, turn out 'thin'. Strategic behaviour

practice by a number of factors other than distance, such as geographical position, size of smokestack, meteorological conditions (wind speed, wind direction, etc). See Tietenberg (1985).

132.   See Tietenberg (1996:339-41), which gives an illustrative numerical example of EPS and APS.

133.   There will be a fixed number of permits available at receptor $R$ as defined by the ambient standard. Due to supply and demand, more sources will demand emission permits in cities or industrial areas. Therefore, the concentration permit price will be higher there than in areas with fewer sources.

and difficulties in identifying potential sellers and buyers may further raise transaction costs in a thin market.[134] Transaction costs are thus likely to be lower when the number of markets is kept small.[135]

### 3.7.2 PO, NO and MPO

The challenge in terms of the number of markets has been met by three alternative trade rules that combine elements from both APS and EPS. These trade rules seek to create only one market based on a few chosen receptor sites.

Trade takes place with emission permits, and the source location is incorporated through an individual and administratively set trade ratio before trade begins. This trade ratio individually defines the exchange rate between emissions reduction (from the selling source) and emissions increase (from the buying source).

Thus, if a polluter wants to establish itself or to increase its emissions, it must ensure that one or more other polluters reduce emissions to such an extent that no concentration standards are exceeded. To ensure that standards are met at receptor sites, the authorities must base their individual trade ratio judgments on well-developed dispersion models.[136]

The three trade rules, which will be examined in turn, are:[137]

1 Pollution Offset (PO)
2 Non-degradation Offset (NO)
3 Modified Pollution Offset (MPO)

Pollution Offset (PO) allows trading of emission permits as long as no concentration standards are exceeded at receptors in the regulated area. In this way, the PO system does not require, as was the case in the APS, that the regulator calculates a distribution of permits that will maximize the number of allowable permits at each receptor so that the concentration level will match the allowed standard. In principle, an arbitrary distribution rule like grandfathering can be used, because sources can always obtain additional permits from the environmental authority as long as the standard is not violated at any receptor point. PO will therefore be cost-effective after trade, regardless of the initial

---

134. See Klaassen (1996), which introduces a model with 547 receptors in the context of trade among 38 countries.

135. In principle, the APS covers an infinite number of markets because each source affects an infinite number of receptors in a given regulated area. More detailed discussions of the APS are found in Baumol and Oates (1988: 183–85) and Tietenberg (1985:60–64).

136. Surveys indicate that sufficient local monitoring of receptors for an average American city requires 9–10 monitoring stations, Ludwig et al. (1983).

137. The concepts of pollution offset, non-degradation offset and modified pollution offset were first introduced by Krupnick, Oates and Van de Verg (1983), Atkinson and Tietenberg (1982) and McGartland and Oates (1985), respectively.

distribution of permits, because the free access to 'excess' permits will lead to full exploitation of concentration capacity at each receptor.

On the other hand, this 'first-come-first-serve' principle means that PO cannot be used to improve environmental quality. Polluters can use 'excess' permits for nothing at receptors where environmental quality exceeds the standard, thereby diminishing environmental quality. Even though no ambient standards are violated, this option may be problematic for two reasons. First, there is a risk that sources may affect receptors without monitors or that sources will build high smokestacks so that emissions are transported by local winds to receptors outside the regulated area. Second, environmental groups have traditionally opposed any deterioration in environmental quality. At present, this situation has changed somewhat due to improved monitoring techniques and dispersion models. Many environmental groups now actively promote the use of economic instruments in environmental regulation.[138]

The two other trade rules, the NO and the MPO, were both introduced to remove the risk of a decrease in environmental quality by setting a requirement for the trade ratio. They are similar to the PO except for the addition of trade restrictions. The NO rations the excess permit rights with an emission constraint: no increase in emissions may take place after trade. That is, the buying source is never allowed to emit more than the selling source has reduced – not even in the cases where no concentration standards are exceeded. The MPO is designed so that concentration contributions at the relevant receptors do not increase after trade. Under this rule, the selling source must reduce its emissions to such an extent that the increase in emissions caused by the buying source does not cause increased concentration at any of the relevant receptors. So far, the costs associated with using NO and MPO have been estimated in only two surveys. These concern the reduction of certain particulates in the St. Louis region and Baltimore, respectively, and suggest that the NO is more effective at reducing costs.[139]

Although these trade rules beyond any doubt reduce costs below those that would be incurred under the traditional CAC approach, they still present problems. The degree to which NO and MPO are effective depends on how close the initial distribution of permits is to the maximum of allowable permits at all the receptors – the closer, the better. Further, these rules may lead to significant transaction costs because a buying source may have to engage several selling sources in order not to violate the threshold limits. As the administratively set trade ratio depends on how far the sources are located from the receptor, it may – as was the case with the APS – be hard for sources to orient themselves in the market.[140]

---

138.   See Chapter 5 concerning this change in attitude among environmental groups.

139.   See Atkinson and Tietenberg (1984) and McGartland and Oates (1985).

140.   Stavins (1995). Such administrative distortions can block an active market with simultaneous and multilateral trades, which would allow all increases and reductions among sources in relation

### 3.7.3 Summary

The choice among the five permit market systems is not easy. APS can guarantee both cost-effectiveness and environmental quality at relatively low administrative costs after working out a dispersion model, but transaction costs to polluters are high. In the three 'second-best' trade rules, PO, NO and MPO, administrative costs and transaction costs are both high. These difficulties lead us to consider the potential use of a 'third-best-solution', namely the EPS, for policy-making. As Tietenberg laconically puts it: 'one way to deal with the spatial complexity of pollution control is to ignore it'.[141]

The five permit markets are summarized in Tables 3.1 and 3.2 below:

*Table 3.1: The design of five tradable permit systems for incorporating source location*

| DESIGN | EPS | APS | PO | NO | MPO |
|---|---|---|---|---|---|
| **Standard** | Emissions | Concentration | Concentration | Concentration and emissions | Concentration |
| **Trade ratio** | Predefined (one-to-one ratio) | Predefined (dispersion model ratio) | Individually defined for each trade (dispersion model ratio) | Individually defined for each trade (dispersion model ratio) | Individually defined for each trade (dispersion model ratio) |

*Source:* Tietenberg (1985;1993), Krupnick, Oates and Van de Verg (1983), Atkinson and Tietenberg (1982), McGartland and Oates (1985), Klaassen (1996), and Baumol and Oates (1988).

to the concentration standards. The claim, that a concentration norm must not be violated before trade in each individual trade, is a far stronger condition than a simultaneous and multilateral setting, in which multiple trade activities will equalize each other and create balance (Atkinson and Tietenberg 1991).

141.    Tietenberg (1985:64). As Chapter 4 shows, the use of PO, NO and MPO has in general been unsuccessful in the US whereas the EPS has been applied successfully. A number of dynamic problems arise under the PO, NO, and MPO systems. For example, if an area without pollution adopts the MPO system, economic development is, in effect, banned (McGartland and Oates 1985:222). So, in certain instances, a redefinition of the standard may be relevant so that it is less stringent than the existing level of environmental quality.

*Table 3.2: Theoretical assessment of five tradable permit systems for incorporating source location*

| Permit Markets | Cost-effective | Environmental quality*) | Transaction costs | Administrative costs | Individual approval |
|---|---|---|---|---|---|
| **EPS** | No | Below | Low | Low | No |
| **APS** | Yes | Identical | High | Medium | No |
| **PO** | Yes | Identical | High | High | Yes |
| **NO** | No | Above | High | High | Yes |
| **MPO** | No | Above | High | High | Yes |

*) Actual ecosystem protection compared with target level.

## 3.8  COMPARATIVE METHOD

Is it possible to transfer experiences from politics and policy design from one country to another? Is it, for example, possible to apply knowledge gained from the US experience with permit markets to a Danish or European setting? What is the justification for using a comparative method?

In principle, it seems necessary to analyse all similarities and differences because countries vary. For example, the US political system is dominated by lobbyism and many special interest groups in a two-party system (without much party discipline, however). In contrast, the Scandinavian countries are dominated by corporatism and only a few central interest groups in a multi-party-system. How is it possible then to transfer experience between these two different political systems? Is it possible to justify the selection and comparison of only a few variables in a most complex reality?

In answering this question, the discussion in Section 3.8.1 will present the traditional view of the comparative method, as represented by Lijphart (1975), which holds that all similarities and differences should be investigated. The discussion in Section 3.8.2 will counter this approach by presenting Yin's (1989) innovative way of viewing the comparative case study as an experiment.

### 3.8.1  Traditional Approach: Most Similar and Most Different

Lijphart (1975) represents the traditional approach.[142] First, all similarities must be identified so they can be assumed constant. Second, all differences must be found, and their occurrence must be explained. As such, the Scandinavian countries are ideal for comparison because they are similar in most ways, making it easier to reduce the number of possible explanations for the differences. This is not so easy, however, when comparing such different countries

---

142.  See Lundquist (1980) for a traditional comparison between the US and Sweden. See also Vogel (1987).

as the US and Denmark.

The analysis begins by choosing a causal relationship such that the variation in the dependent variable is maximized and the variation in the independent variable is minimized so that the variation in the remaining independent variables can be used to explain the differences. This choice avoids the situation in which the dependent variable shows no variation, because then nothing can be explained. In this way, according to Lijphart, comparable cases are those in which the most similar variables are chosen as independent variables, whereas the most different variables are chosen as dependent variables.

The resulting variation in the dependent variable, then, forms the basis for an explanation. As such, the researcher can focus on the connections between variables with significant variation and try to explain why this variation takes place. However, this way of dealing with the comparative method is extremely cumbersome and difficult to handle. An infinite number of potentially related variables, and a universe of possible outcomes, make any result questionable.

### 3.8.2  Comparative Method as Experiment

Traditional case study is defined as 'an empirical inquiry that: investigates a contemporary phenomenon within its real-life context; when the boundaries between phenomenon and context are not clearly evident; and in which multiple sources of evidence are used'.[143] These points are examined in more detail and contrasted with elements of three other dominant research strategies: historical analysis, statistical analysis, and case study as experiment. It will be argued that the 'case study' combined with the 'experiment' approach is the most appropriate tool for this book. These two approaches are listed with the approaches of 'history' and 'statistics' in Table 3.3.

In contrast to a case study, historical analyses deal with events that have taken place in the past. Statistical analyses (or surveys) concern quantifiable data where the number of observations is large. An experiment differs from a case study by its laboratory setting. The experiment controls the context and separates a phenomenon from reality by varying only a few variables.

But the case study also concerns non-quantifiable (or qualitative) data, such as interviews or written statements, and thus makes it possible to investigate motivations and perceptions behind an action, such as the incentives for forming an environmental organization. Case studies are found both in political science, for studying international relations, for example, and in economics, for investigating the structure of an industry. In both cases, quantifiable data are insufficient to explain strategic motives.

In general, case studies have been the preferred strategy for explanatory research, that is when 'how' or 'why' questions are being posed, when the investigator has little control over events and when the focus is on a contem-

---

143.   Yin (1989: 23).

porary phenomenon within a real-life context.[144] To 'explain' a phenomenon is to stipulate a set of causal links about it, which case studies do through sets of logical statements. When Lijphart uses this method in a comparative context, however, the logic becomes flooded by the complexity of the analysis.

*Table 3.3: Comparison of four research strategies*

| | **COMPONENTS** | | | |
| | Contemporary phenomenon | Real-life context | Boundaries between phenomenon/context | Multiple sources of evidence |
| --- | --- | --- | --- | --- |
| **STRATEGIES** | | | | |
| Case Study | + | + | − | + |
| History | − | + | − | + |
| Experiment | + | − | + | + |
| Statistics | + | + | − | − |

*Notes:*
+ indicates that the component is included.
− indicates that the component is excluded.

Yin (1989) offers an alternative to this messy, traditional approach to comparative analysis, arguing that a universe is not needed to explain local phenomena. Yin's point is that the single case is analogous to a single experiment in that the number of observations is one. A theory specifies a clear set of propositions and the circumstances within which the propositions are believed to be true. To confirm, challenge, or extend a theory, the case can be used to assess whether its propositions are correct, or whether some alternative set of explanations should be considered. In this way, the case can provide a significant contribution to knowledge and theory-building and can help to re-focus future investigations in an entire field.[145] Consequently, when several cases are empirically tested against the theory, a multiple-case study simply means that an experiment is conducted several times over.

The actual test of the theory is deductively carried out by pattern-matching with the experimental approach.[146] This logic is used to compare an empirically based pattern to the theoretically predicted one. If the patterns coincide, the result does not reject the theory, and it becomes stronger the more confirming cases that are investigated. If a case does not confirm the theory, a rival theory may be reinforced or new theoretical propositions and explanations may be

144.   Yin (1989:13).

145.   Yin (1989:47 and 53). See also Maaløe (1993) for a review of theory-testing and theory-building which is used for developing an explorative integrative approach.

146.   Yin (1989:109).

developed. Such new knowledge ensures the continuation of scientific progress.

The comparative method used in this book is not as clear-cut as described above. It is in fact a combination of both deductive and inductive elements. The starting point is a theoretical model, but the choice of theory and the observations that follow have been influenced by induction. As such, the approach has been shaped by a dynamic interplay between theory and reality. However, as in a pure theory-testing model, the final choice of theory guides the collection of data. In this way, the theory contained in the evaluation model (Section 3.10) will guide the collection of data in the US and Denmark. The experiences in the US with permit markets and in Denmark with a $CO_2$ tax are considered as multiple experiments. The use of economic rationality allows theory to be used both in an explanatory and an explorative (predictive) way. First, the success and failure of applied policies is explained, and second, the potential for introducing new cost-effective and politically attractive policies in both a European and an American setting is predicted.

## 3.9 CONCLUSION

The chapter reviewed the similarities and differences between the tax and the permit market, listed potential market failures in the permit market, and discussed the administrative problems of incorporating source location. It was suggested that the complexity of the trade rules for defining and enforcing property rights, when source location is incorporated, would create substantial administrative costs, and this pointed to the option of ignoring source location.

Then the political argument for the use of a grandfathered permit market and the design of a revenue-neutral auction was further developed. Target levels, such as the Danish case of a 20% $CO_2$ reduction or the US case of 50% $SO_2$ reduction, may be achieved at very low costs for industry when the *MC* curve is linear in the relevant range. The use of this assumption regarding marginal costs offers some important insights for comparing the sizes of costs in a tax and a permit market approach. In the Danish $CO_2$ case, under this assumption, the tax solution is nine times more costly for polluters than is the permit market, and a grandfathered permit market would be cheaper than the existing Danish $CO_2$ tax (which has been proposed to rise sixfold). In this case – when shifting from the actual $CO_2$ tax in Denmark to a permit market – private industry would save one-third of its present costs. Similarly, in the case of the US, it is, under the assumption of linear marginal costs, one-third as costly for industry to use a grandfathered permit market than tax payments without any refund systems.

As the market can be initiated by grandfathering, so can the auction. The potential use of revenue-neutral auctions in relation to discriminative (multi-priced) and non-discriminative (single-priced) designs was discussed. The results pointed towards the use of a non-discriminative auction to secure a single price signal to the market. Finally, because the American, Danish and European cases can be considered multiple experiments testing the same theoretical approach, it is possible to transfer the US experience to a European setting and vice versa.

## 3.10  EVALUATION MODEL

An evaluation model will be used to discover whether a grandfathered permit market is workable in practice. The model is constructed below in four parts. Parts I and II are descriptive whereas Parts III and IV are explanatory.[147]

The design of the market will determine the performance of the market. Part I describes the design whereas Part II describes actual performance.

The design may result in market failure due to economic, administrative and political distortions. These three distortions may explain why performance turned out good or bad. Part III offers an evaluation of how distortions have influenced market performance.

### I  Design

The design of the permit market is described by using a set of five variables. The first variable is a set labelled *target level*. It contains information about the pollutant and the reduction goal; the period in which the program is applied; the program's location; and the potential cost savings from using a permit market rather than, for example, a traditional CAC approach for achieving a given target level.

The second variable is the *target group*. It contains information on who can take part in the trading; the number of sources; the concentration of permit holdings among sources; and the variation in marginal reduction costs.

The third variable is labelled *distribution rule*. This variable defines how the permits are distributed.

The fourth variable is that of *trade rules*. A trade rule is a restriction on trade that limits the property rights conveyed by a permit. Some trade rules may be necessary for reaching the defined target level and for ensuring that no ambient standards are violated while trade takes place, that is that 'hot spots' are not created.

The fifth variable, connected to the trade rules, is labelled *control system*. The control system defines how the regulator intends to monitor and sanction violations of the rules.

### II  Performance

Permit market performance in practice is, following the independent variable of design, characterized by a set of four effect variables.

The first variable is labelled *trade activity*. It contains the number of trades;

---

147.   This subsection draws heavily on Svendsen (1998a)

the price generated by the market; and whether a high concentration of buyers or sellers poses a risk of incomplete competition and strategic behaviour.

The second variable is *cost savings*. It contains information on the cost savings resulting from trade and the trade option compared to the situation without trade.

The third variable is labelled *innovation*. It reveals dynamic information about market-stimulated innovation and investments in new reduction technology.

The fourth variable is *environmental impact*. It indicates whether any impact can be measured at present, and, if so, whether any receptors are violated.

## III Evaluation

In explaining why actual market performance turned out as it did, a set of four variables is used in the evaluation.

First, *competitiveness* in the market is necessary to avoid strategic behaviour.

Second, *property rights* to the permits must be defined and enforced by the administrator to make the market work.

Third, *transaction costs* must be kept low to allow trade in the market. These may include costs such as bargaining costs, broker compensation, fees, the expense of collecting information relevant to the transaction, and the expense of finding a trade partner and acquiring administrative approval.

Fourth, *lobbyism* among rational organized interests must be taken into account. These groups may distort market performance by trying to influence the design and the definition of property rights in their redistributional favour.

The evaluation model is summarized in Table 3.4.

This model is applied in Chapter 4, which evaluates the US experience with permit markets in relation to the first three evaluation variables of competitiveness, property rights and transaction costs.

The fourth evaluation variable, lobbyism, is empirically investigated in Chapter 5, which continues the discussion of the US experience. The discussions in these chapters lead to the final investigation in Chapter 6. Here, part I in the evaluation model is used to design a potential $CO_2$ market in Denmark and in the European Union.

*Table 3.4: Evaluation model for permit markets*

---

**I DESIGN**
**Target level**
  pollutant
  standards
  period
  location
  potential savings
**Target group**
  number
  concentration
  marginal reduction costs
**Distribution rule**
**Trade rules**
**Control system**

**II PERFORMANCE**
**Trade activity**
**Cost savings**
**Innovation**
**Environmental impact**

**III EVALUATION**
**Competitiveness**
**Property rights**
  definition
  enforcement
**Transaction costs**
**Lobbyism**

---

# 4　US Permit Markets

## 4.1　OVERVIEW

The purpose of this chapter is to create a systematic overview of permit markets in the US.[148] Eight US programs using permit markets in environmental regulation are reviewed in terms of economic and administrative distortions for performance.

This chapter traces the competitiveness of the US permit markets, investigates the definition and enforcement of property rights, and presents information regarding associated transaction costs. It is shown that trade rules and administrative requirements have been essential because the pollutants dealt with have local impacts. The trade rules have been designed so as to avoid 'hot spots', or violations of ambient standards. These rules are thought to determine the size of transaction costs, that is all the costs of a permit transaction associated with both the sources and the regulator's activities.[149]

In general, most attempts to incorporate source location have failed due to the need for individual administrative controls. Therefore, the recommendation to US and European policy-makers is to ignore source localization and the risk of creating hot spots, as has been done in the more recent, improved designs.

The eight US permit markets have been implemented at two different levels. Four of them have been implemented on a national level by the US Environmental Protection Agency (EPA); the other four have been implemented on the state level. They can be grouped according to air or water pollution. Sources fall into two main groups: point sources and non-point sources. Point sources are readily identifiable and measurable, such as pipes or ditches. Non-point sources are neither readily identifiable nor measurable, such as urban rainwater run-off or run-off from agricultural irrigation.[150]

All four programs on the national level and one on the state level are connected with air.

The first is the Emission Trading Program (ETP), which has dealt with a

---

148.　There are numerous other small-scale experiments taking place in the tradable permit system in the US (see for example Elman et al. 1992 and Carlin 1992). However, the eight programs chosen here are by far the biggest and most ambitious.

149.　The trade rules for incorporating source location were analysed in Section 3.7. Two surveys indicate that a permit market without restrictions on trade will result in extensive trade (see Russel 1981 and Maloney and Brady 1988).

150.　Federal Water Pollution Control Act (Clean Water Act), 33 U.S.C.A §§ 502(14) and 1362(14).

number of air pollutants since 1974. The second (lead trading) concerns the trading of lead used in gasoline; it was started in 1982. The third (CFC and halon trading) aims to meet the target levels for ozone-depleting substances. The fourth, the Acid Rain Program (ARP), is very large and regulates $SO_2$ emission from electric utilities all over the US. The ARP uses an interesting reserve mechanism for direct sale and an annual auction. The fifth program, which is administered at the state level, is the Regional Clean Air Incentives Market (RECLAIM) in the Los Angeles (California) area. It was initiated to regulate $NO_x$ and reactive organic compounds. Both the ARP and RECLAIM started in 1994. Their designs are largely based on experience from previous programs.

The three remaining programs concern water pollution and operate at the state level. They are the Fox River (Wisconsin), Dillon Reservoir (Colorado) and Tar-Pamlico River Basin (North Carolina) programs. A general overview of these eight is provided below in Table 4.1.

*Table 4.1: The US experience with permit markets, 1974–1998*

| Program | Target level | Period | Location | Target Group |
|---|---|---|---|---|
| **I. AIR** | | | | |
| **ETP** | National Standards | 1974–? | US | Industry |
| **Lead** | Lead phase-out | 1982–1987 | US | Refineries |
| **CFC/Halon** | CFC/Halon phase-out | 1989–1996 | US | Industry |
| **ARP** | 50% $SO_2$ | 1990–2000 | US | Electric utilities |
| **RECLAIM** | 75% $NO_x$, 60% $SO_x$ | 1994–2003 | California | Industry |
| **II. WATER** | | | | |
| **Fox River** | State Standards | 1981–? | Wisconsin | Paper/pulp mills |
| **Dillon** | State Standards | 1984–? | Colorado | Point/non-point |
| **Tar-Pamlico** | 36% nutrients | 1991–2004 | North Carolina | Point/non-point |

*Source:* Compiled by the author from Tietenberg (1985), Hahn and Hester (1989a;1989b), Dennis (1993), Broadbent (1993) and EPA (1992a).

The design and performance of the eight programs are compared in the sections that follow to see if any general pattern in the design variables can explain the programs' performance. In cases where parallel information under the different programs is not available, only available information is listed.

# I. Air

The US Environmental Protection Agency (EPA) has defined two sets of air pollution standards, namely the National Ambient Air Quality Standards (NAAQS) and technology-based standards. The NAAQS have been set for seven air pollutants specified in the Clean Air Act of 1970:[151] 1) $SO_x$ (sulfur oxides), 2) $NO_x$ (nitrogen oxides), 3) particulates, 4) CO (carbon monoxide), 5) HC (Hydrocarbons, also referred to as volatile organic compounds (VOCs)), 6) lead and 7) ozone.[152]

The NAAQS target levels were, in many areas, more stringent than actual air quality. Still, they were supposed to have been met for all the specified pollutants in 1975.[153] The Clean Air Act divided the US into 247 geographical areas for the purpose of controlling air quality. Many areas, especially the urban ones, did not meet the NAAQS on schedule.

An attainment area is one of these areas that meets the NAAQS for a specific pollutant, whereas a non-attainment area is one that does not meet a particular NAAQS. The 1977 Amendments to the Clean Air Act required individual states that were in violation of one or more of the standards to develop State Implementation Plans (SIP) and thereby demonstrate which measures they would take to reach the target levels.[154]

---

151.    The original Clean Air Act of 1970 included ozone and lead as well. The law recognized two main types of air pollutants: criteria and hazardous pollutants. 'Criteria' refers to the fact that the act requires the EPA to produce 'criteria documents' to be used in setting NAAQS. Unlike the criteria pollutants, small doses of 'hazardous' toxic pollutants can produce serious health effects. The seven hazardous pollutants listed are asbestos, beryllium, mercury, vinyl chloride, benzene, radionuclides and arsenic. Whereas criteria pollutants exist virtually everywhere and affect large numbers of people, hazardous pollutants are found only in certain locations (Tietenberg 1985:2–4).

152.    $SO_x$ is a corrosive gas produced when fossil fuels are burned. $NO_x$ is produced when fossil fuels are burned at very high temperatures. Electric utilities, industrial plants and transportation vehicles are the main sources for $SO_x$ and $NO_x$ emissions, which may return to the earth from the atmosphere as acid components of rain or snow. Particulates are particles of solid or liquid substances in a wide range of sizes, which typically are produced together with $SO_x$ and $NO_x$. CO is a colourless, odourless, poisonous gas, slightly lighter than air, that is produced by the incomplete burning of carbon in fuels (a complete burning will result in $CO_2$). HC, like CO, represents unburned fuel, but is not toxic in the same way. It is a major pollutant because under the influence of sunlight, it combines with $NO_x$ to form photochemical oxidants or smog. The word smog is created by combining 'smoke' and 'fog' and consists of a complex mixture of secondary pollutants including ozone (an unstable, toxic form of oxygen), $NO_2$, peroxyacyl nitrates, aldehydes, and acrolein. Smog causes eye and lung irritation, damage to vegetation, offensive odour, and thick haze (Findley and Farber. 1992:97–98).

153.    In contrast to this national air pollution approach, the Clean Water Act of 1972 delegates the setting of water quality standards to the individual states because the effects from water pollution in general are more localized.

154.    Until the Clean Air Act of 1990, states chose their own way of demonstrating continuous efforts for reaching the NAAQS. Most states chose to use the trade rules for permit markets recommended by the EPA. The new Clean Air Act of 1990 now makes it obligatory, in some cases, for states to use permit markets in dealing with their hot spot areas (see Elman et al. 1992).

The second set of standards consists of three technology-based ones. They define control-technology for each of the seven air pollutants and represent the traditional CAC approach to regulating emission levels, in which no trade is allowed to circumvent the standards. The three technology-based standards are the Lowest Achievable Emission Reduction (LAER) standard, the Best Available Control Technology (BACT) standard and the Reasonable Available Control Technology (RACT) standard. LAER is the most stringent standard, BACT is the next most stringent, and RACT is the least.

The technologies satisfying the BACT and LAER requirements are determined by the states on a case-by-case basis. To prevent states from giving in to industry pressure, the US Congress defined a national floor for LAER and BACT by introducing the New Source Performance Standard (NSPS). Neither LAER nor BACT can be lower than NSPS, or they will automatically be replaced by NSPS. Together with the trade rules in question, the technology-based standards serve as means for reaching the NAAQS.

The 1970 Clean Air Act Amendments distinguish between existing, new and modified sources. Existing sources are those that existed when the trade systems started in the mid-seventies. All sources built since then are new. Modified sources are alterations of existing ones that have led to significant increases in emissions.

The two groups of standards are intertwined. The relevant technology-based standard depends both on area status (attainment or non-attainment) and source type (existing, modified or new).

When determining which technological standard to apply, the regulator first must determine whether the maximum ambient standard, the NAAQS, for a given pollutant is exceeded. If so, the area is designated a non-attainment area. If not, the area is designated an attainment area. This distinction has implications for which technology-based standard is applied. In a non-attainment area, a new source faces the most stringent technology-based standard, LAER. In an attainment area, a new source faces the less stringent BACT. The same is the case for a modified source.

Existing sources are better off. In a non-attainment area, an existing source faces the least stringent RACT. In an attainment area, the existing source faces no standard. However, states are obliged to maintain existing air quality. This is normally done in both attainment and non-attainment areas by using permit markets. Even though the resulting state standards can vary a lot, they are typically no more stringent than RACT and may be less.[155] In general, new and modified sources must meet more stringent technology-based standards than existing sources do. This stricter limit on emissions from new sources is an effort to reduce overall emissions.

---

155.   Hahn and Hester (1989a:370).

## 4.2 EMISSIONS TRADING PROGRAM

The Emissions Trading Program (ETP) is extremely complex and severely marked by regulatory changes and ad hoc solutions. The four trade rules in the program gradually evolved as administrative emergency solutions to problems that arose from the conflicting goals of economic growth and pollution control. In short, the trade rules make it possible for new or modified sources to locate in 'hot spot' areas, which would otherwise have been closed to them.

### 4.2.1 Design

#### 4.2.1.1 Target level
Target level is defined in terms of the ambient and the technology-based standards listed above in Section 4.1.

The potential cost savings from trade are high. Using a permit market, rather than a traditional CAC approach for reaching the ambient target levels gives the theoretical potential of saving up to 90%.[156]

#### 4.2.1.2 Target group
The target group consists of any major stationary source that otherwise would have been controlled under CAC regulation because of emissions of one of the criteria pollutants. Only sources within the target group may take part in the market. The differences in marginal reduction costs for the different pollutants are substantial.[157]

#### 4.2.1.3 Distribution rule
Whenever a source reduces its actual emission below the emission limit, the source can apply to the control authority for certification of the 'emission surplus' as an Emission Reduction Credit (ERC). An ERC can be described as currency. The trade rules of the ETP govern how the ERCs can be spent. To receive certification, the emission reduction must be surplus, enforceable, permanent and quantifiable.[158] This distribution rule corresponds to grandfathering, because historical emission rights are handed over for free; no financial transfers to or from the government are involved. In practice, this distribution rule will depend on sources' emission rates, capacity utilization and operating hours, and will be determined on a case-by-case basis. For attainment areas, grandfathering is based on the lower of the actual or allowable emissions. In non-attainment-areas, grandfathering is based on the emissions from the SIP.

The existing CAC infrastructure is the basis on which permits are historically grandfathered in the market. The only difference is that now it is possible to

156.  See GAO (1982).
157.  Ibid.
158.  Tietenberg (1985:7).

trade and exchange permits. No announced devaluation of permit value takes place. As the next section shows, reductions take place by trade rules that require the selling source to reduce more emissions than the buyer gets the right to emit.

### 4.2.1.4  Trade rules

The ETP consists of four trade rules, or ways in which sources are allowed to trade their ERCs: netting, offset, bubble and banking.[159] Trades must be for the same pollutant, and interstate trading is allowed only as long as the requirements of the more stringent state are met.[160]

Netting was introduced in 1974. Netting is optional and available only to modified sources. It allows these sources to avoid the more stringent technological standards applied to new sources, that is, LAER in non-attainment areas and BACT in attainment areas. Netting means that new emissions from plant modification are met with an equal decrease in emissions from another source within the same plant. The trade is, by definition, internal, and the trade-ratio, when defined as the amount of reduced emissions divided by the increase in new emissions, is one.[161]

In contrast, the offset rule applies to new sources. It was introduced in 1976. Offsetting is mandatory for new sources both in non-attainment areas (when meeting LAER) and in attainment areas (when meeting BACT). The offset rule allows plants to locate new sources only if they can offset their new emissions by reducing emissions from existing sources by even larger amounts. This offset can be obtained through internal trading, as in the netting case (among different smokestacks within the same plant), but also through external trading (between two independent plants). Under the offset rule, the technology-based standards cannot be avoided and replaced by trade.

The bubble rule applies to existing plants with several emission sources. Introduced in 1979, it is optional for existing plants when trying to meet RACT (in non-attainment areas) and state standards (to prevent any significant deterioration) in attainment areas. Its purpose was to give existing sources the same trade options as were available to new sources under the offset rule.[162] An

---

159.  The following description is based on the rules that the EPA stated in 1986 in its final ETP policy (EPA, Emissions Trading Policy Statement: General Principles for Creation, Banking and Use of Emission Reduction Credits, 51 Fed. Reg. 43,814, 43,829 1986).

160.  Note that states are not required to use the trade rules. They are free to change the trade rules or invent their own to meet the NAAQS. However, virtually all 50 states do allow some emission trading activities (Hahn and Hester 1989a:369).

161.  Modified sources choose not to use netting, then offsets are mandatory in non-attainment areas and the LAER cannot be avoided by trade (Hahn and Hester 1989a:370).

162.  Bubbles originally allowed only trade between existing sources in attainment areas. In 1982, the bubble policy was revised and extended to non-attainment areas. Also, all proposals for bubbles had to be submitted by states to the EPA for approval. In 1981, the EPA began to approve general 'bubble rules' that enabled states to approve bubbles themselves. Several states now have such rules.

imaginary bubble is placed over the multi-source plant so that emission levels for the various smokestacks may be adjusted in a cost-effective manner such that the aggregate limit is not exceeded.

According to these rules, when modifying a source, existing plants only have to meet the standards for existing sources (RACT in non-attainment and state standard in attainment areas), not the standards applied for modified or new sources.[163] But the bubble concept differs from netting in three important respects. First, it does not require that technology-based standards on individual smokestacks are met; only the total emissions from the plant count. Second, the bubble can be used for external trade. Third, the trade ratio will typically be higher for bubbles than for netting so that more must be reduced than newly emitted.

In the earlier phases of the ETP program, that is before 1986, the general focus was on emissions reduction.[164] Regulators chose the 'easy' solution and demanded that emissions not be allowed to increase rather than performing ambient tests. Typically, emissions were reduced because regulators set the trade ratio so that target levels for concentration could be reached.

As a result, in many non-attainment areas, the starting position for trade was already above the threshold for allowed concentration – one or more receptors had been violated. The regulator's goal, consequently, has been not just to fix environmental quality, but to improve it. The early ETP system, therefore, most resembles Non-degradation Offset (NO) because it does not allow emissions to increase after trade; rather it calls for an asymmetrical trade-ratio, in which emissions are reduced more than the new increase. In other words, the potential for dispersing pollution, as promised by the models, is not realized because environmental quality is fixed by an inappropriate focus on reducing emissions rather than on concentration.

At present, bubble rules, formulated by the EPA in 1986, mandate that the trade ratio should be set at 1:1.2 at least, so that emissions be cut back by at least 20%. Most important is that an ambient test, that is a test to show that the trade has no significant negative impact on air quality, may also be required. In general, an ambient test applies when the pollutants are particulates, $SO_2$, CO or lead. For VOC and $NO_x$, no such test is required. The test requires air quality modelling unless the emissions increases are below certain minimum levels, or unless sources are located within 250 metres distance and certain other conditions are met.[165] In the cases where an ambient test is applied, the ETP resembles the Modified Pollution Offset (MPO) because no increase in concentration contributions is allowed after trade. This attempt to fix the existing air quality

163.  Whether it is allowable to use bubbles and external trade for significantly modified existing sources in non-attainment areas and attainment areas, and thereby avoid new source standards, depends solely on state practice.

164.  Tietenberg (1985:86–89).

165.  Klaassen (1996).

level at its pre-trade level means again, as in the NO case, that administrative approval must be obtained for each trade.

The final trade rule, banking, is not really a 'trade' rule, but rather a 'store' rule. It allows existing plants to save or 'bank' an ERC for subsequent use (in the bubble, offset, or netting programs). It was introduced together with the bubble policy in 1979, and the EPA has established guidelines for banking programs. However, states must set up their own rules and administer the rules governing banking themselves.

Only offsets are mandatory, and they are applied only to new sources. Under the offset rule, new sources cannot avoid LAER by trading in non-attainment areas or BACT by trading in attainment areas. Netting and bubbles are optional so that modified sources may use netting, and existing sources may use bubbles, thus avoiding the most stringent technology-based standards by trade.

The four trade rules and their role in the ETP are summarized in Table 4.2 and Table 4.3.

*Table 4.2: ETP trade rules*

| Trade rules | Year established | Source covered | Trade ratio*) | Trade |
|---|---|---|---|---|
| *Netting* | 1974 | Modified | 1 | Internal |
| *Offset* | 1976 | New | $\geq 1$ | Internal/External |
| *Bubble* | 1979 | Existing | $\geq 1.2$ | Internal/External |
| *Banking* | 1979 | Existing | – | Internal/External |

*) Ratio is defined as reduced emission/increased emission.
*Source:* Based on Hahn and Hester (1989a:368–71; 1989b:114–36); Tietenberg (1985:2–9 and 117).

*Table 4.3: Area, source, technology standard and trade rules in ETP*

| Area* | Source | Technology Standard | Trade Rule | Mandatory? | Replace Standard by Trade?** |
|-------|--------|---------------------|------------|------------|------------------------------|
| N-A | New | LAER | Offset | Yes | No |
| N-A | Modified | LAER | Netting | No | Yes |
| N-A | Existing | RACT | Bubble | No | Yes |
| A | New | BACT | Offset | No | No |
| A | Modified | BACT | Netting | No | Yes |
| A | Existing | (State) | Bubble | No | Yes |

*Notes:*
* N-A = Non-Attainment
A = Attainment
** Including use of banked permits.

*Source:*  Based on Hahn and Hester (1989a:368–71; 1989b:114–36); Tietenberg (1985:2–9 and 117).

### 4.2.1.5  Control system

The control system for the ETP builds on the CAC control mechanisms with regular inspection and traditional legal prosecution. Each time a firm violates the rules, it is moved up into a more stringent control category and monitored with more frequent inspections. Violations of the rules, when detected, result in fines.

The states must continually demonstrate their efforts to comply with the NAAQS. If they fail to do so, the EPA may take over the regulation. For example, EPA has warned the local regulators in the Los Angeles area in California that such action may be taken if violations of the NAAQS continue.

### 4.2.2  Performance

#### 4.2.2.1  Trade activity

In the period 1974–1986, the number of actual trades has been approximately 8,000 in the netting program, 3,000 in the offset program, and 250 in the bubble program. There have been approximately 100 cases in the banking program.[166] The existence of trade activity and the substantial cost savings that have been realized to date seem to prove that the ETP works, but the number of trades has

166.   For accounts on trade activity, see Hahn and Hester (1989a:373; 1989b:119–36; 1987:49–50), Tietenberg (1985:7–9 and 50), Bohm and Russel (1985:427–28), Raufer and Feldman (1987:17–21), Pearce and Turner (1990:118).

been disappointingly small. The volume of emissions trading has averaged below 1% of the potential that could have been traded.[167] Furthermore, most trade activity has been internal. External trade amounts to only about 10% of all offsets and about 2% of all bubbles, and netting is by definition internal. With respect to publicly owned electric utilities, many either made or received external trade offers, but none of the offered trades were realized.[168] These plants have only made use of internal trading opportunities. This pattern is especially disappointing because the potential benefits from trade are larger for external trades than for internal trades. Most trade seems to have taken place in California; approximately 90% of all offsets have occurred there.[169]

How defined has the price signal been? Out of 200 known offset trades in the Los Angeles basin, trading prices are known for 48. Prices range from less than $100 to over $700 per ton per year from reactive organic gases (ROG) with a slightly smaller range for $NO_x$.[170] Prices exhibited wide variation over time. For example, the lowest price for ROG in 1991 was $43 while the highest was $712.[171] These facts confirm that the market has been 'thin' and that the price signal has been diffuse.

### 4.2.2.2  Cost savings
Since 1975, cost savings formed about 4% of the total reduction costs.[172]

### 4.2.2.3  Innovation
No exact estimates of investments in the development of new knowledge and technology associated with the ETP are to be found, but the program is believed to have encouraged technological progress to a limited degree. Broad scale innovation, however, has not taken place because of the availability of relatively cheap emission control opportunities and industry's slow response to the ETP.[173]

### 4.2.2.4  Environmental impact
The effect on environmental quality has been neutral, both in terms of emissions and ambient air quality.[174] Hot spots still exist.

---

167.   Hahn (1989b:102).
168.   Tietenberg (1985:53ff).
169.   Anderson et al. (1990:16).
170.   ROG is the acronym currently used in Los Angeles for reactive hydrocarbons (HCs).
171.   Foster and Hahn (1994:9–11).
172.   Klaassen (1996).
173.   Klaassen (1996).
174.   Hahn and Hester (1989a:375)

### 4.2.3  Evaluation

#### 4.2.3.1  Competitiveness
The precise number of sources potentially involved in the ETP is not known, but the number is very high because all major stationary sources in the US may participate. As such, the market structure can be assumed to be competitive.

#### 4.2.3.2  Property rights
In summary, the target level is defined in terms of ambient standards, and the trade rules are defined so that reduction is accomplished by trade ratios larger than one and by more stringent technological standards for new sources than for existing sources. As such, the ETP regulation clearly favours existing sources. Existing sources can use the bubble both for internal and external trade and can enjoy, as such, the most flexibility. However, their incentive to trade is less because they face the most lenient standards.

The main trade restrictions in relation to the transfer of full property rights can be subdivided into six groups: *i*) emission reduction credits (ERCs) are the only currency; *ii*) stringent technology based standards are required for new sources; *iii*) new sources cannot use bubbles; *iv*) banking has not been well implemented; *v*) the trade ratio is typically more than one; and *vi*) permits are arbitrarily confiscated. Let us look at each of these six groupings in detail.

*i)  Emission reduction credits (ERC) are the only currency*
ERCs are the only legal currency in the ETP, which means that permits from plants that have been closed are confiscated without compensation. It is not possible to store these, and it is only possible to trade reductions, not permits as a whole. In this way, permits can be obtained only after emissions are reduced or when buying a plant and taking over existing permits.[175]

*ii)  More stringent standards are required for new sources*
Besides the fact that new sources must ensure that existing plants reduce emissions by more than emissions are increased, they also are forced to invest in the newest technology. This is because a more stringent standard is in effect for new sources. As a result, a new source cannot be established by the purchase of permits alone. This limits the demand for permits; the amount of permits bought and sold would rise if LAER (BACT) controls were not required for new sources in non-attainment (attainment) areas.

*iii)  New sources cannot use bubbles*
Furthermore, bubbles are only allowed for existing facilities, not new ones. Only an existing facility can avoid the LAER standard by trading emissions internally or in the area covered by the bubble. This is in line with the more

---

175.  Raufer and Feldman (1987: 27).

stringent standards for new sources. New plant construction is consequently reduced and so is the demand for permits.

### iv) Banking has not been well implemented
In general, banking and the right to store permits have not been well implemented. As of 1986, the EPA had approved banking rules for Oregon, Missouri, Rhode Island, and the Puget Sound in Washington. Eight additional areas had adopted and submitted banking rules to the EPA for approval. Only the bank at Louisville, Kentucky (one of the eight areas with adopted rules) is active still. Very few restrictions apply to the use of banked credits, and 18 firms have deposited credits worth 26,000 tons per year of pollutants. The bank has also mediated 9 external and 19 internal offsets. Other banks have been inactive for several reasons. For example, the bank in Rhode Island is located in an attainment area, so there is only a small demand for permits. Strict limitations are placed on the use of banked credits in other areas. This is mainly a problem of administrative practice; banking facilitates a smoothly functioning market by maintaining a public ledger that enables buyers to locate potential sellers easily.[176]

### v) The trade ratio is typically more than one
The facts that the trade ratio may be changed arbitrarily by administrators, that new sources in non-attainment areas are subject to more stringent standards, and that the bubble concept is in effect for existing plants, only result in incomplete transfers of property right. For example, the trade ratio for offsets discriminates against new sources in non-attainment areas because administrators have so far claimed that external trade should ensure a continued reduction in emissions. This restriction encourages sources to save emission reductions for later expansion, where the ratio will be one-to-one, rather than engaging in external trade. If the trade ratio were one-to-one for any trade and the same standards were in effect for existing and new sources, permit rights would be fully transferable.

### vi) Permits are arbitrarily confiscated
Administrators tend to confiscate emission credits if they are not sold immediately. The situation may be compared to a private market in which the state confiscates the product if a buyer is not found straight away.[177] Current administrative practice does not, therefore, encourage the creation of emission credits. Holding permits is risky. For example, the probability of confiscation or sudden administrative devaluation of permit value is likely to increase if air quality is worsened or politicians choose to tighten target levels. Time limits on the validity of banked ERCs also create the potential for confiscation.[178]

---

176.   Hahn and Hester (1989b:130).
177.   Tietenberg (1985:191).
178.   Hahn and Hester (1989b:130).

All these barriers to trade are caused by ill-defined property rights. Plants cannot dispose freely of their permits, and there is uncertainty regarding the permits' future value. Understanding these problems is crucial to understanding the emission trading that has taken place so far. New sources have the greatest incentive to use emission trading since they are subject to the most stringent limits. Existing sources enjoy most flexibility in using emission trading, but have less incentive to do so since they are subject to less stringent limits.[179]

The trade restrictions listed above illustrate how the transfer of property rights has been limited in the ETP. Full transferability of property rights would require the removal of legal and administrative barriers. In particular, the following conditions would be needed: no individual approval would have to be undertaken; the currency would be permits and not reduction credits, so that, for example, permits from 'shutdowns' would be tradable; technology-based standards would not be used; new sources would be allowed to use bubbles; the trade-ratio would consistently be one-to-one; banking and the right to store permits would be implemented; and administrators would be prohibited from intervening arbitrarily and changing the value of permits in circulation.

In a simultaneous and multilateral setting without individual approval, the multiple trade activities are meant to equalize each other so that one trade that would violate an ambient standard is neutralized by other counterbalancing trades. If trade still threatened to lead to the violation of ambient standards, this situation could be avoided by announcing a devaluation of permit value over a well-defined period of time and by defining the trade direction so that no hot spots would be likely to occur. These points have been incorporated in more recent air programs, as described in the next sections.

Enforcement under the permit systems has been insufficient. Even though polluters face significant fines for violations, fines have in general not been assessed due to complicated procedural rules.[180] Because control has been based on regular inspections and traditional legal prosecution, it has been possible to cheat. Furthermore, local authorities may try to protect firms in their regions by allowing violations.

### 4.2.3.3 Transaction costs

In the early phases of the ETP, it was doubtless difficult to find a potential trade partner. For example, Pacific Gas & Electric, a utility company in California, sponsored a study at the cost of $56,000 in the early eighties to find offsets in the San Francisco Bay area. After 10 months of searching, only one source was willing to sell, even though more than 200 major sources had the ability to offer ERCs, and the outcome was not favourable. Pacific Gas & Electric lost $70,000

---

179.   Ironically, the rules for not trading shutdown permits and for more stringent standards for new sources prolong the life of old, heavy polluting sources, for example the ten most restrictive states in the US were exposed to 27% more $SO_2$ emission among utilities than they would have been without restrictions (see Maloney and Brady 1988).

180.   Tietenberg (1985).

in option money when the regulatory agency disallowed the offsets it was going to purchase; the project was cancelled.[181]

More recent trends of transaction costs in the ETP are available from California. ETP trade activity in the Los Angeles basin has been analysed carefully in a study by Foster and Hahn (1994). They find that half of all proposed trades fall through during the negotiation process, which is marked by considerable uncertainty. To avoid the search process, a plant may trade internally or obtain a list of credits deposited in the permit 'bank' established by the local regulator and thereby identify a potential trade partner. A source may also use a broker. Brokerage fees are levied in proportion to the value of the trade at a rate that can vary between 4% and 25%.[182]

The administrative process of approving trades is slow. It takes at present between 5 and 12 months; in the early years of the programs, it took up to 29 months.[183] Furthermore, significant administrative fees have been attached to a trade. In the ETP, buyers and sellers have had few opportunities to identify each other independently; therefore consultants and brokers have received substantial fees for their assistance in the search for available permits.

Fees to the regulator can amount to $2,900 per trade, and additional fees are levied for certifying ERCs ($1,700), banking them ($900), and reissuing them in smaller units ($900). Also, costs ranging between $7,500 and $15,000 can be incurred for preparation of the substantial supporting documentation required. The joint transaction costs for two partners to bring about a trade is thus typically about $25,000. The transaction cost may easily exceed the permit price. If an ambient test is needed with air quality modelling, then even further costs are imposed on the contracting sources. But most troubling of all, the administrative approval process creates a significant element of uncertainty. Only about 20% of all trades have been fully approved as proposed. Of the remaining 80%, half were rejected out of hand, and the other half were subject to a variety of downward revisions.[184] Determining how much the selling source has to reduce emissions and which benchmark the reduction should be measured against is problematic.

Overall, due to the individual approval procedures in the NO and MPO systems, the ETP experience displays a picture of confusion and high transaction costs which has lead to low, sequential and bilateral trade activity, where individual trades take place at different points in time and where sources cannot trade with more than one trading partner simultaneously.[185] Because the emission permit price varies with location and has to be settled by authorities, it is difficult for buyers and sellers to orient themselves in the market. The results

---

181.   Raufer and Feldman (1987:28–29).
182.   Foster and Hahn (1994:21–22).
183.   Opschoor and Vos (1989) and Foster and Hahn (1994:22).
184.   Foster and Hahn (1994:22–23).
185.   See Atkinson and Tietenberg (1991)

from this section are summarized in Table 4.7 at the end of this chapter.

## 4.3 LEAD TRADING PROGRAM

The lead trading program ran as a national program over a clearly defined six-year period from 1982 until 1987. It was introduced to facilitate a drastic phase-out of lead in gasoline produced by the oil refineries.

Lead has been added to gasoline to increase the octane level and to prevent engine 'knocking' since the 1920s.

### 4.3.1 Design

#### 4.3.1.1 Target level
Health effects of airborne lead – along with the fact that leaded gasoline can cause the catalytic converters in cars to malfunction – made the EPA react in 1974.[186] The EPA limited the allowable lead content in gasoline to 1.7 grams per gallon beginning January 1, 1975 and tightened the standard to 1.1 grams per gallon in 1982, 0.5 grams per gallon in 1985, and 0.1 grams in 1986.[187]

This was virtually a phase-out. Given that 0.1 grams is the minimum lead content that many older cars require to protect their engine valve seats, the EPA did not allow lead rights trading after the upper limit of 0.1 grams was reached in 1987.[188]

In this way, announced devaluations of the lead permit were implemented. The regulator gradually tightened the technological standards for the amount of lead added. No estimates on potential cost savings for the program are available.

#### 4.3.1.2 Target group
The target group for this program was all major refineries in the US. The definition was broad including anyone who manufactured gasoline. In 1985, there were 195 'real' refineries in the market, so the number of participants was already quite high.[189] However, the number grew much higher due to the broad definition of refineries. Unintentionally, the program permitted facilities blending alcohol into leaded gasoline to claim and sell lead rights based upon their activity. This new industry of 'alcohol blenders' increased sharply in number from 1984, but generated only a small quantity of lead rights.[190]

---

186.   EPA, Regulation of Fuel and Fuel Additives: Lead Phase Down, 49 Fed. Reg. 31,032 (1984).

187.   Anderson et al. (1990:24–25).

188.   See Hahn and Hester (1989a:381) and Anderson et al. (1990:26).

189.   GAO (1986:11). The EPA also applied restrictions on lead content of imported gasoline and gasoline components beginning in 1982, so from then importers were treated in the same fashion as refiners (Anderson et al. 1990:24).

190.   By the end of 1984, there were about 100 'alcohol blenders'. The 'free credits' combined with banking made the number of alcohol blenders grow to over 900 by late 1985 (Nussbaum

Refineries were technologically stratified by age, and the geographical development of the industry had followed movements in population. So, older refineries tended to be located in the east and newer ones tended to be located on the west coast. As such, significant differences existed in marginal reduction costs for lead.

### 4.3.1.3  Distribution rule

The lead permits were implicitly grandfathered because a refinery that added less lead than the upper limit to its petrol could sell this difference. So, the initial distribution of rights was determined by the amount of leaded gasoline produced by a refinery and the standard per gallon. The lifetime of each permit was three months or one calender quarter. In the succeeding quarter, fewer lead permits were distributed, according to the phase-out scheme.

The rights to add specified quantities of lead to gasoline could then be traded among refineries and importers. It was anticipated that some small refiners would face a particularly hard task in meeting the standards. An important concern was, consequently, to make it easier for smaller producers to meet the target levels. The EPA therefore set a less stringent standard for small refineries than for large refineries. This attempt to give small refineries more time to modernize their equipment was successful. No refineries asked for extra time.[191]

### 4.3.1.4  Trade rules

Refineries were allowed to trade lead permits in an EPS system, that is on a one-to-one ratio. Here, the EPA undertook an analysis to show that the actual market structure and the reduction in lead concentrations would not cause any hot spots. As it was, no hot spots occurred.[192] So, by ignoring the spatial dimension, transaction costs were kept low. Sources were allowed to trade freely and simultaneously, and had only to fill out a simple orientation form for the EPA registering the trades.

To ease the phase-out, the EPA established a market in lead rights effective from November 1, 1982. Until then individual refineries had to meet standards expressed as the average lead content (grams of lead per gallon of gasoline produced in each calendar quarter). Once the market in lead rights was established, refineries and importers were allowed to sell lead rights as long as their individual quarterly average of the actual used lead amount plus rights sold (or minus rights bought) did not exceed the regulatory limit. The trade took place on a one-to-one ratio, so that the selling source did not have to reduce more than the buyers could increase. However, trading could not be used to avoid the

1992:34–37). For example, an alcohol blender who adds 10% ethanol to leaded gasoline at the maximum level would generate a lead credit at the value of 10% of the total lead content per gallon per year. (Anderson et al. 1990:26).

191.   Hahn and Hester (1989a: 381) and Nussbaum (1992:38).

192.   Nussbaum (1992:35).

Californian standards for lead content which were more stringent than the general EPA standards.[193]

Initially, the value of the lead permits was devaluated every quarter and no banking was allowed. However, in late 1984, the EPA decided to allow the banking of lead rights from 1985 through 1987 (withdrawals being allowed from the second quarter of 1985). Banking thereby enabled lead rights that would normally have expired at the end of the quarter to last until the end of 1987.[194]

### 4.3.1.5  Control system

The control system was kept simple and was undertaken by a central authority. The information reported from buyers and sellers made it possible to cross-check the trade activity and to see if any refiner had violated the rules. This 'double-sided' reporting system gave buyers and sellers a strong incentive to report correctly.[195] Enforcement of the rules by the EPA was largely confined to analysis of, and reaction to, the reported data, because continuous monitoring of an individual refiner was extremely expensive.[196]

Every quarter, refiners and importers were required to report their trades, banking deposits, withdrawals and balances, along with gasoline production volumes. The forms were very simple, consisting of one page of summary information and two lists: first a list of the names of trade partners and the quantities traded; and second a list of any physical transfers of lead additives to or from anyone other than lead additive manufacturers.[197]

### 4.3.2  Performance

### 4.3.2.1  Trade activity

After a hesitant start, trade activity rose rapidly. In the first 'whole' trade year, 1983, less than 1% of rights were traded, but this number increased rapidly. By 1985, more than half of the refineries had participated in trading. A typical quarter now involved more than half of the refineries in trade, during which 20% of total permits were traded.

After banking was introduced in 1985, more than 35% of the permits were banked. Trade activity increased further, and in the last trade year of 1986, trade increased from 20% in the first quarter to 60% in the second quarter. Prices of

---

193.   See Hahn and Hester (1989a).

194.   Anderson et al. (1990:26).

195.   EPA experienced some start-up problems with its computer systems to control banking and trading activity (Nussbaum 1992:37).

196.   Anderson et al. (1990:29).

197.   This second list included not only physical transfers of the lead additives but also sales of gasoline components or unfinished gasolines to which lead had already been added (Anderson et al. 1990:28).

rights were precise and increased from 0.75 cents to about 4 cents per gram of lead after banking was allowed.[198] In conclusion, a well-functioning market evolved with precise price signals.

### 4.3.2.2  Cost savings
The cost savings due to trade activity were substantial, amounting to $300 million, or roughly about 20% of total lead refining costs.[199]

### 4.3.2.3  Innovation
The tougher standards on lead content forced car manufacturers to develop 'low-lead' engines, just as, in the early seventies, they had been forced to turn to catalytic converters for controlling carbon monoxide and hydrocarbons.[200]

### 4.3.2.4  Environmental impact
The environmental impact was an unusually sharp and rapid decrease in lead pollution. One might have expected that refineries in the west – with the newest technology – would sell lead rights to the east and create hot spots. However, a worst-case analysis by the EPA showed that if eastern refineries bought up the permits in circulation, the actual lead concentration on the east coast would have been 1.16 grams per gallon in contrast to the maximum standard set at 1.1 grams – only a slight difference and not enough to be considered a hot spot. No hot spots occurred.[201]

### 4.3.3  Evaluation

### 4.3.3.1  Competitiveness
The refineries varied greatly in size. There were many small refineries representing a low share of total production. They usually played an important role in regions where transportation costs were too high for the larger, more efficient refineries to locate. About 100 of the 195 refineries produced 90% of total output in a rather even way.[202] Hence, concentration was relatively low, and the market was competitive.

### 4.3.3.2  Property rights
Lead trading was largely unrestricted. The lead trading program conveyed well-defined property rights to refiners and importers of gasoline. The devaluation period was clearly defined and was not supplemented by asymmetrical trade ratios. Making or importing one gallon of gasoline generated the right to use or

198.   Hahn and Hester (1989a:387).
199.   Klaassen (1996).
200.   Nussbaum (1992:29).
201.   Nussbaum (1992:35).
202.   Nussbaum (1992:29–31).

sell an amount of lead equal to the currently imposed upper limit.

Because many of the 'alcohol blenders' and small refineries did not know how to fill out the forms properly, some illegitimate credits were sold, often through another small and new industry, that of lead brokers. The EPA tackled these illegal trades by issuing notices of violations to all parties involved and letting them sort out the cases, which then, typically, could be settled administratively. Very few cases went to court. Frequently, the problems were caused by a small refiner with a small quantity of rights. The small violators therefore had a small effect on the overall performance of the program.[203]

### 4.3.3.3  Transaction costs

Transaction costs were low. Source location was ignored and no administrative approval process was imposed when a lead permit was traded or banked. Refineries only had to report their trades in a simple form at the end of each quarter.[204] Another advantage was that well-established gasoline markets already existed among refineries beforehand, so they knew each other and could make new deals relatively easily.[205]

These results are summarized in Table 4.8 at the end of this chapter.

## 4.4  CFC/HALON TRADING PROGRAM

Chlorofluorocarbons (CFCs) and halons are ozone-depleting substances. The ozone ($O_3$) layer in the stratosphere shields the earth by absorbing harmful, ultraviolet radiation from the sun.

CFCs and halons are used as aerosol propellants and in cushioning foams, packaging and insulating foams, industrial cleaning of metals and electronics components, food freezing, medical instrument sterilization, refrigeration for homes and food stores, and air conditioning of automobiles and commercial buildings. The major known effect of increased ultraviolet radiation is an increase in skin cancer. Other potential effects, such as suppression of human immunological systems, damage to plants, and eye cancer in cattle, are suspected.[206]

The Montreal Protocol of 1987 therefore targeted the production and consumption of both CFCs and halons.[207] To meet the target levels for these ozone-depleting substances in the US, the US implemented a nation-wide

---

203.  Nussbaum (1992:37–38).

204.  See Hahn and Hester (1989b).

205.  See Hahn and Hester (1989a).

206.  Tietenberg (1996:388–89).

207.  For information regarding international transfers, see Klaassen (1996). Chlorofluorocarbons are hydrocarbons with some or all of the hydrogen atoms replaced by chlorine and fluorine atoms. Halons are hydrocarbons where the hydrogen atoms have been replaced by at least one bromine atom and possibly chlorine and fluorine atoms.

tradable permit market system, which first allowed trade in 1989.

### 4.4.1  Design

#### 4.4.1.1  Target level

Production of CFCs and halons was to be stabilized by 1992 at its 1986 level and to be reduced by 50% by 1998. These target levels were tightened in 1990, and finally in 1992, a total phase-out scheme was settled. CFCs were to be phased out in 1996, and halons were to be phased out in 1994.[208] It is not permissible to trade CFC permits for halon permits and vice versa.

This scheme was similar to the quarterly phase-out scheme in the lead program, but renewals took place on an annual basis. Not much is known about the program because information of this kind is considered confidential concerning firms and their production methods.[209] Earlier models suggested that the costs for this kind of permit market could be 40% lower than those under CAC regulation.[210]

#### 4.4.1.2  Target group

Permits were distributed both for production and consumption. CFC and halon production permits were distributed to 7 producers, whereas 17 consumption permits were distributed to both the 7 producers and 10 importers.[211] The system was designed with two types of permits in order to limit both domestic production and consumption effectively.[212]

Significant differences in marginal reduction costs exist.[213]

#### 4.4.1.3  Distribution rule

Permits are specified in kilograms for one year and are grandfathered as production or consumption rights on the basis of 1986 production and import levels. They are renewed every year.

#### 4.4.1.4  Trade rules

Until 1990, trades took place on a one-to-one ratio. In the 1990 Clean Air Act (Title VI), the trade ratio was raised by 1%, that is a seller of permits had to reduce one per cent more than the amount by which emissions would increase after the trade. This was to ensure a net environmental gain from trade.[214] Still,

---

208.   EPA (1993).

209.   Interview, January 18, 1995: D. Lee, Ozone Hot Line, EPA.

210.   Palmer et al. (1980:vi).

211.   Klaassen (1996). For administrative reasons, no permits were distributed to the consumers themselves as they numbered up to 10,000 (Hahn and McGartland 1989).

212.   Hahn and Stavins (1993:11).

213.   Interview, January 18, 1995: D. Lee, Ozone Hot Line, EPA.

214.   Elman et al. (1992:13).

trade might roughly be said to take place as in the EPS and on a one-to-one basis because the trade ratio is so close to one.

Importers require only consumption permits and exporters can obtain additional consumption permits to avoid the US rules. Banking is not allowed. International trading of production permits is permitted in keeping with the Montreal Protocol. A US company may sell production permits internationally when approved by the EPA. It also may buy permits from outside the US as long as the relevant administration of that nation certifies that the number of production permits has been reduced by a corresponding amount.[215]

### 4.4.1.5 Control system
Transfers within the US have to be reported to the EPA. The reporting includes information about parties involved, type of pollutant, control period and permits remaining after the transfer.[216] The EPA only checks to see if the seller has sufficient permits to justify the transfer, and the EPA responds within three working days.

Producers and importers are obliged to report their production and import levels to the EPA every calendar quarter. The EPA is responsible for checking whether the companies have sufficient permits to carry out the transfers; for responding to requests for additional permits; for resolving policy issues; for inspecting; for reviewing quarterly reports and guides; and for carrying out compliance and enforcement activities.[217]

### 4.4.2 Performance

### 4.4.2.1 Trade activity
Through 1991, there were 34 participants in the market, and 80 external trades took place among firms.[218] The number of internal trades is unknown, as are the permit prices.

### 4.4.2.2 Cost savings
It is very difficult to judge the cost savings of the program since information regarding costs is confidential. But as of September 1993, roughly 10% of total permits had been traded. Demand increased somewhat when more stringent 1994 production caps had to be met, but estimates are not available. Furthermore, it is not known to what extent the high concentration of production has affected price.[219]

---

215. Elman et al. (1992:13). The EPA rule is that consumption of CFCs or halons within a firm must equal production plus imports minus exports.

216. Klaassen (1996).

217. EPA (1992b).

218. Hahn and Stavins (1993:11). Also, a small number of international trades have taken place.

219. Klaassen (1996).

### 4.4.2.3  Innovation

No official data are available on innovation because this information is confidential. However, the phase-out has clearly forced producers to employ substitutes for CFCs and halons and to use new technology. It is therefore reasonable to assume that significant innovation has taken place.

### 4.4.2.4  Environmental impact

Hot spots did not seem to occur because of the drastic reductions in emission.[220] Actual production levels are lower than allowable levels, so improvement in environmental quality has been achieved earlier than scheduled in the phase-out program.

### 4.4.3  Evaluation

### 4.4.3.1  Competitiveness

The market is highly concentrated. The two top producers, Du Pont and Allied Signal, account for 75% of total domestic CFC production.[221]

Performance has been good overall, in spite of the fact that market structure threatens competitiveness.[222]

### 4.4.3.2  Property rights

The CFC/halon program is in most ways similar to the lead trading program. Property rights are well-defined even though the target level has been raised rather unexpectedly a couple of times following international conferences. Nor is banking allowed.

The trade ratio is almost one-to-one, except for the rule of 1% extra reduction, and the control system seems very effective, with self-reporting every quarter and extremely high fines for violation of the rules.

So far, about 10 violations of the rules have been detected, and they were attributable to ignorance regarding the rules. Fines are so high ($25,000 per kg) that enforcement is not a problem.[223]

### 4.4.3.3  Transaction costs

Administrative approval procedures are minimized like those in the lead trading program. Transaction costs have been low and the spatial dimension has been ignored. These results are summarized in Table 4.9 at the end of this chapter.

---

220.  Klaassen (1996).
221.  Hahn and McGartland (1989:597).
222.  Hahn and Stavins (1993:12).
223.  Klaassen (1996).

## 4.5 ACID RAIN PROGRAM

The last of the four national permit markets is a historical experiment in environmental regulation, namely the Acid Rain Program (ARP). It is initiated by the EPA and calls for major reductions of sulphur dioxide ($SO_2$) which, together with nitrogen oxides ($NO_x$) causes acid rain. As will be seen, it builds in many ways on earlier experience with the other three programs.[224]

### 4.5.1 Design

#### 4.5.1.1 Target level
The ARP is a consequence of the 1990 Clean Air Act legislation, Title IV. According to this law, major electric utilities all over the US are permitted to trade $SO_2$ permits.[225] The target level is 50% $SO_2$ reduction of the 1980 level by the year 2000.[226] Trade has been allowed since 1990 and the 50% reduction is to take place with a two-step devaluation. In Phase I, which started in 1995, 'dirty' utilities in the mid-west must reduce emissions to 75% of their 1985 level, and in Phase II, which starts in the year 2000, these 'dirty' utilities, as well as the cleaner ones, must reduce emissions to 50% of their 1985 level.[227] So, most of the trading can be expected in the year 2000, when a larger number of utilities will be significantly affected.

The potential cost savings are massive. ICF (1989) concludes that trading will cut yearly reduction costs by about 30%, compared to the costs for a CAC policy. Rico (1995) predicts that reduction costs will be lowered by 50%. The latest estimates are even more optimistic. Burtraw and Swift (1996) indicate that if all potential trades take place, then the program will result in 70% cost savings compared to CAC.

The ARP may be viewed as an extension of the ETP to $SO_2$. The question is whether the ARP – in contrast to the ETP – can be expected to create a well-functioning market. As with the ETP, technology-based emission standards are applied such that more stringent standards (LAER and BACT) are imposed on

224. This subsection draws heavily on Svendsen (1998a).

225. Because $SO_2$ is a regional pollutant for which source localization determines environmental quality, this spatial dimension should in fact be calculated into the tradable permit system, as shown in Section 3.7. The ARP simply chooses to ignore this very complex problem. The only exception in the ARP is the special 'Class I areas' (National Parks, Wildernesses and Forests) where plants may face additional reduction requirements (Kete 1992:85). See also Ferrall (1991), Portney (1990), and Project 88 (1988).

226. The target reduction was much debated. It was based on scientific principles, and set so that the resulting $SO_2$ concentrations would not cause any known danger to health (Interview, November 12, 1994: Claire Schary, Acid Rain Division, EPA).

227. In actual numbers, Title IV of the Clean Air Act is designed to achieve a 10-million-ton annual $SO_2$ reduction from 1980 levels by the year 2000. Of this reduction, 8.5 million tons are to come from electric utilities, GAO (1994:2).

modified and new sources. New sources cannot circumvent these standards by trade, and modified sources can do so only when state practice allows it.

### 4.5.1.2 Target group

As mentioned, the reduction will take place in two phases. Phase I started in 1995 and includes the dirtiest 111 $SO_2$-emitters, those with greater than 100 MW net capacity and 1985 emission rates equal to or exceeding 2.5 lb/mmBtu. In the year 2000, Phase II will involve an additional 900 utilities with greater than 25 MW net capacity and 1985 $SO_2$ emission rates greater than 1.2 lb/mmBtu. In total, about 1000 electric utilities will be covered by the program after the year 2000. The 1000 plants are owned by roughly 200 public utility companies, which will be the trading partners in the market. The target groups and the reduction targets are summarized in Table 4.4.

*Table 4.4: $SO_2$ reduction and target group in ARP*

| Phase | Period | Plant Size | $SO_2$ Emission | Reduction | Number |
|---|---|---|---|---|---|
| 1 | 1995–2000 | > 100 MW | > 2.5 lb/mmBtu | 3.5 mill. ton | 111 |
| 2 | 2000– ? | > 25 MW | > 1.2 lb/mmBtu | 5 mill. ton | 1000 |

*Source:* Lee (1991), Kete (1992).

It was an administrative and political decision to include in the trading program only electric utilities with a net capacity greater than 25 MW. The affected utilities emit about 80% of the total $SO_2$ emission in the US, and they are already heavily regulated on the state level. The target group includes the main emitters and to incorporate smaller sources would be a difficult task for administrators.

In addition to the target group, the ARP allows all other interested participants to take part in the market such as brokers, coal companies and environmental organizations. At a later stage, the EPA plans to allow additional large industrial polluters to optin and take part in the market.[228]

The marginal reduction costs vary significantly among sources in the target group.[229]

### 4.5.1.3 Distribution rule

In starting up the market, the initial distribution rule is grandfathering. In this case, the basis for distribution is the historical use of fossil fuels in the period

---

228. This optin concerns only industrial sources with boilers – not sources that emit from processes that cannot be accurately monitored. The industry is to be allowed to participate voluntarily and optin if they buy and install monitoring equipment (Interview, November 12, 1994: Claire Schary, Acid Rain Division, EPA).

229. ICF (1989) and Rico (1995:119).

1985–1987.[230] By basing the distribution rule on fuel input, utilities that have recently invested in $SO_2$ reduction are not punished by a relatively smaller allotment. If, for example, two utilities use the same amount of fuel, each of them will get the same number of $SO_2$ permits even though one of them has installed a scrubber and, therefore, emits only half as much $SO_2$. Variations in the use of fossil fuels are smoothed out by using an average over the three-year period, from 1985 to 1987.

The battles over the actual distribution of $SO_2$ permits in the Congress have resembled the annual battles over the federal budget, with representatives each attempting to maximize the slice of the national income pie for their constituents. States likely to face the largest cost increases for electricity (for example, Indiana and Ohio) have sought means to force other states to share these costs.[231]

The result of this battle has been an implicit subsidy for the most-polluting utilities, all of which are located in the mid-west. They have been grandfathered, their permits starting in 1995, whereas cleaner utilities will be grandfathered, their permits starting in the year 2000. In this way, the subsidy consists of five years' extra permit value: from 1995 to 2000, permits from the most-polluting utilities can be sold to anyone, including the cleaner utilities.[232]

### 4.5.1.4  Trade rules

The ARP ignores the risk of hot spots created by $SO_2$ emissions; no ambient standards are expected to be violated for two reasons. First, total $SO_2$ emission will be reduced by 50% in a 10-year period (from 1990 to 2000). And, since damage from acid rain is due to cumulative emissions rather than the level of emissions in a given year, fluctuations will neutralize each other. Second, the older and 'dirtier' utilities, which are primarily located in the west, have lower marginal reduction costs than do the newer and cleaner utilities in the east. One can therefore expect eastern utilities to buy permits from western utilities. Since the wind direction is west-to-east, this is likely to improve environmental quality in the eastern areas where the problem of acid rain is most acute and hot spots would otherwise be most likely to occur.

Should an individual utility in the eastern zone want to sell permits, it may

230.  The years 1985–7 are thought to be three representative years without recessions. Utility plants that started operating in or after the 3-year average period, for example in 1989, were forewarned at the introduction of the CAA in 1990 and could then apply for a free standard allocation of permits. If failing to apply before the deadline in 1990, they had to buy their way in (Interview, November 12, 1994: Claire Schary, Acid Rain Division, EPA).

231.  Hausker (1992:555 and 566). Distributional concerns in relation to different areas in the US have played a significant role when designing and passing the program, Rico (1993), Kete (1992), Van Dyke (1991), Krupnick et al. (1990), Bohi and Burtraw (1991;1992) and Bohi et al. (1990). For a discussion of equity considerations and distribution rules, see Tietenberg (1985:100–101 and 110–13).

232.  This subsidy or 'bribe' to the dirty utilities is a selective incentive, an individual reward, for participating in collective action, see Section 2.4.3.

not be allowed to sell them to a source in the western zone because then the ambient standards in the eastern zone could be violated. For example, a utility in New York should not be allowed to reduce emissions and sell its permits to a utility in Ohio. Such trade could decrease the environmental quality in the eastern zone and perhaps violate the ambient standards in the Adirondacks, Canada, and other sensitive non-urban regions.

In this hypothetical case, the State of New York has to make its own decisions, because the EPA will not review individual trades. States will still apply the most stringent technology-based standards for new or modified sources and, as is the case in the ETP, will prohibit new sources from circumventing the standards by trade.[233]

The ARP trade rules can as such be characterized by four features. First, utilities can trade freely under the condition that they comply with local technology-based standards. Second, utilities can store and bank $SO_2$ permits in preparation for sale or use after the year 2000. Banking may consequently result in some fluctuation below and above the cap. Third, the ARP allows the use of 'shut down' credits from closed plants. Fourth, trade takes place on a one-to-one ratio for both new and existing sources.

An extra 'safety valve' mechanism has been added to the ARP in order to stimulate trade and to prevent the price from turning out to be so high that the market does not work. The US Congress has therefore created a special reserve pool in which 3% of the total permit quota is held back. Its purpose is to ensure easily accessible permits for new sources. This pool is distributed through direct sale at a fixed price and through an open auction. The fixed price is $1500, or twice the expected equilibrium price in the market (EPA 1991). Unsold surplus permits are released together with the remaining permits at a yearly auction to the highest bidders.[234]

### 4.5.1.5   Control system

As in the lead program, the sources themselves must report the trades to the EPA, which only checks the aggregated annual figures. Because electric utilities are large and already heavily regulated units, it is furthermore possible to use a continuous-emissions-monitoring system (CEMS), which monitors both $SO_2$ and $CO_2$ emissions. All affected utilities must pay for and install the CEMS themselves. The cost of such a monitor is about $120,000 annually.[235] The CEMS gives the EPA accurate data on tons emitted and makes it possible to run the ARP effectively from the federal level.

The EPA has developed a computer-controlled bookkeeping system for this

233.   Interview, November 12, 1994: Claire Schary, Acid Rain Division, EPA.

234.   The special reserve pool and the $SO_2$ auction linked to the ARP are both described in Section 4.5.4.

235.   Interview, July 2, 1997: Kevin Culligan, Acid Rain Division, EPA. See also Ellerman et al. (1997:31). The use of CEMS for monitoring $CO_2$ emissions is reconsidered in Chapter 6 in a discussion of control systems in potential $CO_2$ markets.

specific control task and has combined it with an efficient penalty system. If two electric utilities trade permits, they are obliged to inform the EPA, which then registers the transaction. If one of them has superseded its permit, a fine of $2000 per ton $SO_2$ is assessed, and the extra tons emitted must be reduced the following year.[236]

A 'CAC mentality' exists nonetheless in the EPA because a company must still submit 'compliance plans' describing how much it plans to emit, how it will meet the goal and how it will obtain the necessary allowances. This extra layer of regulation is strangely superimposed on the program's otherwise simple, yet sufficient requirements.[237]

A possible loophole in the legislation is created by the fact that many companies own plants that are subject to both Phase I and Phase II. This may give a perverse incentive to increase the use of plants subject only to Phase II requirements and, by that, to create more permits for their own use, sale or banking. The EPA is currently implementing regulation to avoid this situation and is checking up on the emission figures to prevent shifting. If significant transfers occur, then the EPA requires permits created for that purpose to be surrendered.[238]

### 4.5.2 Performance

#### 4.5.2.1 Trade activity
Market activity has succeeded in generating prices. Between 1994 and 1996, the EPA recorded 1,902 trades in the market, involving the transfer of over 34 million permits. Out of these, 741 trades were external and 1161 trades were internal. The number of transfers increased steadily from 215 in 1994 to 1,074 in 1996. Nearly 90 % of Phase I affected units have participated.[239]

In the March 1997 spot auction, the clearing price was $107.[240] The price

---

236.  Sources must report emissions and trade activities to EPA before January 30 every year. If any limits are exceeded, then the source must submit a new report on March 1 at the latest, and must pay any penalties by enclosing a cheque (Interview, November 12, 1994: Claire Schary, Acid Rain Division, EPA).

237.  Hausker (1992:557). The process of approving the compliance plans must slow down the transaction process. Some decisions would be better made as events unfold, for example plant, dispatch, maintenance and construction schedules could be affected by the price and availability of permits. There is no reason for the EPA to approve how utilities plan to comply. The approval rule is a result of a conflict within the administration. Early EPA drafts suggested even harsher provisions suggestive of CAC regulation, but this was opposed by the Office of Management and the Council of Economic Advisers. Hausker believes the puzzling compromise to be provoked by unreformed 'Stalinists' in EPA who still believe in CAC as the one and only way of dealing with pollution (*Ibid*).

238.  See Rico (1993).

239.  Interview, May 7, 1997: Melanie Dean, Acid Rain Division, EPA and EPA (1997b).

240.  EPA(1994b:8–9) and EPA (1997a). Another remarkable trend in the market is the development of more sophisticated types of trades such as permit swaps, fuel bundling, forward contracts, and options trading. Permit swaps have taken place between utilities without any exchange

generated by the market is somewhat higher than the price generated by the auction. The most active brokerage firm (Cantor Fitzgerald in New York) calculated its average spot market price at $110 over the month of March 1997.[241]

### 4.5.2.2  Cost savings

Actual cost savings are estimated to be 40% compared with CAC. The potential 70% savings have not been realized yet, in particular because not all external trades have yet taken place.[242] The incentive to minimize costs has grown stronger in recent years as a result of competitiveness in electricity production and strong pressure from consumers for lower prices.[243]

Another indicator is the clearing price from the March 1997 spot auction ($107). It is less than one-seventh the market price of $750 that the EPA projected in 1991 (EPA 1991). The costs of participating in the program are thus much lower than expected.

### 4.5.2.3  Innovation

Market prices have dropped drastically due to innovation. Four main reasons may be listed.

First, the emergence of low-sulphur coal is a major low-cost option for compliance. Prices of low-sulphur coal have dropped 40% in real terms between 1983 and 1993 due to improvements in the productivity of surface mining. Second, a reduction in the cost of rail transport of low-sulphur coal has lowered rates as much as 50%. This is due to major investments in new infrastructure and to innovations. Third, the technology of blending low- and high-sulphur coal has been improved. Fourth, the costs of installing and maintaining a new scrubber have fallen by 50% during the early nineties. Other options such as energy conservation, efficiency management and electricity despatching have also played a role.[244]

---

of cash. Fuel bundling, combining the sale of fuel with permits, has been offered by coal companies to help the utility offset the burning of higher sulphur coal. Also forward contracts and options have occurred. A forward contract means that a purchaser can agree to buy a number of permits for delivery in the future at an agreed-upon price, whereas an option means that a party can negotiate to buy the right to a specific number of allowances over some time period. See EPA (1997a).

241.   Interview, May 7, 1997: Melanie Dean, Acid Rain Division, EPA.

242.   Burtraw and Swift (1996:10415). One southeastern utility estimates having saved $300 million through trading. GAO (1994:4).

243.   See Section 5.6.

244.   Klaassen and Nentjes (1997:399), Burtraw and Swift (1996:10419), Burtraw (1996), GAO (1994:4), and interview, September 22, 1994: Dallas Burtraw, Resources for the Future. Bohi (1993) projected for 11 states (or 85% of phase I permits) that two-thirds of the utilities would switch to low sulphur fuels, one-sixth would install scrubbers, and one-sixth would buy permits.

#### 4.5.2.4  Environmental impact

In 1995, phase I utilities emitted 40% less than their permits allowed them to. This is a dramatic overcompliance that provides an opportunity for earlier ecological recovery.[245] This extra reduction has probably taken place because utilities are risk averse and like to hold a reserve. No hot spots have been created by the program so far.[246]

### 4.5.3  Evaluation

#### 4.5.3.1  Competitiveness

No strategic behaviour is known to have occurred. The large number of market participants and the low concentration of permits are believed to have created a competitive market.[247]

#### 4.5.3.2  Property rights

Utilities are fully allowed to bank permits, to shut down plants and use the related permits, and to take each of these actions without individual approval. Furthermore, the CEMS control system in the ARP makes it possible to enforce property rights clearly.

However, the risk of sudden regulatory intervention is present in the ARP. Permits may be confiscated without compensation or may be devaluated without notice. Note that the distributed permits do not represent a permanent right. A permit gives the right to emit one ton per year and is subject to renewal every year by the regulator.

The Clean Air Act states clearly that the EPA or the Congress is authorized to terminate or limit the use of permits without compensation.[248] Such regulatory uncertainty connected to the future value of the permits is difficult to quantify and incorporate in the permit price. A critical concern then is whether the electric utilities have the full property right to dispose of the $SO_2$ permits. If not, the future value of the permits will become uncertain and utilities will then hesitate to participate. In other words, the question is whether authorities will tend to use the constitutional right to confiscate permits in practice.

Arbitrary regulatory interventions are not likely to occur in the near future for two reasons. First, even though authorities reserve the right to formalize the property right of the permits, it seems unlikely that unannounced confiscations will take place in the short and well-defined devaluation period, given that both environmental groups and utilities have approved the program.[249] Second, the influential and well-organized utilities will resist permit confiscation, and so

---

245.  Burtraw and Swift (1996:10414).
246.  Interview, November 12, 1994: Claire Schary, Acid Rain Division, EPA.
247.  See Schmalensee (1989), Hesse (1989) and Bohi et al. (1990).
248.  Clean Air Act of 1990, Title IV, §403(f).
249.  These political attitudes are described and explained in Chapter 5.

will any other holder of permits, for example, speculators. In general, the favourable political climate, the definition of a devaluation period, and the absence of significant trade restrictions all suggest that electric utilities in practice may gain the full property rights of the grandfathered $SO_2$ permits.

However, administrative procedures for dealing with the property rights from the gains from trade are not settled yet. The Public Utility Commissions (PUCs) must publish administrative practice rules for determining how to treat costs and revenues from trade, as soon as possible.[250] There is one PUC in each state and the 50 PUCs are organized under the Federal Energy Regulatory Commission (FERC). The FERC has not yet settled the rules.[251] This uncertainty inhibits trade because the PUCs are waiting for utilities to trade, whereas the utilities are waiting for the PUCs to describe how their costs and revenues will be treated.[252]

Until now, the manner in which the gains from individual trades are treated has been determined by the PUCs on a case-by-case basis. The trend is unfavourable at the moment. Bohi (1993) has summarized the stated policies in 11 states (85% of phase I permits). All 11 states have mandated that gains from trade go to ratepayers. However, this will encourage utilities to keep permits for their own use rather than undertaking cost-minimizing strategies. A major problem at the state level is, therefore, that capital gains will not go to shareholders who, then, will not be willing to take risks.[253] A better solution would be for the gains to be counted as capital gains, rewarding shareholders and encouraging trade activity.

The market is very effectively enforced by the CEMS, run by the EPA as a central authority. Due to the CEMS, self-reporting, and computer controls, it is hardly possible to cheat. High fines, almost twenty times the market price, ensure that it does not pay to run the risk of being caught cheating.

### 4.5.3.3 Transaction costs

Transaction costs are low because sources report their trades directly to the EPA, which only checks the aggregated annual figures. Also, as shown in the next section, the price signals from the annual $SO_2$ auctions lower transaction costs. Brokerage fees lie around 5% which, compared to other tradable permit systems in the US, is low.[254]

---

250.   Rico (1993).

251.   GAO (1994).

252.   Also, new PUC staff are elected every 4th year, so they hardly have time to figure out the rules and to find out what is going on (Interview, November 12, 1994: Claire Schary, Acid Rain Division, EPA).

253.   Bohi (1993). See also Bohi and Burtraw (1991).

254.   Klaassen (1996).

### 4.5.4 EPA's Emission Trading Auction

A so-called Special Allowance Reserve is withdrawn from the total number of permits in circulation for direct sale and auctions. As seen above in Table 4.4, the total $SO_2$ market in the ARP is divided into two phases.

During Phase I (1995–1999), the Special Allowance Reserve amounts to 175,000 permits, or 3.1% annually of the total. Out of these, 25,000 permits are reserved for direct advance sales and 150,000 permits are reserved for spot and advance auctions. In Phase II (2000–), 250,000 permits, or 2.8% annually of total, are to be set aside for the special reserve. 50,000 permits are earmarked for direct sales, 200,000 permits are earmarked for the auctions. The auctions and direct sales will continue to run until the EPA assesses that the demand is too small.[255] To maintain the quotas on total $SO_2$ emissions in the ARP, new units must obtain permits from existing sources or through the EPA auctions and direct sales programs.[256]

The rules are such that direct sales from 1993 through to 1999 are all advance sales, that is the permits sold are not usable until seven years after purchase. Starting in the year 2000, both spot and advance sales will take place. A spot sale means that the permit is usable in the year of purchase. The price is fixed at $1500 indexed to inflation. Permits not sold at direct sales will be offered at auctions the following year.[257]

These auctions are revenue-neutral and are used to distribute about 2% of the permits.[258] As of February 1998, the auction has been used five times at the Chicago Board of Trade (CBOT). The process of linking such auctions to the ARP was initiated in 1992 when the EPA delegated the administration of its annual permit auctions to CBOT.[259] The CBOT is only to handle the administrative aspects of the auctions and is not to be compensated by the EPA nor

---

255. Interview, January 23, 1995: Kevin Smith, Acid Rain Division, EPA.

256. The direct sale option was requested by private independent power producers (IPPs). IPPs represent 7% of the total production in the US electricity industry, NIEP (1994:2). They were fearful that the public utilities would not sell to them because they were competitors (Hausker 1992:568). Title IV of the Clean Air Act Amendments, therefore, requires that the EPA ensures priority for certain new independent power producers (IPPs) in the direct sale. The fear among IPPs – that no permits would be available to them in the market – has disappeared by now, and the IPPs see many possibilities in the permit market (Interview, January 25, 1995: Liza Mackey, NIEP, Washington D.C). A symbiotic relationship now exists. Public utilities have been eager to support and purchase electricity from IPPs because they thereby avoid the risks involved in constructing their own plants; it gives them extra flexibility. The IPPs are expected to provide more than half of the new electricity production over the next 10 years (Hoffman 1994:56).

257. EPA (1992c).

258. Each permit (or 'allowance') entitles a source to emit 1 ton of $SO_2$ during or after the year specified in the permit serial number. Permits may be bought, sold or banked like any other commodity.

259. CBOT was chosen after an objective selection process because of its demonstrated ability in handling and processing financial instruments and using transactional information systems (EPA 1992).

allowed to charge fees.[260]

The US Congress chose to use the auction as a mechanism to stimulate the $SO_2$ market for two reasons. First, the auction ensures the availability of permits and makes it possible for new sources to buy their way into the market. Second, the auction gives a clear price signal for $SO_2$ permits to the market, where permits are traded privately among firms, and may thereby reduce transaction costs.

When the auction mechanism was considered in Congress, two important political concerns influenced the final design. First, the US administration was obliged to pursue a policy of 'no new taxes' – any proposal for a revenue-raising auction was politically unacceptable. Therefore, the zero-revenue proposal was adopted. Second, the fraction of permits withheld for auction had to be small. The utilities resisted larger withholdings despite the refund of revenue.[261] They feared losing control over their own permits if the permits could possibly be bought by others.

According to the theory described in Section 3.5, bidders may have an incentive to bid too low. In this case, did the clearing price turn out to be too low? The answer to this question lies in the actual design of the auction and the results so far.

The annual EPA auction process consists of four separate sales. The first three concern 'public' special reserve permits. These 'reserve' permits are sold before those offered by private holders are sold in the fourth auction. All four auctions are held on the same day in the order listed below:

1   Spot market auction for permits usable in the year of the auction. Starting in the year 2000, this will also include unsold permits from direct spot sales. If the permits are not sold at direct spot sales before January 30 in the year in which they are valid, then they are automatically transferred to the spot auction for that very same year. The spot auction is to be held no later than March 31, every year.

2   Seven-year advance auction for permits usable seven years later. The number seven is chosen so that the first permits, which were sold in 1993, will take effect in the year 2000, when the most stringent reduction requirements apply.[262]

3   Six-year advance auction for seven-year permits not sold in direct sales the previous year. This started in 1994. For example, an unsold direct advance sale permit from 1993 (valid in the year 2000) will still be valid in the year 2000 when sold in the following six-year auction.[263]

---

260.   CBOT have administered the auctions and sales for a period of three years beginning in January 1993, with a possibility for extension. CBOT must not bid for permits in the auctions or transfer any permits among sources (EPA 1992c). All data are coded into computer systems which generate the auction results. The reward that CBOT gets for running the auctions is publicity and a 'green' image (Interview, January 23, 1995: Kevin Smith, Acid Rain Division, EPA).

261.   Hausker (1992:559).

262.   Interview, January 23, 1995: Kevin Smith, Acid Rain Division, EPA.

263.   Interview, November 12, 1994: Claire Schary, Acid Rain Division, EPA.

4 Private auction. The Clean Air Act of 1990 allows any person holding permits to sell them in this auction, which the EPA is required to hold. These permits must be dated for the year in which they are offered (spot) or for seven years (advance) in the future.[264]

These first three auction types concern permits from the special reserve. The number of permits offered at the direct sales, spot auctions, and seven-year advance auctions are provided in Table 4.5.

The four EPA auctions are, in general, discriminative and multi-priced because the permits are sold on a pay-what-you-bid basis.[265] The only difference between the public and the private auctions is that the private permits are sold according to price level, starting with the permits for which private holders have set the lowest minimum prices. The reason for starting from below is to maximize the incentive to sell at a low price.[266]

The three public auction types work in just the opposite way. Reserve permits are first sold at the highest bid price and, thereafter, sold at lower and lower prices until the lowest price that clears the market is reached (or until the number of bids is exhausted). The buyer pays what is bid and the EPA cannot set a minimum price.[267]

*Table 4.5: Permits offered at direct sales and spot auctions and seven-year advance auctions (in 1000s)*

| Year of Purchase | Spot Sale | Advance Sale* | Spot Auction | Advance Auction* |
|---|---|---|---|---|
| | | ...................................*1000s*........................................ | | |
| 1993 | | 25 | 50** | 100 |
| 1994 | | 25 | 50** | 100 |
| 1995 | | 25 | 50 | 100 |
| 1996 | | 25 | 150 | 100 |
| 1997 | | .. | ... | ... |
| 1998 | | .. | ... | ... |
| 1999 | | .. | ... | ... |
| 2000 and after | 25 | 25 | 100 | 100 |

*Notes:*
\* Not usable until seven years after purchase / \*\* Not usable until 1995
*Source:* EPA (1992c)

264. Authorized account representatives must notify the administrator of the EPA auctions of their intent to sell at least 15 business days prior to the auctions. The account representatives must specify the number of permits they are offering and their minimum price requirements (EPA 1992c).

265. In all cases, revenue is rebated to the contributing sources. The same revenue-neutral mechanism applies for direct sale.

266. Interview, January 23, 1995: Kevin Smith, Acid Rain Division, EPA.

267. EPA (1992c).

In the private auction, revenue is returned to the private holders. In the three reserve permit auctions, the EPA returns revenue and unsold permits on a pro rata basis to those units from which the EPA originally withheld the permits.[268] The EPA returns payment from unsuccessful bids and permits from unsuccessful offers.[269]

The private auction has hardly been used as yet. Prices seem to have been set too high by the private groups making the offers. In 1993, only 10 $SO_2$ permits were sold, at the minimum price of $131. In 1994, 400 permits were sold, at $140, in the six-year advance auction, and 800 were sold, also at $140, in the seven-year advance auction.[270] Timing the fourth auction immediately after the first three EPA auctions is probably a bad idea since the market is easily exhausted at the beginning of the program.[271]

There is information on the performance of the three reserve auctions. The results from 1993 and 1994 are depicted in Table 4.6.

Table 4.6 shows that out of 145,000 permits offered for sale at the EPA's spot auction in 1993, 50,000 were sold. The minimum or clearing price was $131. In 1994, 108,000 were offered and 50,000 sold at a higher clearing price, $150. At the seven-year advance auction in 1993, 100,000 permits were sold out of 131,000 offered. The clearing price was $122. In 1994, 100,000 permits were sold out of 147,000 offered. The clearing price was $140.

Bid quantities went down slightly in the 1994 spot auction compared to those in the 1993 auction. The EPA explains this as a result of the shift in the focus of the permit market to phase II compliance, given that most phase I compliance strategies have already been established. The new focus was confirmed by the higher bid quantities in the 1994 advance auction and the higher phase II

268.   In a way similar to the auction program, the EPA apportions revenues from the direct sale of permits on a pro rata basis to those units from which the EPA withheld 'reserve' permits.

269.   Concerning auction deadlines, all EPA auctions are held no later than March 31 of every year, beginning in 1993. They are all held the same day. Data and bids are put into a computer system, which also generates the auction results. Bidders must send sealed offers containing information on the number and type (spot or advance) of permits desired and the purchase price to CBOT no later than three business days prior to the auctions. Direct sales of permits begin on June 1 of each year and continue until all permits are sold or until January 30 (the last day permits may be transferred for purposes of end-of-year compliance). Any individual or organization may purchase permits at the direct sales by submitting the proper application materials which again must specify number and type of permits desired. Upon approval, permits are reserved under the name of the applicant who must tender 50% of the total payment within 6 months of the date on which their request was affirmed. The second half must be paid on or before January 30. Payment defaults will result in a withdrawal of purchase requests. EPA transfers permits only after full payment is received. Applicants are placed on a waiting list where the first-come, first-served rule applies (EPA 1992c).

270.   EPA (1994b).

271.   The timing of the private auction right after the EPA auction has been criticized by the utility associations themselves. For example, the American Public Power Association (APPA) recommends that the private auction be held separately from the EPA auction in order to offer parties a second opportunity to participate in the auction after evaluating market response to the EPA auctions (APPA 1991:1).

average winning bid price. 1994 bid prices were more focused around the average bid price, reflecting a maturing of the permit market.[272] Overall, the auction program appears to be working and generating revenue and price signals.[273]

*Table 4.6: EPA's SO$_2$ auction programs, 1993 and 1994*

|  | 1993 Auctions | | 1994 Auctions | | |
|---|---|---|---|---|---|
|  | Spot[1] | 7-year[2] | Spot[1] | 7-year[2] | 6-year[2] |
| **Total permits offered**\*[3] | 145 | 131 | 108 | 147 | 75 |
| **Permits sold\*** | 50 | 100 | 50 | 100 | 25 |
| **Bid quantities\*** | 321 | 283 | 294 | 489 | 110 |
| **Winning bidders** | 36 | 30 | 17 | 11 | 6 |
| **Maximum winning bid** | $450 | $310 | $400 | $250 | $150 |
| **Average winning bid** | $156 | $136 | $159 | $149 | $148 |
| **Minimum winning bid** | $131 | $122 | $150 | $140 | $140 |
| Total revenue (mill.) | $7.8 | $13.6 | $7.9 | $15.0 | $3.7 |

*Notes:*
\* Rounded figures in 1000s.
1. Permits first usable in 1995.
2. Permits first usable in 2000.
3. Permits offered include both public and private permits. For example, the 1993 spot auction offered 50,000 permits by the EPA and 95,000 permits by private holders.

*Source:* EPA (1994a)

One may now consider whether the price signal to the market was too low and whether the sources had any pre-auction information on equilibrium price. In the market, as of November 1994, SO$_2$ permits could be acquired for $150–160 a piece, or typically about 10% above the minimum prices from the auctions.[274] The market prices are somewhat similar to the average prices from the auctions, which spanned from $136 to $159. These results indicate that the price signal

272. EPA (1994a:11).

273. The actual working of this revolutionary approach has been a surprise. Paul Portney of Resources for the Future puts it this way: 'back in 1988 people would think that you were crazy if you expected systems like ARP and auctions in actual use. Now it is there and it is working in spite of many troublesome regulations and barriers to trade' (at the seminar 'Why So Little Participation in the SO$_2$ Allowances Auction?' (Resources For the Future, December 7, 1994)). New competitive initiatives in electricity production – like the one taking place in California – are expected to stimulate market activity even further. (See Section 5.6 and Svendsen 1995b).

274. Interview, November 12, 1994: Claire Schary, Acid Rain Division, EPA.

was too low and that sources bid on the basis of their expectations rather than their marginal $SO_2$ reduction costs. This trend continued in 1995 and 1996, though the difference between market and auction spot minimum prices have been somewhat reduced.[275]

Most bidders seemed to have had information about the market price and therefore tried to get the permits cheaper in the auction than in the market. Other bidders, much fewer in number, seemed to have had less knowledge about the market price and therefore to have paid too much in the auction compared to the market.[276]

When the price signal is too low, the number of trades in the market is reduced because potential buyers want to buy at the low auction minimum price while sellers want to sell at the existing market price. This two-price signal from the current auction is confusing to market agents. The deviance creates higher transaction costs compared to the single price signal in the alternative non-discriminative design. Presumably, the degree of uncertainty that exists in the immature market would be reduced in a more mature one.[277] However, in the future, the difference between the auction and the market price will probably persist because the market price is rapidly changing. In time, new production and scrubber technologies will be developed, more low-sulphur energies will become profitable. And soon this is the reason why it is so important that the auction every year generates a single and precise price signal to the market. If the only difference in practice is the number of price signals, then a non-discriminative auction with a single price signal would be the most attractive solution.

The results of this section are summarized in Table 4.10 at the end of this chapter.

---

275.   Interview, May 7, 1997: Melanie Dean, Acid Rain Division, EPA. See also Joskow and Schmalensee (1996) and Hansjürgens (1998).

276.   If this difference between auction and market prices persists, 'cross-trading' is and stays an attractive option, that is it pays to buy 'cheap' permits in the auction and then sell them in the market afterwards. The downward bias in price may create additional inefficiencies, for example if state public utility commissions use the EPA market clearing prices to value the permit 'assets' of the utilities they regulate (Cason 1993:181).

277.   The short-term character of the auctions may complicate utilities' long-term planning. Present administrative procedures favour short-term trades. The PUC approval process may only accept short-term transactions and the likelihood of prudence review will increase in a long-term market. This is problematic because the need for long-term planning is obvious. When building a new plant for example, it may be necessary to count on a 10- to 20-year stream of permits – or the equivalent in banked permits. The auction should be designed so that it is possible to buy long-term permits. This would provide the market with important long-term permit price signals (Hausker 1992:561). But such a transfer of property rights may not be easy in the political arena because environmental groups are likely to raise concerns that new information on damage associated with $SO_2$ may justify further reductions (see Chapter 5).

## 4.6 RECLAIM

Southern California is renowned for its smog. The major cause is the unique meteorology and topography of the region: the Los Angeles basin is ringed by mountain ranges within which emissions are trapped. Air stagnation typically lasts two weeks or more and, when coupled with high temperatures, makes conditions ideal for the formation of smog.[278]

### 4.6.1 Design

#### 4.6.1.1 Target level
A permit market was chosen as a low-cost solution out of necessity. California's economic slow-down in recent years made business, workers, and ultimately politicians resistant to high-cost approaches, such as CAC regulation. It was also considered important that the permit system allow economic growth and, at the same time, guarantee environmental quality in a more flexible way than CAC regulation could. Most importantly, it was chosen to provide sources an incentive to develop new and cost-effective means to reduce emissions.[279] In this way, the district found that the cost savings from a permit market far outweighed the opportunity costs or added incentives for facilities to shut down and leave the basin.[280] So, on October 15, 1993, the district adopted the Regional Clean Air Incentives Market (RECLAIM), which in most ways resembles the design of the ARP.[281] It covers the Los Angeles valley or basin, which is an area of roughly 500 square miles.

The target levels concern $SO_2$ and $NO_x$.[282] No inter-pollutant trading is allowed. Overall average rates of reduction are 8.3% for $NO_x$ and 6.8% for $SO_x$ per year. Because RECLAIM runs for a 10-year period, from 1994 until 2003, the final devaluation of permits will result in an overall reduction of 75% in $NO_x$ emissions and a 60% reduction in $SO_2$ emissions.[283] Because RECLAIM only began operating in 1994, it is probably still too early to judge its performance but its design can be evaluated. RECLAIM must first and foremost respect local impact standards, which are more stringent than the national

278.  This is also why Los Angeles has more severe pollution than more heavily industrialized cities like New York or Chicago (Johnston 1994:44).

279.  See Seligman (1994:18).

280.  Broadbent (1993:9).

281.  This 'mini' Acid Rain Program can work alongside the nation-wide program for $SO_2$ trade among utilities because all utilities in the district run on gas and, therefore, do not emit any $SO_2$ (Interview, November 12, 1994: Claire Schary, Acid Rain Division, EPA).

282.  The district is also considering the possibility of introducing a market for reactive organic compounds (called ROGs) which come from sources such as coating and solvent operations (Johnston 1994:45).

283.  Broadbent (1993:9). See also Dwyer (1993), Fromm and Hansjürgens (1996) and Polesetsky (1995).

ambient standards because of the severe smog problems. Potential cost savings are estimated at 42% compared to those from CAC regulation.[284]

### 4.6.1.2  Target group

The target group is defined by the amount of emissions. If a plant emits or emitted 4 tons $SO_2$ and/or $NO_x$ per year or more in 1990 or any subsequent year, it is included in the target group. Only mid-sized and large-sized businesses are included; all small businesses are excluded and they are therefore subjected to the traditional CAC regulation. Approximately 400 facilities are regulated in the $NO_x$ program and approximately 40 facilities are regulated in the $SO_2$ program.

Facilities not initially included in the program will have the ability to optin if it is technically feasible for them to do so.[285] Again, as in the ARP, significant differences in marginal reduction costs are predicted across sources.

### 4.6.1.3  Distribution rule

Permits are grandfathered and determined by the highest annual emissions from a source during the period 1989–1992. Note that due to a slow-down in economic growth, many plants have emission levels that are as much as 50% lower than they were in 1989.[286] Permits are renewed annually.

### 4.6.1.4  Trade rules

The trade rules are similar to the ones used in the ARP: banking is allowed, permits from shut-downs can be used, and trades take place on a one-to-one EPS basis. RECLAIM ignores the spatial dimension. However, as was also the case with the ARP, wind-direction and geographical location may lead to a specific situation in which a trade may be forbidden by the local regulator. For this purpose, the L.A. region has been divided into an eastern and a western zone. For example, a new source in the western zone may only be allowed to buy permits from another source in the western zone, whereas a new source in

---

284.  SCAQMD (1993).

285.  Broadbent (1993:9). It is still very expensive to buy monitoring equipment for private firms, even though the prices have started falling (Interview, November 12, 1994: Claire Schary, Acid Rain Division, EPA).

286.  Seligman (1994:20–21). The South Coast Air Quality Management District (SCAQMD) justified the excessive distribution for three reasons. First, economic growth after a recession should be allowed. Increases would also have occurred under CAC regulation. Declining emissions caps will eventually force plants to trade and eliminate the problem of 'paper credits'. Second, RECLAIM has added Non-Tradeable Credits (NTCs) to plants which had higher production and emissions in 1987 or 1988 than in the subsequent four-year period. These NTCs can be used during the first three years of the RECLAIM program and were meant to ease the transition. Third, almost 60% of emission permits will be calculated using emission factors (engineering estimates) rather than through the monitoring of actual emissions. This technical concern makes calculation more uncertain and leaves room open for actual emission to exceed measured emission so that sources may receive too many permits (*Ibid*).

the eastern zone may be allowed to buy permits from both.[287]

Another interesting feature is that RECLAIM allows trading of mobile source emissions reduction credits through the scrapping of old cars. This creates the potential problem of attracting cars fit only for the scrapyard to the basin in order to be sold in the emissions credit market. Strict administrative control is needed to prevent this situation.[288]

### 4.6.1.5  Control system
Monitoring takes place through high-technology methods, such as continuous-emission-monitoring systems (CEMS) for major sources and continuous-process-monitoring systems (CPMS) for smaller sources. The latter can track emission-related parameters, such as fuel flow and hours of engine operation.[289]

### 4.6.2  Performance

### 4.6.2.1  Trade activity
It is known that one substantial external trade took place in June 1994. Union Carbide's Torrance plant sold 1,700 $NO_x$ permits to Anchor Glass Container Corporation at a total value of $1.2 million. The average price was $700 per ton.[290]

### 4.6.2.2  Cost savings
No data are available yet.

### 4.6.2.3  Innovation
No data are available yet.

### 4.6.2.4  Environmental impact
Even though substantial emissions reduction will take place, the risk of hot spots is not rejected so easily in the case of RECLAIM because ozone can be

---

287.   Seligman (1994), Polesetsky (1995) and Atkinson (1994).

288.   Seligman (1994:21).

289.   SCAQMD (1993).

290.   Johnston (1994:50). The number of internal trades is not known. Note, as Krupnick and Burtraw (1994) point out, that many external trades are not necessary to show that a program is performing – or will perform – well. First, trade can take place internally, either within a plant or across plants owned by the same company. Second, companies can reduce their demand for permits by adjusting production processes, capital investment and retirement plans. Third, the SCAQMD has issued 'excess' permits in the initial years of the program to keep political opposition and prices down. This excess supply will be eliminated over time and market activity may pick up. Also, the trade option gives, in itself, flexibility. Sources know that if they get into trouble meeting the target levels, then they can use the trade option rather than having to invest in major modifications of the production process or the control technology (Interview, September 22, 1994: Dallas Burtraw, Resources For the Future). Finally, the price signals from the  market can warn about rising reduction costs (Interview, February 10, 1995: D. Downing, Technology Assessment, US Congress).

generated by $NO_x$ emissions. Ozone is a toxic pollutant and has effects that include lung scarring and decreased lung function. Moreover, $NO_x$ emissions are often accompanied by emissions of carcinogenic toxics, such as formaldehyde, while $SO_2$ emissions are accompanied by hydrogen sulphide, which can cause asphyxiation and nervous system damage.[291]

The South Coast Air Quality Management District (SCAQMD), however, argues that the permit program will not increase the problem of hot spots for five reasons. First, the average per capita exposure in L.A. will decline as the emissions cap tightens. Second, the alternative of technology-based regulation, that is CAC regulation, provides no guarantee against such hot spots since sources can increase emissions freely through process changes or by increasing operations without buying permits. Third, the prices of permits are expected to rise sharply, so that it will soon become less attractive to buy them. Fourth, new plants are subject to more stringent technology-based standards. Fifth, the projected localized increases of ozone concentrations are expected to occur in areas where ozone concentration is well below the limits. Therefore, the SCAQMD does not see any risk.

### 4.6.3   Evaluation

#### 4.6.3.1   Competitiveness
The 440 agents in the market represent 80% and 65% of all $NO_x$ and $SO_2$ emitting stationary sources, respectively, located in the basin. This corresponds to 17% of total $NO_x$ emissions and 31% of total $SO_2$ emissions. The concentration of permits among the 440 agents in the market is thought to be low.[292]

#### 4.6.3.2   Property rights
The life of a permit is limited to one year. Because the number of permits is reduced every year, target companies scramble frantically for permits. This raises total transaction costs.[293]

The transfer of property rights is limited, as it is in the ARP.[294] It is impossible to promise that the SCAQMD will not change the rules of the program in the future. However, as was the case in the ARP, confiscation is not likely to happen within the near future.

The enforcement system for larger sources (CEMS) is the same as the one used in the ARP. It works very well, in contrast to the CMPS system for smaller

---

291.   Seligman (1994:22).

292.   Broadbent (1993).

293.   See Krupnick and Burtraw (1994).

294.   The rules of RECLAIM state that 'an RTC [RECLAIM Trading Credit] shall not constitute a security or other form of property' and 'nothing in District rules shall be construed to limit the District's authority to condition, limit, suspend or terminate any RTCs or the authorization to emit which is represented by a Facility Permit'.

sources. Here, the calculation of emission factors is quite uncertain. The margin of error in prediction may exceed 50%, for example a source reported to emit 149 tons of $SO_2$ per year, with the right to emit 100 tons per year, cannot be penalized.[295]

Moreover, reporting is in the hands of industry, so the potential for fraud is also a concern. It is possible for firms to tamper with meters or under-report data on fuel consumption. Trading provides an extra incentive to cheat since under-reported emissions can be sold in the market.[296] Periodically, the regulator will inspect smaller sources that have not installed CEMS and will audit emission records and reporting activities. The formula for penalties is linked to the amount exceeded. As in the ARP, violating sources' allocation for the following year is reduced to make up for previous excesses. In addition, all penalties must be paid before the permits will be reissued.

### 4.6.3.3 Transaction costs
No data are available yet.

The results of this section are summarized in Table 4.11 at the end of this chapter.

## II: Water Pollution

US federal and state regulators share in the clean-up of polluted waters in the US. Ambient water quality standards are established by the individual states and must be approved by the EPA. Even though the standards are often based on EPA guidelines, these do not represent national standards but rather those for adoptation to local conditions. The reason is that water pollution generally has a stronger local impact than air pollution does.[297]

The point sources fall into one of three categories. They may be 1 municipal dischargers, known as publicly owned treatment works (POTWs); 2 direct industrial dischargers, which discharge directly into a water source; or 3 indirect industrial dischargers, which discharge into municipal sewers that flow into POTWs.

New water-pollution sources must meet more stringent technology-based standards than those applying to existing sources. For direct industrial discharg-ers, minimum standards are described by best practicable control technology currently available (BPT), best available technology (BAT) and best conventional pollutant control technology (BCT). These standards and their use corre-spond to those required by the Clean Air Act, that is LAER, BACT, RACT.

In other words, a new source must meet the most stringent BPT, whereas

---

295. Seligman, (1994:21).
296. Dennis (1993).
297. Bartfeld (1992).

existing sources meet BAT or BCT.[298] Even though the sources may have to meet an aggregate limit as a group, individual sources must still comply with the technology-based standards. In one program (Fox River), even more stringent rules apply.

In addition to the local definition of technology-based standards, another main difference between water-pollution policy and air-pollution policy is that water standards are applied to classes of dischargers only, not to attainment or non-attainment areas. A discharger within a given class must comply with the technology-based standard applicable to its specific class.

However, when technology-based standards are not sufficient to achieve ambient water quality standards, the EPA must apply more stringent controls, known as 'water-quality-based-effluent' limitations, to specific plants. These limitations are based on a nexus between discharge quality and received water quality. To date, however, the EPA has focused on developing guidance for technology-based control levels.[299]

The types of pollutants entering streams, lakes and oceans include organic wastes or 'nutrients' (phosphorus and/or nitrogen), toxic chemicals and other hazardous substances, heated water, and sediments. But permit markets have, in practice, been used for controlling organic wastes only.[300] Because the Clean Water Act allows point/non-point source trading, both trade between point sources and trade between point and non-point sources have taken place. Non-point sources require a different set of solutions from those of point sources because non-point source pollution is diffuse and highly variable, depending on factors such as climate, soils and land use practices. Thus, if no easily identifiable outlet is present, the way to control, for example, agricultural sources, is by changing land use practices.[301]

The experience with permit markets in water pollution control is discussed below. Only point sources are regulated in the Fox River program (Section 4.7), whereas the Dillon and Tar-Pamlico programs (Sections 4.8 and 4.9) also allow for limited trade between both point and non-point sources.

---

298.   Bartfeld (1992:7).

299.   Ibid.

300.   Organic waste is the main water pollutant, and potential hot spots caused by these are less dangerous than those created by toxic or hazardous pollutants. Organic wastes decompose by bacterial action. They are commonly measured in units of biochemical oxygen demand (BOD), or the amount of oxygen needed to decompose them. Fish and other aquatic life need oxygen, and the amount of dissolved oxygen in a water body is, therefore, one of the best measures of its ecological health. If too much of the oxygen is spent in decomposition of organic waste, certain types of fish no longer can live there and are replaced by pollution-resistant fish, such as carp, which are considered less desirable. Eutrophication, or the 'dying of lakes', is a natural process resulting from the addition of nutrients and sediments. Over time, lakes become shallower and biologically more productive, eventually evolving into swamps and finally into dry land. Normally this takes thousands of years, but humans greatly accelerate the process when they add nutrients such as fertilizers and detergents. (Findley et al. 1992:133).

301.   See Bartfeld (1992:10).

## 4.7 FOX RIVER PROGRAM

In 1981, Wisconsin introduced a discharge trading program for controlling biological oxygen demand (BOD) on a 45-mile stretch of the Fox River (from Lake Winnebago to Green Bay).[302] The heaviest concentration of paper mills in the world lies along the banks of the Fox River.

### 4.7.1 Design

#### 4.7.1.1 Target level
The target level of water quality is expressed as 5 parts per million (ppm) of dissolved oxygen. This level ensures enough oxygen to sustain fish life and to allow recreational activities on the rivers.[303] At this stated target level, a permit market has the potential of reducing CAC costs by about 80%.[304]

#### 4.7.1.2 Target group
The program concerns two types of point sources: paper and pulp plants and municipal waste-treatment plants. Fifteen paper/pulp plants and 6 municipal waste-treatment plants are engaged in the program.[305] Because the sources are either newly built facilities or were substantially upgraded between 1977 and 1980, substantially different treatment costs across plants are unlikely.[306]

#### 4.7.1.3 Distribution rule
The plants have been grandfathered five-year permits that define their wasteload allocation. The initial distribution is based on production figures from 1970, when no one could have anticipated the regulation associated with the 1972 Clean Water Act.[307] The initial distribution of permits sets a single limit on the total discharge from a plant rather than a number of limits on individual waste sources within a plant, so there is no opportunity for internal trading.[308]

---

302.  BOD is a key measure for water pollution, referring to the demand for dissolved oxygen imposed on a water body by organic effluents.

303.  Oates (1984:16).

304.  O'Neil et al. (1983).

305.  Oates (1984:15).

306.  David and Downing (1992:10).

307.  Interview, February 10, 1995: E.L. David, Natural Resources, Wisconsin.

308.  Hahn and Hester (1989b:392). The need for permits varies through the year with river flow and temperature, that is the rivers' capacity to assimilate the emissions. For example, during the dry summer season, emissions are more damaging (water flow is low and temperatures are high). The program, therefore, uses variable permits that depend upon both water flow and temperature. Such 'flow-temperature' permits require sources to adapt their levels of discharges to river conditions (Oates 1984:16).

#### 4.7.1.4 Trade rules

High transaction costs are to be found in the Fox River trading program. The attempt to introduce an MPO system and to define trade ratios, so that the ambient standards for oxygen level are not exceeded after trade, has resulted in massive administrative requirements.[309]

The trade ratio is defined with respect to two stationary 'sag points' along the Fox River, each of which is located behind a dam. At these points, the oxygen level reaches its minimum. By using a theoretical model of the river that indicates the impact that a unit of emissions from each source will have on the dissolved oxygen level at the sag points, the trade ratio is calculated so that the target level at the sag points is not violated.[310]

Several restrictions limit the transfer of permits. Trading is only allowed if the buying source is new, if it increases its production or if it is unable to meet its discharge limit despite optimal operation of its reduction measures. Also, the plant must demonstrate – to the satisfaction of the regulator – that the increase is needed.

The incentive to trade permits is further weakened because permits are valid for only five years. Sources lose the rights to their permits after they expire, and it is unclear how permits will be redistributed following expiration. Banking of permits is not allowed.[311]

#### 4.7.1.5 Control system

The control system is based on administrative reviews. Approval must be obtained before the trade takes place, and modification of a permit holding requires a minimum of 175 days, a significant shortening of the already limited life of a permit.[312]

### 4.7.2 Performance

#### 4.7.2.1 Trade activity

Trade activity has been low. At the end of 1994, only one trade had occurred.[313] This trade was not a 'real' trade in the traditional sense because it involved a direct industrial discharger which decided to become an indirect discharger by linking to a municipal waste-treatment plant.[314]

The paper/pulp plants have had no difficulty in meeting their permit limits. They have started recycling more of their waste water and using less water-

309.  Hahn and Hester (1989b:393).

310.  Oates (1984:16).

311.  Hahn (1989b:98).

312.  Hahn and Hester (1989b:393).

313.  Interview, January 20, 1995: John Caletti, Wisconsin Water Division, Permit Section.

314.  Interview, February 10, 1995: D. Downing, Technology Assessment, US Congress.

intensive production processes.[315]

### 4.7.2.2  Cost savings
No data are available.

### 4.7.2.3  Innovation
No data are available. Because no significant emission trade have been registered, innovation motivated by the program itself has probably been insignificant.

### 4.7.2.4  Environmental impact
The environmental impact is neutral because the program has been virtually inactive.[316]

### 4.7.3  Evaluation

### 4.7.3.1  Competitiveness
The target group is probably not competitive because the paper/pulp plants are an oligopoly in the product market. Therefore, municipal utilities may not act in a cost-effective way in the permit market.[317] The regulator may attempt to act as anti-trust authority so to secure competitive and non-strategical behaviour. However, it is a hard task to prove that one plant refuses to sell to another plant as a way of reducing competition.

### 4.7.3.2  Property rights
Property rights are limited by five significant barriers to trade. First, transfers must be for at least one year and permits are valid for five years. This means that new holders of permits must hold them for at least one year before selling them. Second, all sources (not only the new ones) are forced to use the newest technology, so sources seek to buy pre-defined technology rather than permits. Third, a source must demonstrate a need for a permit. Fourth, banking is not allowed. Fifth, the future value of the permit is uncertain due to vague signals from authorities.

Enforcement seems not to have been a problem. Since 1981, only one of the 15 paper/pulp plants on the Fox River has been referred for prosecution to the State's attorney general for prosecution for exceeding its water permit limits. That case was settled out of court.[318] No waste-treatment plants have been

315.  David and Downing (1992:10–11).

316.  Another concern with the program is that paper/pulp plant effluents contain toxic organic compounds. Therefore, a potential trade may lead to high local concentrations of toxic materials, causing the trade to be rejected, see Anderson et al. (1990:40).

317.  For further details, see Hahn and Noll (1983), David and Joeres (1983).

318.  David and Downing (1992:13).

prosecuted.

### 4.7.3.3  Transaction costs
The burdensome administrative approval process has presumably created significant transaction costs. With only a few potential participants in the market, transaction costs may have increased for this reason too. On the other hand, most of the paper/pulp plants on the Fox River are members of the Wisconsin Paper Council through which information can easily be exchanged.[319]

The results of this section are summarized in Table 4.12 at the end of this chapter.

## 4.8  DILLON RESERVOIR

The Dillon Reservoir is the source of half of Denver's water, and the local area relies on the income from tourists during both summer (water recreationists) and winter (ski enthusiasts). It is situated in mountainous Summit County, one of the fastest growing counties in the US. To allow for future economic growth and, at the same time, to maintain the desired 1982 level of water quality, the Dillon Reservoir program was developed.[320]

### 4.8.1  Design

#### 4.8.1.1  Target level
Implemented in 1984, the program aims to stabilize phosphorous, the reservoir's most problematic pollutant, at its 1982 level[321] by allowing permits to be traded not only between point sources but also between point and non-point sources.

Potential cost savings were huge at the outset because at the time the program was initiated, it was much cheaper to reduce from non-point sources than from point sources.[322] However, trade potential now runs the other way because non-point sources have started buying from other non-point sources or point sources.[323]

---

319.  Ibid.

320.  The Northwest Colorado Council of Governments concerned a group of local representatives from the county, towns, special districts, ski areas, and mining interests, as well as representatives from the state, the EPA, and the Denver Water Board. Self-named 'the Phosphorus Club', this group proved to be intensely committed to finding a solution to the reservoirs' water-quality problem. They met every week for an extended period of time, evaluating technical and administrative innovations for addressing the problem (Zander 1991:47). The final result was a recommendation of the existing Dillon permit market.

321.  WQCC (1984:4).

322.  Hahn and Hester (1989b:395).

323.  Interview, January 20, 1995: Bruce Zander, Colorado Water Management Division.

#### 4.8.1.2 Target group
The most important point sources are four municipal waste water treatment plants and one industrial treatment plant. Important non-point sources are septic systems and urban run-off.

#### 4.8.1.3 Distribution rule
The initial distribution rule is grandfathering, based on 1982 production levels and the holding capacity of the reservoir.[324] The program includes a 'growth margin' or surplus in its initial distribution of permits to accommodate development through 1990.

#### 4.8.1.4 Trade rules
In the Dillon Reservoir program, a stringent NO system – like the one partially used in the ETP – is at work. Trade between point and non-point sources is allowed on a two-for-one basis, that is, one extra pound of phosphorous emitted from a point source requires a two pound reduction from a non-point source. This is so because a margin of safety is needed in the quite uncertain control of non-point sources.

Emissions are thus intended to be reduced through trade. In theory, the trade is supposed to take place by allowing point sources to install controls at existing non-point sources and then to receive the permits created in return. However, only one trade has occurred to date. The trade ratio itself is simple, but installing control equipment in somebody else's firm might be troublesome.[325] As in the Fox River program, point sources must use the latest technology before they are allowed to trade.

#### 4.8.1.5 Control system
Control is based on irregular inspection. Furthermore, every three years, a central authority independent of local interests (the State Water Quality Control Commission) is required to review and set the discharge distribution.[326]

#### 4.8.2 Performance

#### 4.8.2.1 Trade activity
So far, one trade has taken place in the Dillon Reservoir program. It was in 1988. The Breckenridge Sanitation District received extra phosphorus credits for sewering a subdivision that, until then, had been serviced by individual septic systems. At the moment, two other trades are being considered between non-point sources, this means that the credits obtained will be used to offset

---

324.  EPA (1987).
325.  Interview, January 20, 1995: Bruce Zander, Colorado Water Management Division.
326.  Ibid.

other non-point sources, not point sources.[327]

### 4.8.2.2  Cost savings
No data are available, but in retrospect, the waste-load allocations set in 1984
– which included growth margins – were set too high. Economic growth has
declined and innovation has flourished, so it is unlikely that any more trades
will take place among point sources.

Still, the program has brought enterprises together for meetings and common
decisions. For example, the waste-water treatment plants in total have reduced
their discharge to only 2% of the allowable basin-wide load.[328]

### 4.8.2.3  Innovation
Sources have experimented and innovated in spite of the fact that they have not
used the trade option.

### 4.8.2.4  Environmental effect
The environmental effect has been positive because sources operate below the
upper limits.

### 4.8.3  Evaluation

### 4.8.3.1  Competitiveness
The market is not fully competitive. A future concern for the functioning of the
market is that five firms will dominate. These five need to be followed closely
by the regulator to avoid strategic behaviour. If possible, the number of market
participants should be increased.

### 4.8.3.2  Property rights
Property rights have been transferred to a higher degree in the Dillon Reservoir
program than in the Fox River program. The only significant restriction on trade
is the requirement that all sources must use the latest technology.

A traditional enforcement system based on inspection seems to work satisfactorily.

### 4.8.3.3  Transaction cost
No data are available yet.

The results of this section are summarized in Table 4.13 at the end of this
chapter.

---

327.  Bartfeld (1992:40).

328.  Bartfeld (1992:39). The four POTWs discharging into Dillon reservoir now boast some of
the highest phosphorus removal efficiencies in the US.

## 4.9  TAR-PAMLICO RIVER BASIN

In 1988, the Pamlico-Tar River Foundation (PTRF), a citizens group, asked for the basin to be classified as a nutrient-sensitive watershed. In response to this request, the state of North Carolina designated the entire Tar-Pamlico watershed as nutrient-sensitive in 1989. The state also developed a nutrient management strategy to combat increased nutrition loads that threatened the valuable fisheries in the Pamlico River.[329] A significant portion of the $NO_x$ and phosphorus loading results from non-point source run-off associated with agricultural practices, which dominate the 5,400 square-mile watershed.[330]

### 4.9.1  Design

#### 4.9.1.1  Target level
The Tar-Pamlico program contains a series of stepped-down annual nutrient limits for the sources involved. The net effect of the program was to reduce nutrient loads approximately 36% by the end of 1994, based on 1989 levels.[331] This five-year reduction was only the first phase of the program. Phase II of the program runs from 1994 to 2004, during which further reductions are planned to take place. The phase II target level is being negotiated.[332] No estimates for potential cost-savings are available.[333]

#### 4.9.1.2  Target group
A group of sources formed the Basin Association. There are 19 POTWs and 2 industrial dischargers in the Tar-Pamlico watershed, of which 12 POTWs and 1 industrial source are members of the association.[334] These 13 covered by the program are jointly responsible for achieving a total nutrient target level. They incur substantially different marginal treatment costs for nutrients.[335]

The program also involves non-point sources, which follow the so-called 'best management practices' (BMPs) in agriculture. Agricultural BMPs used in the Tar-Pamlico Basin include grassed waterways and animal waste treatment lagoons.[336] Forestry operations are also included to the extent that they represent a monoculture, typically pine trees, planted in rows that are fertilized like a crop.[337]

---

329.  Levitas and Rader (1993:14).
330.  Bartfeld (1992:40–41).
331.  Levitas and Rader (1993:17).
332.  GUC (1994).
333.  Bartfeld (1992:41).
334.  Interview, February 13, 1995: R. Dodd, Research Triangle Institute.
335.  Interview, February 16, 1995: R. Elks, Greenville Utilities, North Carolina.
336.  Bartfeld (1992:41).
337.  Interview, February 16, 1995: R. Elks, Greenville Utilities, North Carolina.

### 4.9.1.3  Distribution rule
The allowable emissions in the actual calendar year are grandfathered and can be traded.[338]

### 4.9.1.4  Trade rules
Within the aggregate limit, association members may trade among themselves on a one-to-one trade ratio. The Basin Association must fund the development of a nutrient model of the basin. It must also offset excess discharges with payments into a non-point source control fund.[339] Point/non-point source trading is allowed, just as in the Dillon program.

The Tar-Pamlico program also presents a fixed cost for non-point source control in contrast to the Dillon program. Association members can pay the fixed price of $56 per kilogram of extra nutrient emitted to cover necessary non-point source controls.[340] Sources that are not members of the association are eligible to participate in the trading program at a slightly higher rate. Their discharge limits will be adjusted, based upon a rate of $62 per kilogram of extra nutrient discharged. In this way, a trade mechanism is combined with a tax solution. Tax revenue is then invested in reduction measures among non-point sources and is administered through an existing state agricultural cost-share program that provides money to local soil and water conservation districts. The aim is to implement BMPs for reducing nutrient loadings.

If the Basin Association members exceed their total quota, they must pay the tax per extra unit and thereby fund the necessary investments in BMPs for non-point sources.

### 4.9.1.5  Control system
The monitoring mechanism is based on self-reporting. Each source must weekly conduct a certified laboratory test and submit the results to the regulator. To prevent cheating, regulatory inspections occur on an irregular and unannounced basis. Any cheating is punished by fines and loss of professional certifications and may jeopardize the agreement itself. If a source pays a tax to receive a permit, it is important to make sure that the reduction from non-point sources actually takes place. The Basin Association is not legally responsible for non-point source control.[341]

---

338.   Ibid.

339.   Bartfeld (1992:41–42).

340.   The figure of $56 is based on costs associated with non-point source control in a neighbouring watershed, the Chowan River Basin. This figure is presumably set very high and may as such, result in greater environmental improvements than the target level.

341.   Bartfeld (1992:42).

### 4.9.2  Performance

#### 4.9.2.1  Trade activity
No trades have yet taken place, and no money has flowed into the fund. The association has not reached its upper quota limit due to low-cost operational and capital improvements that were implemented at the POTWs.[342]

#### 4.9.2.2  Cost savings
No data are available.

#### 4.9.2.3  Innovation
While innovations have been used to meet the target levels, it is less necessary to innovate in this case because of increased flexibility. Sources can always buy permits from each other or pay a tax if they should get into trouble.

#### 4.9.2.4  Environmental impact
The environmental effect has been good. Association members have, without trading, implemented a substantial, gradual reduction in the amount of nutrients discharged.

### 4.9.3  Evaluation

#### 4.9.3.1  Competitiveness
The 13 actors differ substantially in size and the market is non-competitive. A few actors have sufficient market power to act strategically.[343]

#### 4.9.3.2  Property rights
As in the Dillon program, a well-designed program without unnecessary trade restrictions has been defined. However, no trade has yet been provoked.

Enforcement has been based on a combination of irregular inspections, self-reporting and a system of fines. No penalties have been imposed so far and the control system seems to work as intended.

#### 4.9.3.3  Transaction costs
Transaction costs are probably low because of the self-regulatory nature of the program. The close relationship between the sources makes information about trade and innovation options easily available. However, due to the lack of trade, this suggestion is subject to uncertainty.

---

342. Interview, February 13, 1995: R. Dodd, Research Triangle Institute. An engineering study from 1991 of Basin Association member facilities has indicated that most plants could meet required nutrient reductions through relatively inexpensive operational changes rather than through expensive capital investments. See Bartfeld (1992:41).

343. Interview, February 16, 1995: R. Elks, Greenville Utilities, North Carolina.

These results are summarized in Table 4.14 at the end of this chapter.

## 4.10 CONCLUSION

The purpose of this chapter is to explain which economic and administrative distortions have reduced the performance of permit markets in practice.

Economic distortions due to incomplete competition seem not to have been any problem so far. Tietenberg (1985:142) suggests that the reason for this is that the initial distribution rule used in the trading programs is close enough to the cost-effective distribution to prevent any serious impediment to competition. Another plausible explanation is that trade has been limited in the programs with critical market structures (CFC/halon program, Fox River, Dillon Reservoir, Tar-Pamlico).

Administrative distortions, on the other hand, have played a main role in explaining actual performance so far. In Section 3.7 it was shown that any attempt to incorporate source location is likely to create substantial transaction costs because of the required trade restrictions and extensive administrative approval processes. All eight US programs reviewed here tried to deal with the hot spot problem either by using one of the trade rules or simply by ignoring it.

The US programs were initiated by grandfathering.[344] With respect to the air pollution programs, the ETP, on the national level, has dealt with a number of air pollutants since 1974. In the early phase of the ETP, regulators tried to improve environmental quality and remove hot spots by setting high trade ratios so that target levels for concentration could be reached. This system resembled the NO trade rule the most because it called for an asymmetrical trade ratio at which the seller's emissions were reduced much more than the buyer's emissions were allowed to increase. Since it was not possible to know the trade ratio in advance, this requirement created much uncertainty about the value of a trade; and no stable market prices were created.

Since 1986, an ambient test has been applied for most of the pollutants. In the cases where this test has been carried out, the ETP resembles the MPO trade rule because no increase in concentration contributions were allowed after trade. This attempt to fix the existing air quality level at its pre-trade level still meant administrative approval for each trade and substantial transaction costs in a market with varying prices depending on the location of the trade partners. The rules did not allow the plants to dispose of their permits freely, failed to transfer property rights, and created a high degree of regulatory uncertainty.

The purpose of the lead trading program was to phase out the lead content in gasoline. Refineries were allowed to trade lead permits in an EPS system, that is, on a one-to-one ratio, though trading could not be used to avoid California's

---

344. For summary information on the design, performance and evaluation of each program, please refer to the evaluation tables at the end of this chapter.

standards for lead content. Before the program started, EPA undertook an analysis that took into account the actual market structure and concluded that the program would not result in any hot spots. And as predicted, no hot spots occurred. It was thus possible to ignore the spatial dimension and keep transaction costs low while still achieving the goals of the program.

The CFC/halon trading program aimed to phase out CFCs in a similar way to the phase-out scheme in the lead trading program. Again, the drastic reductions in emissions made the occurrence of hot spots, following trade activity, highly unlikely. Therefore, as in the lead trading program, trade was allowed on an EPS basis and the spatial dimension was ignored, resulting in low transaction costs.

The ARP addressed $SO_2$ emissions from electric utilities. It also ignored the risk of hot spots. The ambient standards were not expected to be violated anywhere for two reasons. First, total $SO_2$ emissions were to be reduced by 50% over a 10-year period (from 1990 to the year 2000). Second, old and 'dirty' utilities (with low marginal reduction costs) were situated in the mid-west. Because the wind blows from west to east, the environmental quality was expected to be improved in the critical east coast areas. Utilities were therefore allowed to trade in an EPS system without individual approval procedures, as was the case in the lead trading program and the CFC/halon trading program. However, trade was supposed to take place in one direction only, so that a utility in the east could be forbidden to sell permits to a utility in the mid-west by the local regulator. Transaction costs were kept low.

Another important innovation in the ARP was the design of the US EPA's new revenue-neutral auction for $SO_2$ permits. This auction was discriminative, that is, the source paid what it bid. The results from the two first annual auctions showed that it worked well. However, it could be improved by using a non-discriminative design, in which the source only pays the clearing price. A shift to a non-discriminative design would send a single price signal to the market. Therefore, if the auction mechanism is to be used, for example in a Danish or European $CO_2$ market, the results of this analysis suggest the use of a non-discriminative design.

RECLAIM dealt with air pollutants in California. It was similar to the ARP in design. Again, hot spots were not expected by the regulators at the outset because of substantial reductions in emissions, because of high expected prices on permits and because the projected localized increases of ozone concentrations were located in areas that are substantially within concentration limits. Transaction costs were, therefore, expected to be low. Note, however, that the L.A. region was divided into a western and an eastern zone for purposes of this program. To protect the critical western zone, new sources there would not be allowed to buy permits from the eastern zone.

The first of the three water pollution programs is the Fox River program, in which an attempt is made to introduce an MPO system; trade-ratios are to be defined so that the ambient standards for oxygen level are not exceeded after trade. These efforts have resulted in massive administrative requirements for individual approval and massive transaction costs. No trades have yet occurred.

In the Dillon Reservoir program, a simplified NO system is established: a specific trade ratio is defined for reducing phosphorous. Trade is to take place between point and non-point sources on a two-for-one basis, that is one extra pound of phosphorous emitted from a point-source requires a two-pound reduction from a non-point source. The program is thus designed so that emissions will be reduced by trade. The extent to which administrative approval procedures and transaction costs have influenced market activity is yet unclear because, while the trade ratio, in itself, has been fixed and simple, only one trade has occurred.

In the Tar-Pamlico program, the participants can trade on a one-to-one basis. Point/non-point source trading is allowed, so that sources can pay a fixed cost per kilogram of extra nutrient emitted to cover necessary non-point source controls. Transaction costs would probably be low because of the self-regulatory nature of the program and because the sources know each other. However, no trades have taken place and no money has flowed into the fund yet. The reason for this seems to be the fact that the sources already operate below their upper discharge limits.

In conclusion, the ETP and Fox River programs were influenced by complicated rules and individual approval procedures that created high transaction costs and prevented trade. In both these cases, it was cheaper for sources to make their own reductions rather than trade. By contrast, the lead trading program, the ARP and the CFC/halon trading program (where substantial trade activity took place) together with RECLAIM, the Dillon Reservoir program and the Tar-Pamlico program (where it is still too early to judge performance), were far less restricted.

In this way, the successful programs in the US avoided individual administrative control procedures by using well-defined property rights and reduction schemes that allowed the risk of creating hot spots by trade to be ignored. These designs are obvious models for policies regarding pollutants without spatial impact, for example $CO_2$. Many aspects of the design of the ARP, in particular, can be recommended for the creation of a $CO_2$ market and a $CO_2$ auction in Denmark and the EU.

What were the political reasons for designing these successful programs? Why were early programs like ETP and the Fox River program severely restricted? There is hardly any doubt that the regulators' original intention was to define property rights and minimize restrictions on trade. But it was difficult to convince other parties of the potential environmental benefits from using markets and letting go of traditional individual control. Whereas Chapter 4 focused on the design and resulting performance of permit markets in the US, Chapter 5 shows that these specific choices of policy designs in the US have been the result of political decision-making and lobbyism.

*Table 4.7: ETP*

| | |
|---|---|
| **I DESIGN** | |
| **Target level** | Comply with national standards for ambient air quality. |
| pollutant | $SO_2$, $NO_x$, particulates, CO, HC. |
| standards | Ambient national standards: NAAQS, and technology-based emission standards: RACT, BACT, LAER. |
| period | 1974 – ? |
| location | US (implemented by individual states). |
| potential savings | 90% compared to CAC. |
| **Target group** | CAC-regulated industry. |
| number | Major industrial sources all over the US. |
| concentration | Low. |
| marginal reduction costs | Huge variation. |
| **Distribution rule** | Individual review, grandfathering. |
| **Trade rules** | Netting, offset, bubble and banking. |
| **Control system** | Uses CAC infrastructure. |
| **II PERFORMANCE** | |
| **Trade Activity** | Low – only 1% of potential trade realized. |
| type | Mainly internal trades. |
| price signal | Diffuse. |
| **Cost savings** | 4% of total reduction costs. |
| **Innovation** | Low. |
| **Environmental effect** | Neutral. |
| **III EVALUATION** | |
| **Competitiveness** | High. |
| **Property rights** | |
| definition | Not well-defined. Many restrictions on the use of permits. |
| enforcement | Unsatisfactory. Traditional control; it is possible to cheat. Court rules should be simplified and enforcement should be by central authorities independent of local interests. |
| **Transaction costs** | High. |
| **Conclusion** | Poor performance. Markets are competitive but property rights have not been defined or enforced satisfactorily and transaction costs are high. 1 only emission reduction credits (ERCs) are currency; the currency should be permits, 2 stringent technology-based standards are required for new sources; technology-based standards should be removed, 3 new sources are not permitted to use bubbles; new sources should be permitted to use bubbles, 4 banking has not been implemented; banking should be implemented, 5 the trade ratio is typically more than one; the trade-ratio should, in general, be 1:1, 6 permits are arbitrarily confiscated; the regulator should not be allowed to arbitrarily change the value of permits. |

*Table 4.8: Lead trading program*

---

**I DESIGN**

| | |
|---|---|
| **Target level** | Phase-down lead content in gasoline to 0.1 grams per gallon. |
| pollutant | Lead. |
| standards | Progressively more stringent standards for amount of added lead . |
| period | 1982–1987. |
| location | US. |
| potential savings | No data. |

| | |
|---|---|
| **Target group** | Manufacturers of gasoline. |
| number | 195 refineries, 900 alcohol blenders. |
| concentration | Medium. |
| marginal reduction costs | High variation. |

| | |
|---|---|
| **Distribution rule** | Grandfathering. |
| **Trade rules** | Banking and one-to-one trade so that source location is ignored. Trade cannot be used to avoid the more stringent Californian standards for lead content. |
| **Control system** | Buyers and sellers report trade activity every calendar quarter to the EPA, which can cross-check the data. Administrative settlements of violations. |

**II PERFORMANCE**

| | |
|---|---|
| **Trade Activity** | High. |
| type | Both external trade and banking. |
| price signal | Precise. About 4 cents per gram of lead. |

| | |
|---|---|
| **Cost savings** | About 20% of total lead refining costs. |
| **Innovation** | High among car manufacturers. |
| **Environmental effect** | Positive. |

**III EVALUATION**

| | |
|---|---|
| **Competitiveness** | High. |

| | |
|---|---|
| **Property rights** | |
| definition | Well-defined devaluation scheme and simple trade rules that ignore source location. |
| enforcement | Good. Close double-checking by a central authority, the EPA. |

| | |
|---|---|
| **Transaction costs** | Low. |
| **Conclusion** | Well-designed program with a competitive market and a well-defined and enforceable trade system that keeps transaction costs low. |

---

*Table 4.9: CFC/Halon trading program*

---

**I DESIGN**

| | |
|---|---|
| **Target level** | Phase-out CFCs in 1996 and halons in 1994. |
| pollutant | CFCs and halons. |
| standards | Progressively stricter standards for production /consumption. |
| period | 1989–1996. |
| location | US. |
| potential savings | 40% compared to CAC. |

| | |
|---|---|
| **Target group** | Producers and importers of CFCs and halons. |
| number | 7 producers and 10 importers. |
| concentration | High. |
| marginal reduction costs | High variation. |

| | |
|---|---|
| **Distribution rule** | Grandfathering, based on 1986 production and import level. |
| **Trade rules** | No banking. Nearly one-to-one trade (1% reduction). Exports held free. |
| **Control system** | Buyers and sellers obliged to report production, imports and trade activity every quarter to the EPA which can cross-check the data. High fines ($25,000 per kilo). |

**II PERFORMANCE**

| | |
|---|---|
| **Trade Activity** | Substantial. 80 external trades through 1991. |
| type | Presumably both external and internal. |
| price signal | Confidential. |

| | |
|---|---|
| **Cost savings** | Confidential. |
| **Innovation** | Presumably high due to the trade option when substituting away from CFCs and halons. |
| **Environmental effect** | Positive. |

**III EVALUATION**

| | |
|---|---|
| **Competitiveness** | Low. |

| | |
|---|---|
| **Property rights** | |
| definition | Well-defined devaluation scheme and simple trade rules that basically ignore source location. Banking not allowed. Some regulatory uncertainty because the target level has quickly been tightened to a phase-out. |
| enforcement | Good due to high fines that deter cheating. |

| | |
|---|---|
| **Transaction costs** | Low. |
| **Conclusion** | A reasonably well-designed program that may be improved. Enforcement is good and transaction costs low, but the market may not be competitive. Also, banking should be allowed, and the regulator should make announcements about the reduction scheme as soon as possible. |

---

*Table 4.10: ARP*

## I DESIGN

| | |
|---|---|
| **Target level** | 50% $SO_2$ reduction of the 1980 level by the year 2000. |
| pollutant | $SO_2$. |
| standards | Technology-based standards (LAER, BACT, RACT). |
| period | 1990–2000. Trade started in 1990 and devaluation in 1995. |
| location | US. |
| potential savings | 70% compared to CAC. |
| **Target group** | Electric utilities. |
| number | 1000 plants owned by 200 companies. Optin for others. |
| concentration | Low. |
| marginal reduction costs | High variation. |
| **Distribution rule** | Grandfathering, based on average fuel-input, 1985–1987. |
| **Trade rules** | Allows banking, use of 'shut-down' credits, and one-to-one trade. Eastern and western zone. Special Allowance Reserve (3% of permits annually) withheld for direct sale ($1,500) and open auction. Auction is discriminative and revenue-neutral. |
| **Control system** | Automatic monitoring system (CEMS) and $2,000 fine per ton excess $SO_2$ which must be offset the following year. |

## II PERFORMANCE

| | |
|---|---|
| **Trade activity** | High. 1,902 trades involving over 34 million permits (1994–96). |
| type | 741 external and 1161 internal. |
| price signal | Price per ton $SO_2$ was in March 1997: $107 in spot auction and $110 in spot market. |
| **Cost savings** | 40% compared to CAC. Market price in 1997 about seven times lower than expected. |
| **Innovation** | High. |
| **Environmental effect** | 40% overcompliance in 1995. No hot spots and environmental improvement. |

## III EVALUATION

| | |
|---|---|
| **Competitiveness** | High. |
| **Property rights** | |
| definition | Well-designed property rights with a devaluation scheme and simple trade rules that ignore source location. |
| enforcement | High fines and an effective monitoring system (CEMS), run by EPA as a central authority, make it unprofitable to exceed emission limits. So, no need for 'compliance' reporting. |
| **Transaction costs** | Low. |
| **Conclusion** | Well-designed program that creates a competitive market. Property rights are well-defined and enforcement is excellent. Transaction costs are small. However, the treatment of gains from trade is uncertain in some cases. To reward shareholders and trade activity, gains from trade should be counted as capital gains in general. Also, auction design should be changed to a non-discriminative and single-priced system and new sources should not face more stringent technology-based standards. |

*Table 4.11: RECLAIM*

---

**I DESIGN**

| | |
|---|---|
| **Target level** | 60% $SO_2$ and 75% $NO_x$ reduction of the 1994 level by the year 2003 (devaluation annually). |
| pollutant | $SO_x$ and $NO_x$ (ROGs planned). |
| standards | Technology-based standards (LAER, BACT, RACT). |
| period | 1994–2003. |
| location | L.A. basin, California. |
| potential savings | 42% compared to CAC. |
| **Target group** | Industry. |
| number | 40 plants in $SO_2$ program and 400 plants in $NO_x$ program. |
| concentration | Low. |
| marginal reduction costs | High variation. |

**Distribution rule**  Grandfathering, based on highest annual emissions in the period 1989–1992.

**Trade rules**  Allows banking, use of 'shut-down' credits, one-to-one trading and the offset of emission from old scrapped cars. L.A. Region divided into two trade zones.

**Control system**  Automatic high-tech monitoring systems CEMS (large sources) and CPMS (small sources). The formula for penalties is linked to the amount of excess. No permits are reissued before penalties are paid, and excess must be offset the following year.

**II PERFORMANCE**

**Trade Activity**  Too early to report. 1 substantial trade occurred in the first 6 months.

| | |
|---|---|
| type | External one-to-one trade. |
| price signal | $700 per ton $NO_x$. No price signal for $SO_2$ permits yet. |
| **Cost savings** | No data yet. |
| **Innovation** | No data yet. |
| **Environmental effect** | Some risk for creating hot spots because smaller sources have non-exact monitoring equipment. |

**III EVALUATION**

| | |
|---|---|
| **Competitiveness** | High. |
| **Property rights** | |
| definition | Lifetime of a permit limited to one year. Technology-based standards for new sources still in effect. |
| enforcement | Good for larger sources (CEMS) but not satisfactory for smaller sources (CMPS). |
| **Transaction costs** | No data yet. |
| **Conclusion** | Well-designed program and well-defined property rights. Potential for successful performance. New sources should not face more stringent technology-based standards. Need for better monitoring systems for smaller sources, and permits could be devalued in for example 5-year-steps rather than every year. |

*Table 4.12: Fox River program*

---

**I DESIGN**

| | |
|---|---|
| **Target level** | Maintenance of 5 parts per mill. (ppm) of dissolved oxygen. |
| pollutant | Nutrients (BOD). |
| standards | Technology-based standards. |
| period | 1981–? |
| location | Wisconsin. |
| potential savings | 80% compared to CAC. |
| **Target group** | Paper/pulp plants and municipal waste treatment plants. |
| number | 15 paper/pulp plants and 6 municipal waste-treatment plants. |
| concentration | High. |
| marginal reduction costs | No significant differences. |
| **Distribution rule** | Grandfathering. Based on production in 1970. |
| **Trade rules** | Trade ratio calculated so target level at sag points is not violated. Trading only allowed if buying source is new, increases its production or is unable to meet its discharge limit despite optimal operation of its reduction measures. Also, buying source must demonstrate 'need' for permits. Banking not allowed. Transfers must be for at least one year. |
| **Control system** | Traditional inspection system. |

**II PERFORMANCE**

| | |
|---|---|
| **Trade Activity** | Low. Only one trade. |
| type | Administrative. |
| price signal | None. |
| **Cost savings** | No data. |
| **Innovation** | Probably limited. |
| **Environmental effect** | Neutral. |

**III EVALUATION**

| | |
|---|---|
| **Competitiveness** | Low. |
| **Property rights** | |
| definition | Restrictions on the use of permits: 1 transfers must be for at least one year (permit is only valid for five years); 2 all sources are forced to use newest technology; 3 a source must demonstrate a 'need' for a permit; 4 banking is not allowed; 5 regulatory uncertainty due to vague signals from authorities. |
| enforcement | Satisfactory; traditional inspection systems. |
| **Transaction costs** | High. |
| **Conclusion** | The market is not competitive, transaction costs are high and property rights to permits are severely restricted. To ensure competitive behaviour, regulator must closely follow market agents. The present design may be adjusted: 1 by defining property rights for any period and ensuring renewal; 2 by eliminating technology requirements; 3 by removing the required demonstration of permit 'need'; 4 by allowing banking; 5 by providing more precise, regulatory signals and easier approval processes. |

---

*Table 4.13: Dillon Reservoir program*

---

**I DESIGN**

| | |
|---|---|
| **Target level** | Stabilize phosphorous at its 1982 level. |
| pollutant | Phosphorous. |
| standards | Technology-based standards for water. |
| period | 1984–? |
| location | Denver, Colorado. |
| potential savings | $773,000 per year. |
| **Target group** | Point sources (industrial/municipal waste treatment plants). |
| | Non-point sources (septic systems and urban run-off). |
| number | 1 industrial and 4 municipal waste treatment plants. |
| concentration | High. |
| marginal reduction costs | Substantial differences. |

**Distribution rule** — Grandfathering, based on 1982 production and holding capacity of the lake.

**Trade rules** — Trade ratio 2:1 between non-point and point sources. Sources must use latest technology before trade is allowed.

**Control system** — Inspection. Point sources must install controls at non-point sources.

**II PERFORMANCE**

| | |
|---|---|
| **Trade Activity** | Low. Only one trade. |
| type | Administrative. |
| price signal | No. |

**Cost savings** — No data.

**Innovation** — No data.

**Environmental effect** — Positive without trade.

**III EVALUATION**

**Competitiveness** — Low.

| | |
|---|---|
| **Property rights** | |
| definition | Well-defined. Only restriction is that sources must use latest technology. |
| enforcement | Satisfactory; traditional inspection system. |

**Transaction costs** — No data.

**Conclusion** — Property rights are well-defined and well-enforced but the upper emission limit has been set so high that the trade option has not been used. Also, to secure competitiveness in the market, the number of participants should be increased or the agents should be followed closely by the regulator. Finally, there should be no technological requirements.

*Table 4.14: Tar-Pamlico River basin*

---

**I DESIGN**

**Target level**              Gradual 36% reduction of nutrients at the end of 1994 from
                              1989 level.
  pollutant                   Nutrients (phosphorous and/or nitrogen).
  standards                   Technology-based.
  period                      1991–2004.
  location                    Tar Pamlico River Basin, North Carolina.
  potential savings           No estimates.

**Target group**              The Basin Association which consists of point sources and
                              non-point sources.
  number                      1 industrial and 12 municipal treatment plants (POTWs) and
                              numerous non-point sources (agriculture and forestry).
  concentration               High.
  marginal reduction costs Significant differences.

**Distribution rule**         Grandfathering; based on calendar year.

**Trade rules**               One-to-one trading ratio or payment of $56 per kilogram
                              nutrient into a fund for offsetting non-point sources.

**Control system**            If quota is exceeded, association members must pay the fund
                              tax. Monitoring is based on self-reporting combined with
                              irregular inspection. Association members are not respon-
                              sible for the non-point source control.

**II PERFORMANCE**

**Trade Activity**            No trade so far.
  type                        –
  price signal                No.

**Cost savings**              No data.

**Innovation**                No data.

**Environmental effect**      Good because of substantial discharge reduction.

**III EVALUATION**

**Competitiveness**           Low.

**Property rights**
  definition                  Well-defined. No trade restrictions.
  enforcement                 Good combination of irregular inspections, self-reporting
                              and fines for violations.

**Transaction costs**         No data.

**Conclusion**                Well-designed. However, competitive behaviour must be
                              ensured.

---

# 5   Lobbyism: US Interest Groups

## 5.1   OVERVIEW

This chapter provides a political explanation for the designs of US permit markets analysed in Chapter 4. How has the lobbyism of the main political actors influenced environmental regulation in the US? What kind of regulation do the three main political actors in the US prefer at present and why?

The first two main groups of political actors are the regulated parties themselves, that is the public electric utilities and private industries. The third main faction is the environmental group, which traditionally has opposed industrial interests on environmental issues. Section 5.2 explains the performance of previous permit markets as the result of political opposition from environmental groups which, until lately, maintained a symbolic goal of zero pollution. Section 5.3 explains the puzzling choice of a discriminative auction in the ARP as the result of lobbyism among electric utilities. Section 5.4 then discusses organizations representing the three main actors and the preferences reflected by these organizations. The question posed is the following: 'if there is to be regulation, what kind of regulation would you prefer?'

Section 5.5 compares the results to the political hypotheses developed in Chapter 2 and attempts to explain deviations from the theoretical expectations. Both private business and environmental groups demand permit markets. Surprisingly, electric utilities promote the idea of permit markets and deregulation. This attitude is explained by an analysis of the dawning competition in the US electricity sector (Section 5.6). This analysis is important in relation to the simultaneous development of a single market for electricity in the EU, a market in which similar attitudes may emerge.

## 5.2   SYMBOLIC GOAL OF ZERO POLLUTION

Political attitudes explain why some programs have been more heavily opposed than others. The role of US environmental groups and their change of attitude, from strong scepticism to promotion of market-based ideas, has been decisive. Historically, environmental groups have maintained a symbolic goal of zero pollution. Such groups claimed, in general, that legitimizing pollution and creating 'licenses to pollute' were immoral. They maintained that the air is not for sale at any price and that a price mechanism is, therefore, not fitting for abating pollution.[345]

As such, the ETP and the Fox River program were severely opposed by environmental groups because they were seen to have legitimized pollution without ensuring any significant reduction. This opposition persuaded the regulators to weaken the definition of property rights. Property rights were satisfactorily defined in the cases of lead and CFC trading, where the pollutants were phased out over short periods of time. This seems to be the main reason why these programs have not been severely opposed and restricted: the goals of zero pollution and future control over the environment were both in line with the prevailing attitude among environmental groups.

Lately, there has been a major change in attitude. Environmental groups no longer maintain a target of zero pollution; instead they promote markets where substantial reductions in emissions are taking place (and thereby offer significant improvements in environmental quality). The ARP, RECLAIM, Dillon Reservoir and Tar-Pamlico programs all contain substantial emission reduction goals and have therefore in general been approved and promoted by environmental groups. Furthermore, control systems have lately been based on automatic monitoring equipment, which makes it impossible for sources to cheat. Therefore, it has been possible for the regulator to define and enforce property rights and minimize trade restrictions.

Environmental groups now actively promote the use of economic instruments for pollution control. This change in attitude has been the main reason for the absence of excessive administrative control and trade restrictions in recent programs like the ARP and RECLAIM.

## 5.3  CHOICE OF AUCTION DESIGN

Why did the US Congress choose a discriminative auction design for the ARP instead of a non-discriminative auction one? The answer is not obvious. The actual choice of a discriminative design is questionable and suggests that lobbying and cartelization among existing utilities provoked the current format of the US $SO_2$ auction.

The existing utilities wanted to hand over only about 3% of their permits to the Special Allowance Reserve. The design of the program itself has thus probably been an attempt to create a barrier to entry. As explicitly stated by the US Congress, the purpose of the actual design was to maximize revenue.[346] By doing so payments would be redistributed from new to existing sources. New sources (that is 'potential competitors') were, in this way, disadvantaged. Not only would they have to buy their way into the market, the payment they made would be redistributed to the existing utilities (as a payment in proportion to the

---

345.   See Hahn (1989b:110–12) and Raufer and Feldman (1987:7). See also Nelson (1990) who interestingly links the 'sin' of polluting to the perception of God in nature.
346.   Hausker (1992:568).

devaluation), the very ones they were competing against.

If this was the intention, reality has turned out very differently. Bids have followed expectations, that is information on the actual market price, to such an extent that the auction average price is at the same level as the market price. In other words, the discriminative auction hardly creates more revenue than the non-discriminative one. If the auction in practice does not fulfill the objective of imposing more costs on new sources than those imposed by an alternative non-discriminative design, then it must be possible to convince the existing cartel of utilities that a change would be more favourable to them. A non-discriminative design would give everybody more flexibility because a single and precise price signal would lower the negotiation costs when trading $SO_2$ permits.

## 5.4 PRESENT ATTITUDES

Let us look at the utilities, private firms and environmental groups in turn. The interest groups and their present attitudes towards environmental regulation will be presented.[347] The general question addressed in this section is: if there is to be regulation, that is, a target level that must be met, what kind of regulation would the participants then prefer?

### 5.4.1 Public Electric Utilities

US public electric utilities are organized into three associations: the Edison Electric Institute, the American Public Power Association, and the National Rural Cooperative Association.

#### 5.4.1.1 Edison Electric Institute (EEI)

Founded in 1933 as the association of investor-owned utilities, EEI represents 174 investor-owned electric utility companies operating in the US and covered, in 1994, 75% of total public electricity production.[348] It has a staff of 300. Nebraska is the only state which does not have any independent power producers (IPPs).[349]

The EEI generally favours grandfathered permit systems because they – in contrast to CAC regulations – give flexibility.[350]

---

347.   This subsection draws heavily on Svendsen (1998d). If no other source is indicated, all data on organizations, members, and staff are collected from Schwartz and Turner (eds.) (1995) and Russel et al. (eds.) (1994).

348.   EEI (1994a).

349.   EEI (1994b).

350.   Interview, December 15, 1994: John Kinsman, Edison Electric Institute (EEI), Washington D.C.

### 5.4.1.2 The American Public Power Association (APPA)

Founded in 1940 with a staff of 60, APPA now represents 2000 public-owned utilities (utilities owned by municipalities). APPA covers 20% of total public production (half from federal power agencies).[351]

The APPA generally favours permit markets because they allow utilities to fulfill their environmental objectives at least cost.[352]

### 5.4.1.3 The National Rural Cooperative Association (NRCA)

Founded in 1942, the NRCA represents 1000 public-utility cooperatives, those owned by the customers themselves. The NRCA represents 5% of total public production.[353] It has a staff of 500.[354] The general attitude is clear-cut. If there is to be any program, then a grandfathered permit market is definitely, and by far, the best way. It provides a maximum of flexibility and minimizes costs.[355]

### 5.4.2 Private Industry

There are two major organizations that speak for business as a whole. They are the US Chamber of Commerce and the National Association of Manufacturers. A third important organization is to be found among private electricity producers, namely the trade association, National Independent Energy Producers.

### 5.4.2.1 US Chamber of Commerce

The Chamber of Commerce was formed in 1912 on the recommendation of President Taft, who saw the need for a central organization to give Congress the benefit of the opinions of the business community on national problems and issues affecting the economy. The Chamber is the world's largest business federation, with more than 200,000 companies and a staff of 1,350. The general attitude is clearly in favour of permit markets and against the use of CAC regulation. The Chamber is interested in being assigned a target level by the regulator after which the decision-making on how to reach this goal is left to the sources themselves. A permit market is the most flexible and cost-effective solution.[356]

---

351.   EEI (1994a) and APPA (1994).

352.   Major (1992:38). A major concern in the design of the market itself is that the EPA should provide all possible information needed when the market is in its infancy. The availability of information is especially important to the smaller members, which do not have the staff or resources to research ownership and prices (ibid).

353.   EEI (1994a).

354.   NRCA (1993).

355.   Interview, January 12, 1995: Ray Cronmiller, The National Rural Cooperative Association (NRCA), Washington D.C.

356.   Interview, January 23, 1995: Charlie Ingram, The US Chamber of Commerce, Washington D.C.

### 5.4.2.2  National Association of Manufacturers (NAM)

Established in Cincinnati 1895, the NAM represents 12,500 companies and has a staff of 180. The general attitude towards regulation is that if there is to be regulation, then business would choose a permit market because of the flexibility. Business has to be responsive to demand, and often traditional regulation prevents this by making complicated and rigid rules. Simplicity is the keyword. The ARP is an example of a well-designed program which business would like to take part in.[357]

### 5.4.2.3  National Independent Energy Producers (NIEP)

The trade association National Independent Energy Producers (NIEP) was formed in 1986 in Washington D.C. The NIEP represents the Independent Power Producers (IPPs). There are 3,321 independent power projects in operation, accounting for 51 GW or 7% of the total electricity production in the US. The NIEP has promoted full competition in the electricity industry and its general attitude towards environmental regulation is consistent with that of other private industries. The NIEP is also in favour of a permit market.[358]

### 5.4.3  Environmental Groups

Three groups have dominated the discussion on the role of economic instruments in environmental regulation: first and foremost, the Environmental Defence Fund (EDF); second, the Natural Resources Defence Council (NRDC); and third, the Sierra Club.

### 5.4.3.1  Environmental Defence Fund (EDF)

Founded in 1967, the EDF has 200,000 members and a staff of 140. Its purpose is 'to prevent pollution before it occurs, to increase the effectiveness of environmental regulations, and to build broad new coalitions to protect the environment'.[359] The present attitude of the EDF is clearly in favour of permit markets.

The EDF has recently commented on the ARP as 'a powerful example of law reform that should be applied to other pollution reduction strategies'. The identifiable environmental benefits and the fact that the program gives the highest degree of reliability in reaching its emissions reduction objectives are essential.[360] A critical feature is the control system. The ARP requires that all sources install automatic monitoring systems that report directly to the EPA. If sources exceed their permit holdings, heavy fines are automatically imposed on

357.  Interview, January 20 1995: Teresa Larson, National Association of Manufacturers, Washington D.C.

358.  NIEP (1994:2 and 10). Interview, January 25, 1995: Liza Mackey, National Independent Energy Producers, Washington D.C.

359.  EDF (1994:1).

360.  Goffman (1994:2 and 14).

them and the excess amount must be offset the following year. The EDF prefers this type of control system – where any cheating can be easily detected – whereas, they are not comfortable with, for example, the control system used in RECLAIM; it creates too much uncertainty about actual emissions.[361]

### 5.4.3.2  Natural Resources Defence Council (NRDC)

Founded in 1970, the NRDC has 170,000 members and a staff of 156. Its mission is 'to provide the best possible legal defence of the magnificent natural resources – wildlife, forests, waterways and clean air'.[362] The NRDC also prefers permit markets, if well-designed. As such, the NRDC has endorsed the ARP, in part because good monitoring and measurement of $SO_2$ emissions from power plants is technically feasible. But, like the EDF, the NRDC rejects the RECLAIM program because current estimation methods are inadequate. NRDC representatives argue that because permit markets do not work well in all situations, they must be judged on a case-by-case basis: 'To the extent states wish to experiment with trading programs, they should favour limited, carefully-designed programs designed to obtain carefully measured emissions reductions.'[363]

### 5.4.3.3  The Sierra Club

Founded in 1892 by naturalist John Muir to help preserve the beauty of the Sierra Nevada range, the Sierra Club has 650,000 members and a staff of 294. Its purpose is 'to stop relentless abuse of our irreplaceable wilderness lands, to save endangered species and to protect our global environment before our chance to do so disappears for good'.[364] The general attitude toward the choice of instrument in environmental regulation is in favour of permit markets.

The specific choice depends on the details of each emissions trading program, that is a case-by-case evaluation. The goal is to make sure that programs are used to win greater environmental protection. The question is whether emissions trading will help to achieve greater environmental protection at a lower cost or whether it will undo hard-won technology-based regulations (that is CAC). If combined with sharp cuts in permitted emissions, and if strictly monitored and enforced, emissions trading offers an opportunity to blend environmental and economic goals in ways that benefit the environment substantially. For example, the ARP is worth supporting, but this is not to say that every individual trading program deserves support. The Sierra Club has doubts about the RECLAIM program and its potential capability of accomplishing a sufficient reduction to ensure public health and the environment. Any effort to change existing CAC can only be justified if it

361.   Goffman (1994:7).
362.   NRDC (1994).
363.   Driesen (1993:13).
364.   Sierra Club (1994).

achieves significant, new environmental benefits. In conclusion, environmental groups may choose to support permit markets that improve the environment to a greater extent than that achieved with the status quo.[365]

## 5.5 EXPLANATIONS

Can theory, as expressed by the hypotheses proposed in Chapter 2, explain the present attitudes? All main political actors point to a grandfathered permit market as the desirable instrument for environmental regulation in general. Why is there such a striking unanimity in favour of permit markets?

In the case of private business, the choice fits the theoretical expectations. Business will choose the solution that leaves them with a maximum of flexibility, lowest possible reduction cost and a barrier to entry.

In the case of public electric utilities, one would expect these monopolies to follow state regulation and perhaps even demand more CAC regulation or the use of taxes in order to consolidate their position. Unexpectedly, utilities also prefer permit markets and deregulation.

This deviation from the theory can only be explained by two factors. First, the US federal government is too weak – or has not learned how – to use green taxes and create more tax revenue in that way. Second, the US electricity sector is becoming more competitive.[366] So, in spite of heavy regulation, dawning competition and consumer pressure for lower prices may explain why public utilities also favour a permit market. Interference from the regulator creates uncertainty, rigidity, higher prices and dissatisfied customers.

In the case of environmental groups, the earlier focus had been on zero pollution and CAC regulation. It may seem surprising that they now seek cooperation and low-cost solutions for industry.[367] However, this makes sense in relation to theory, because these non-market groups will pursue the collective good of better environmental quality. Environmental groups have, through observation, found a better way of reaching their common goal.[368]

The possible explanations for this rational shift are manifold. The poor environmental results achieved under CAC regulation and arguments from economic literature have had a significant impact. Also, changes occur slowly. For example, fundamental changes in opinion regarding regulation require new expertise among the staff members in the environmental organizations. Seligman also points out that historically it was easier to tell people that we should stop pollution, that is by a CAC approach. It is much more difficult to advocate complicated designs for permit markets where sources may sell and buy. What is going on? Most people do not understand the theoretical background.

---

365. Seligman (1994:4–7 and 27–28).
366. See Svendsen (1995b) and Section 5.6.
367. See Hahn (1989b), Kete (1992) and Seligman (1994).
368. Interview, November 11, 1994: Daniel Seligman, Sierra Club, Washington D.C.

Nelson supplements this reasoning by hypothesizing that the change in environmentalistic attitudes – which often have been left-wing oriented – may have been caused by the fall of communist rule in Eastern Europe. The failure of planned economies may have awakened interest in the use of markets.[369]

The cost savings from making former CAC permits transferable and giving sources their initial, historical free distribution allow industry to reach far more stringent target levels. Environmental improvement is ensured by the devaluation of permits. Environmental groups perceive a need to participate in the negotiation of new reductions and to survey the functioning of the markets.

## 5.6 COMPETITION IN THE US ELECTRICITY SECTOR

Three major networks exist in the US electricity sector: one for the east, one for the west and one for Texas.[370] These networks consist of smaller networks, which in turn are comprised of 'power pools', that is interconnected utilities that trade power with one another. This allows them to reduce their reserve-generating capacity by exploiting the temporarily unused capacity of neighbouring utilities.

The US electric utilities operate with regulated prices calculated to allow a 'fair rate of return'. The concept 'fair rate of return' is dubious and arbitrarily determined by the state public utility commissions (PUCs). Traditionally utilities are not permitted to make cost-minimizing decisions, for example trade pollution permits, in the same way profit-making firms do. The pricing principle is that the rate of return in a utility, $R_u$ (profit $\pi$ divided by the asset or capital base $C$) has to be below a certain allowed rate of return $(R_a)$:[371]

$$R_u = \pi/C \leq R_a$$

This principle encourages investments in capital and places a ceiling on profits which, in itself, is distorting. It thus rewards investments in capital-intensive pollution control equipment, such as scrubbers – which become part of the rate base – more than participation in permit markets.[372] This situation could be corrected by allowing the purchase of permits to be treated as capital investment. It is also relevant whether the revenues from the sale of permits go to ratepayers or shareholders. If these revenues are not shared with shareholders,

369. Interview, November 3, 1994: Professor Robert H. Nelson, Public Affairs, University of Maryland.

370. This subsection draws heavily on Svendsen (1995b).

371. Tschirhart (1984). The liberalization of the US electricity market is expected to strengthen the incentive to take part in the permit markets because a 'fair rate of return' will be defined by supply and demand.

372. Permit trade may in itself serve as an important signal to regulators and consumers that the electric utility activity minimizes costs.

the supply of permits is likely to be too small to be cost-effective.[373]

However, drastic reforms in the US are under way. The US electricity sector is now moving from monopoly to competition, which probably accounts for the shift away from a preference for traditional CAC regulation. To see this, let us take the case of California in the two next sections. Section 5.6.1 will explore the history of the electricity industry in the US. Section 5.6.2 then looks at the recent development of a competitive market for electricity in California. As will be seen, the new competitive situation is created because large industrial consumers demand electricity from suppliers other than the local producer.

### 5.6.1 Natural Monopoly

Traditionally, US utilities have been monopolies, which have been allowed by state regulation to recover all 'prudently incurred' costs and to make limited profits. Regulation was developed in the 1920s to ensure the realization of economies of scale as the demand for electricity rose.[374] Until recently, power suppliers could sell electricity to their local power companies only. About 20 years ago in the US, as a consequence of the oil crisis, fuel prices rose.[375] This made the consumers – especially the industrial ones – dissatisfied, as they had grown accustomed to falling prices.

At the same time, electricity producers in private industries, the so-called 'non-utility generators' (NUGs), wanted the right to sell surplus electricity to other utilities via the electricity superhighway (by 'wheeling' their power through the transmission lines of their local utilities). So, private industrial entrepreneurs promoted competition and free trade. The 1992 Energy Policy Act (EPAct) allowed the Federal Energy Regulatory Commission (FERC) to order utilities to provide wheeling services.[376] The active search for alternatives to local power companies, spearheaded by the California Public Utilities Commission (CPUC), has culminated in the so-called 'CPUC revolution'.

### 5.6.2 Liberalization in California

The CPUC sent a shockwave through the electricity industry in April 1994 when it proposed to phase out California's system of regulated electricity monopolies in favour of a competitive system.[377] If this plan is approved, consumers will be able to purchase their electricity from any producer in the

---

373. Bohi et al. (1990) and Klaassen (1996).

374. Geddes (1992:75). The electric utility sector is over-regulated and tremendously complex both in the US and in Europe. See also Foster (1993) and Swann (1988) for a discussion on regulation of 'natural' monopolies and privatization.

375. For detailed analyses of the oil crisis and of energy price fluctuations, see Linderoth (1993) and Olson (1988).

376. Hoffman (1994:57).

377. Hoffmann (1994:55), Joskow (1997), and Davidson (1998).

State of California by the year 2002. The availability of cheaper power on the electricity superhighway will inevitably draw some local ratepayers to make contracts with producers other than their local ones.

The plan was to begin in 1996. Ratepayers consuming at least 50,000 kilovolts of electricity annually, that is large industrial customers, would have the right to become 'direct access' customers and to contract with distant producers. In the period 1996–2002, smaller and smaller purchasers will gain the same right, until all ratepayers have access.

The utility sector has made three main objections to the California plan.[378] First, opponents of competition in the electricity sector have invoked the metaphor of a morally binding contract between consumers and shareholders. According to this argument, consumers are obligated to pay a price that gives shareholders a 'fair rate of return' on their investments. Utilities, in turn, have a duty to serve all consumers within their service area at a 'reasonable' rate. In fact, however, neither party is morally or legally bound by such a contract. For a homogenous commodity like electricity, a 'reasonable' rate means no more than what the competitors charge, and a fair rate of return means no more than the rate dictated by the forces of supply and demand.

Second, the plan does not include any compensation for local utilities that wheel power. Utilities have argued that ratepayers who wish to bypass local systems should pay an exit fee. While the local utilities own their production and transmission system formally, however, this ownership has been obtained through a system of a monopoly privilege protected by the state.[379] It is questionable whether a company protected from competition by government has the right to impose any such fees.

The state could sell or auction off the electric utilities and let things happen in the market. Buyers and sellers would then be allowed to set up their own lines and arrange matters on their own. This would improve the incentive to develop new knowledge and technology. As Hoffman (1994) and Geddes (1992) note, the history of electricity provision shows that competing transmission systems will be economically viable. Until monopolization in the 1920s, electric utilities often competed vigorously with one another with parallel transmission and distribution systems. A return to this competitiveness would enable the most effective outcome.

Third, utilities have argued that allowing ratepayers to bypass their local utility in favour of cheaper power would leave local capacity stranded and unprofitable. Moreover, in upholding their duty to serve all potential customers, the local utilities would maintain standby capacity indefinitely in case any bypassing rate-payers opt to return to their local systems.

The 'stranded investments' argument has suddenly appeared in the light of

---

378.  Hoffman (1994) and Michaels (1992). See also Joskow (1992) and Houston (1992) for critiques of present regulation along the same lines.

379.  Hoffman (1994:59).

potential competition. It was not presented earlier, for example when industrial customers decided to produce their own electricity, to move to other service territories or to shut down operations. Such actions would mean the same thing to the utilities as losing customers to competition. Since utilities have never received reimbursement in these cases, why should they suddenly receive compensation in the case of competition?

The three arguments have had their effect.[380] The CPUC intends to charge exit fees for switching to direct access. State utilities will be compensated for any 'stranded costs' they may have. The level of this fee has not yet been settled. Unless it is insignificant, it will slow down the process of liberalization and it may even prevent it. Decision-makers in Europe should be prepared for similar objections to competition and similar claims for exit fees.[381]

## 5.7  CONCLUSION

Political distortion was evident in the designs of the eight US permit-market programs. They were all influenced by lobbyism. All eight programs were designed such that firms had to buy their way into the market and to comply with more stringent emission standards. Even the $SO_2$ auction (including the direct sale option) was designed to allocate only 3% of the total permits in circulation and to redistribute as much as possible from new to existing firms in a discriminative and pay-what-you-bid setting.

When the three main political actors were asked what kind of environmental regulation they would prefer, they all asked for a grandfathered permit market. This outcome is supported by theory in the case of private business and environmental groups, but not in the case of public utilities.

Grandfathering is demanded by business because this distribution rule both lowers costs and creates a barrier to entry for new firms. Learning from experience environmental groups have also begun to demand permit markets because the lower costs imposed on industry make it possible to achieve superior environmental results (compared to those experienced under CAC).

It was predicted that the electric utility sector – being a heavily regulated industry – would want to preserve its monopoly by demanding traditional CAC regulation or by supporting the use of green taxes. However, surprisingly, this

---

380.  A special interest group will, as argued in Sections 2.7 and 2.8, use plausibility arguments in its efforts to achieve monopoly and to maximize its slice of the national income pie. Lobbyism also had a strong impact earlier on. The Clean Air Act Amendments of 1977 stated that new electric utilities were not allowed to use low-sulphur coal, which could have had the same effect as the best technological system available! This concern stems from the coal industry and obviously weighed more heavily than the fact that reduction costs were raised (Ackerman and Hassler 1981). This kind of regulation is now prevented by the rule of 'interstate commerce', which is used to preserve competition and free trade among the states in the US.

381.  As Hoffman (1994:62) points out, the arguments in favour of deregulation apply to other regulated utilities with systems of 'pipes' to customers, for example natural gas, heating oil, water, and telephone systems. See also Demsetz (1968) and Broadman and Kalt (1989).

sector has promoted deregulation and permit markets. The reason for this unexpected outcome is the rise of competition in the US electricity sector. In California, pressure from industrial and commercial ratepayers has led to liberalization in the electricity industry.

This process of liberalization is likely to continue. The two main causes are competition from private electricity producers and pressure from industrial ratepayers to get direct access to the most efficient producers. US electric utilities have put forth arguments in opposition to competition in the industry, but these arguments are not sound.

The deregulation program in California has made a significant step in facilitating the purchase of electricity from distant producers. However, one problem with the plan is that the arguments mentioned above have resulted in linking an exit fee to the market in order to compensate local utilities. Local utilities claim ownership of the transmission systems, but this notion of ownership is dubious since the systems were built during a period of state monopoly.

A similar trend is to be expected in Europe. With increased competition, electric utilities in Denmark and the EU may demand permit markets, such as those found in the US for $CO_2$ abatement. Chapter 6 addresses the failure of $CO_2$ taxation and the potential for a $CO_2$ market in Denmark and the EU.

# 6 Potential $CO_2$ Market

## 6.1 OVERVIEW

Is it possible to introduce $CO_2$ markets in Denmark and the EU or are the political, economic and administrative distortions too severe compared to the tax solution? Section 6.2 evaluates the Danish $CO_2$ tax, and Section 6.3 describes an existing 'SNO$_x$ bubble', in which two Danish electricity consortia are allowed to trade $SO_2$ and NO$_x$ permits internally. The political attitudes of organized interests are described in Section 6.4 and explained in Section 6.5. Section 6.6 characterizes the $CO_2$-emitting sources in Denmark, and Section 6.7 discusses economic distortions. Section 6.8 then suggests how to design a Danish $CO_2$ market.

An important concern is the costs imposed on firms if the market does not work and if firms, for some reason, have only the option of $CO_2$ scrubbers. A worst-case scenario is developed in Section 6.9, based on the use of chemical $CO_2$ scrubbers. Section 6.10 investigates political and administrative barriers to applying a common $CO_2$ tax in the EU and describes the option of introducing a grandfathered permit market. It is shown that an appropriately designed initial distribution rule would make it possible to overcome the problems of core action and would encourage relevant parties to engage in permit trading Section 6.11 offers a perspective on the possible development of a global $CO_2$ market. Section 6.12 summarizes the recommendations of this chapter, including the perspectives for a $CO_2$ market in the US.

## 6.2 $CO_2$ TAXATION IN DENMARK

At first glance, it may appear that Denmark is acting against its own interests by aiming at a 20% $CO_2$ reduction of the 1988 level by the year 2005.[382] Denmark's

---

382. This subsection draws heavily on Svendsen (1998b). The very ambitious target level for Denmark matches the appeal from the 1988 Toronto conference 'The Changing Atmosphere' and the 1987 United Nations' World Commission on the Environment and Development report – the 'Brundtland Report' – on global environmental problems and sustainable development, see Danish Ministry of Energy (1990). Concerning the US and the EU, see Thatcher (1994:22). $CO_2$ is emitted when fossil fuels (coal, oil, gas) are burned for energy production or other industrial processes and is considered to be the main cause of global warming. For general considerations of the problems linked to global warming, see Schelling (1992). Svante August Arrhenius (1859–1929), a Swedish physical chemist of wide-ranging intellect, was the first to investigate the greenhouse effect in 1898. He also calculated the changes that would have been necessary to have produced the Ice Ages, and

share of world-wide $CO_2$ emission is no more than 0.3%. The EU share is 15% and the US share is 23%.[383] It does not appear rational for a small country to focus on reducing $CO_2$ rather than aiming to control local and regional pollutants, such as those dealt with by the US permit markets. The acting country benefits most itself from reducing localized pollutants. In contrast, $CO_2$ reduction is a collective good. As such, the theory described in Section 2.4 holds that a small state (with a minute share of the benefits from its contribution) is unlikely to provide that good. Rather, it has a strong incentive to free-ride on larger countries that are willing to provide far more of the collective good than it is feasible for the small country to purchase.

However, $CO_2$ reduction may be rational in a fiscal sense because it justifies a change in tax policy. 'Green' taxation makes it possible to lower income taxes because green taxes, such as $CO_2$ taxation, can cover the resulting fiscal gap. Denmark's fiscal strategy must aim to be cost-effective, to reduce unemployment – by reducing income taxes – and to harmonize the Danish tax structure with that of the other member states in the EU.[384] In this way, green taxes can serve both as fiscal instruments and as an economic incentive to change the behaviour of polluters. A uniform tax set sufficiently high will accomplish a target level of reduction. As has been argued in Chapter 2, organized interests will resist such taxation because it requires that they pay money to the state which cannot be refunded in a politically acceptable way. The capital-intensive losers from the taxation will protest.

A Danish commission has put forth a number of interesting proposals concerning how green taxes may be refunded, including temporary subsidies for environmental investments, reductions in income taxes and VAT, subsidies to employers, a change in devaluation rules, and reduced corporate taxes. However, as the commission itself notices, even if the refund system is revenue-neutral overall for the industries involved, redistributions will take place among industries. Steelworks or electric utilities are particularly vulnerable because they use an enormous amount of the taxed resource. These capital-intensive firms can, therefore, be expected to have small-group advantages for organizing a lobby against taxation, whereas the potential winners from refunding are,

received the Nobel prize in 1903 (Drexel et al. 1991:48).

383.   Larsen and Shah (1994:843). The industrialized countries emit roughly two-thirds of the total global emission. See also Schelling (1992) and Nordhaus (1991). A general review of policies for regulating global $CO_2$ emission is given by Oates and Portney (1992). See also Bierbaum and Friedman (1992), Ingham and Ulph (1991), Jochem (1991), Lyon (1989), Manne and Richels (1992), and Stavins and Hahn (1993). $CO_2$ is well suited for individual emission control because the environmental costs from the substance are independent of source location, in contrast to those from $SO_2$ and $NO_x$ emissions. The harmful effects of $CO_2$ emission are directly connected to the emitted amount, not the concentration. This characteristic simplifies the present analysis since cost- effective involvement of the spatial dimension is associated with utmost difficulty in practice, as seen above in Section 3.4.

384.   Danish Ministry of Finance (1994). See also Goulder (1995) and Parry (1995).

typically, small and numerous firms in the service sector.[385]

It is not immediately clear if the purpose of the Danish $CO_2$ tax is to provide a global collective good, inconsistent with theory, or innovatively to supplement tax revenues, consistent with theory. The $CO_2$ tax went into effect on May 15, 1992, for households and on January 1, 1993, for industry. All Danish households burning fossil fuels are now required to pay the equivalent of US$16 per ton $CO_2$ emitted.[386] VAT-registered firms, however, are required to pay only half the tax ($8).[387]

The Danish $CO_2$ tax cannot achieve the target level for four reasons. First, evidence from the Danish Economic Council (1993) suggests that the present tax is far too low. The Economic Council suggests that it would need to be raised to $50 for the target to be achieved. This $50 tax corresponds to the most expensive technological reduction the petrochemical industry could undertake, as will be described in Section 6.9

Second, it contains a favourable refund system for energy-intensive firms. If the $CO_2$ tax amounts to between 1% and 2% of the firm's refund basis, defined as the firm's total sales inclusive of exports minus total input costs, 50% is refunded. If the $CO_2$ tax payment amounts to between 2% and 3% of the refund basis, 75% of the tax is refunded. If the $CO_2$ tax payment amounts to more than 3% of the refund basis, 90% is refunded. A minimum of $1,540 must, however, be paid in any case. The consequence of this refund system is that firms emitting the most are given the lowest economic incentive to reduce their emission.[388] However, refunds are given on the condition that an energy consultant visits the applying firm and that the firm follows the resulting advice on more efficient energy use. But consultants put a heavy information burden on authorities.

Third, the $CO_2$ tax favours fossil fuel-based energy production by electric utilities because it is levied on electricity consumption and not on fuel inputs. This construction has two major consequences. First, it preserves international competitiveness because exports of electricity are not taxed,[389] and it creates a potential fiscal loss should imports of electricity increase causing revenues from

---

385. The commission is called the Dithmer Commission. See Danish Ministry of Finance (1994:24–25) and Danish Economic Council (1995:82) for further background information. Another interesting idea from Sweden has been a newly introduced $NO_x$ tax. It is based on emission but rebated according to energy produced (KWh) (Lövgren 1994:114–15), which creates a perverse incentive to produce too much energy.

386. All Danish numbers are calculated at the exchange rate of 1:6.1 US$/DKr.

387. Even though the Danish $CO_2$ tax in principle is an emission tax, it is collected as a general fuel tax through existing fiscal channels. This is because so far it has not been technically possible to remove $CO_2$ in a profitable way. (See Section 6.9.)

388. For this reason, the Confederation of Danish Industries laconically encouraged its members – at the introduction stage of the $CO_2$ tax – to increase their $CO_2$ emission so to get higher refunds and thereby save money.

389. Electricity can, in contrast to heat, be transferred profitably over major distances.

general Danish energy taxes on fossil fuels to decrease.[390] Second, utilities get no economic incentive to choose more carbon-neutral fuel inputs. Whether coal or biomass is used has no influence on $CO_2$ tax payments.

The final reason the Danish tax will not achieve the target is that extra costs to the transportation sector imposed by the $CO_2$ tax were zero because other energy taxes were lowered equivalently. The political argument for this was based on border trade with Germany. Lower petrol and diesel prices in Germany would encourage more Danes to fill up on the German side of the border.[391] However, the actual price level in Denmark was so much lower than that in Germany that it was, in fact, possible to impose a $50 $CO_2$ tax on petrol without superseding the German price level. This will be discussed again in Section 6.8.2

Both fiscal and earmarking elements are contained in this $CO_2$ tax reform. The Danish state expects to get a $150 million revenue in 1993 or roughly half of the total revenue springing from the $CO_2$ tax.[392] The other half is earmarked mainly for encouraging the use of less carbon-rich fuels, such as natural gas and biomass. These earmarked activities are not encouraged by economic instruments, but follow from direct state intervention and rule-making. The earmarked portion from taxing private industry is to be refunded as subsidies for energy saving investments.[393] It is not evident who will get the most subsidies and benefit from the refund system. Further, the subsidized firms cannot use the refunded money at will – since it is earmarked for investments in energy-saving installations, it may not be distributed in a cost-effective way. The earmarking system is similar to a CAC setting, in which the regulator sets technology-based standards for each individual firm and does not encourage the firm to make use of its own information.

In conclusion, the refund system for industry and the taxation on electricity consumption for electric utilities create perverse incentives, and the tax is too low. Hence, the tax is unlikely to achieve the $CO_2$ target level. The political deadlock between state fiscal interests and those of the organized interests will be accentuated during economic growth, which brings with it increased energy consumption and increased $CO_2$ emissions. Finally because it is not the economic incentive that drives sources to reduce emission, but direct state intervention corresponding to traditional CAC, the authorities face a serious barrier to using a trial-and-error procedure in adjusting the $CO_2$ tax to the level that would bring about the desired 20% reduction.

390.   Interview April 5, 1994: Flemming Nissen, ELSAM.

391.   Interview, December 11, 1995: Uffe Jacobsen, Copenhagen Business School.

392.   See Comments on the $CO_2$ Tax Proposal (1992). Earmarking systems are also used in other areas. See, for example, Skou Andersen (1994) for a description of water-pollution-related earmarking systems in Denmark, France, Germany, and the Netherlands.

393.   Danish Ministry of Energy (1990).

## 6.3 DANISH SNO$_X$ BUBBLE

Another system of regulating electric utilities operates in Denmark at the
moment. Utilities larger than 25 MW in production capacity and approved by
the regulator before July 1, 1987, are covered by a 'bubble law' and are therefore controlled already.[394] Two bubbles are currently in effect because Danish
public electricity production is organized into two consortia, ELSAM and
ELKRAFT, which lie in the west and east, respectively. These two monopolies
are not interlinked. SO$_2$ and NO$_x$ quotas are distributed between ELSAM and
ELKRAFT according to production capacity. The two consortia are roughly
equal in size.[395]

Two similar quota arrangements in the EU are found in the Netherlands and
in Germany. In the Netherlands, bubbles have been created for four individual
electricity producers and five refineries, for the reduction of SO$_2$ and No$_x$. New
plants must meet more stringent emission standards than existing plants, and
quotas may be altered if electricity demand or imports depart substantially from
their expected levels. In Germany, an air-pollution policy initiated in 1974
allowed the location of a new plant in a non-attainment area if the new plant
replaced an existing plant of the same kind. In the 1980s, further flexibility was
added so that not only the closing down of an existing plant but also its renova-
tion or technical reduction measures could be used to offset added emission
from a new plant. The Dutch design is similar to the two Danish bubbles,
whereas the German offset program is similar to the ETP system in the US.
Transfers have not taken place on market terms with pricing of permits under
any of the European bubble systems. Rather, the bubbles have been administrative arrangements that allow 'internal trading' within firms.[396]

The Danish bubble allows ELSAM and ELKRAFT to transfer both SO$_2$ and
NO$_x$ permits internally.[397] The quotas are fixed every year but are cumulative
over two 4-year periods (1993–1996 and 1997–2000). This means that a quota
in one year may be exceeded by up to 10% as long as cumulative emissions for
the relevant 4-year period are not exceeded – an interesting way of creating
more flexibility for utilities.

Another interesting feature of the Danish bubble is that it is designed to avoid
discouraging exports. Electricity is less competitive when costs from abatement

---

394. Svendsen (1997 and 1994e). Utilities are checked every year by central authorities because
they have to send in a report in which they describe emitted quantities and abatement efforts in
detail. Therefore, the administrative infrastructure is in position for a CO$_2$ permit market or bubble.

395. In 1991 ELSAM had a capacity of 4.010 MW, whereas ELKRAFT had 3.830 MW
(Association of Danish Electric Utilities 1992:25).

396. For more details, see Klaassen (1996) and Schaerer (1993).

397. For new electric utilities, approved by the regulator after July 1, 1987, traditional CAC
regulation applies, as provided by EEC directive 88/609/EØF. This EEC directive is a setback to
CAC regulation because it removes flexibility and gives no economic incentive to reduce emissions
below the fixed, individual standards.

are added. Therefore, to protect exports, the net numbers are considered. If net exports of electricity are negative one year, this deficiency is withdrawn from the quota. When net exports are positive, the surplus is added to the quota. In this way, exports are kept clear of increased production costs resulting from national environmental regulation.[398]

These two internal 'SNO$_x$ bubbles' are hard to evaluate because data are not available. Also, even though actual emissions typically are about 10% under the allowed quota and are expected to be even lower in the future, quotas may be set too high and may be too easy to accomplish. However, this system has enabled utilities to save costs when compared to taxation and has provided increased flexibility. The rules of this bubble system describe precisely how the size of the quota or bubble is to be devalued.[399]

## 6.4   INTEREST GROUPS IN DENMARK

What are the main attitudes among organized interest groups towards the $CO_2$ tax and towards a potential $CO_2$ market in Denmark? Do they match or differ from those in the US?

Interest groups in Denmark are largely unfamiliar with permit markets. This is in contrast to US interest groups, which have experienced these systems in practice. It is therefore not surprising that permit markets are met with more scepticism in Denmark.

According to the theory outlined in Chapter 2, private industry will promote a grandfathered permit market, public electric utilities – as established monopolies – will promote traditional CAC regulation or green taxation, and environmental groups will demand permit markets to achieve as much environmental protection as possible.

### 6.4.1   Private Industry

The Confederation of Danish Industries (DI) is the main representative of the Danish manufacturing sector and has dominated the debate on $CO_2$ taxation. DI was founded in 1992 as the result of the merging two other industrial interest groups; it now represents 4500 firms. Its purpose is to promote the common interests of Danish industry on a regional, national and international scale.[400]

---

398.   Nannerup (1995) investigates this interesting link between environmental policy and trade policy. He shows how less stringent regulation for export industries further distorts national environmental policy.

399.   Flexibility has been reduced to some extent because certain municipalities demanded scrubbers regardless of internal transfers in ELSAM and ELKRAFT. Also, local standards and the risk of creating hot spots have been significant barriers to internal 'trades'. Environmental groups have blocked some internal trades on the grounds that they might create hot spots. (Interview, April 23, 1995: Carsten Mathiesen, DEF).

400.   Hansen et. al (1995:35).

The general attitude towards environmental regulation is that voluntary agreements are the preferred option, and also in the case of CO$_2$ regulation. Industry wants to settle things on its own without state intervention. What DI wants the least is taxation and increased production costs. The permit market offers a solution that lies between these two possibilities. So, if the choice is between a tax and a permit market, the latter is surely preferred.[401]

### 6.4.2 Public Electric Utilities

The Association of Danish Electric Utilities (DEF) represents the public electric utility sector in Denmark. It was founded in 1923 with the purpose of promoting the common interests of producers and distributers of electricity.[402] The general attitude within DEF towards environmental regulation is that economic instruments are preferable.

In the case of CO$_2$, a tax is preferred because there are too few market agents for trade among utilities in Denmark and it is easier to tax fuel input as long as CO$_2$ cannot be removed from emissions.

When asked for an official opinion on the introduction of two CO$_2$ bubbles for ELSAM and ELKRAFT – corresponding to the SNO$_x$ bubbles – a DEF representative answered that they would cause the state to lose revenue. When asked about future competition from the EU and the likelihood that taxation would increase costs of production and lower exports, the DEF representative responded that the tax should be imposed on electricity consumption, as is the case for the actual CO$_2$ tax.[403]

### 6.4.3 Environmental Groups

The Danish Society for Conservation of Nature (DN) was founded in 1911. By the end of 1994, it had 245,000 members. The purpose of DN is 'to take care of nature and preserve rural amenities in Denmark'.[404] The general attitude in DN is in favour of economic instruments. As such, DN promotes a CO$_2$ tax, but is sceptical with regard to a CO$_2$ market. Environmental groups tend to fear the creation of hot spots under a permit market, even though hot spots are not linked to CO$_2$. DN representatives have expressed the opinion that each specific proposal for trade should be considered in detail.[405]

401.   Interview November 20, 1995: Uffe Sønderhousen, DI.

402.   Hansen et. al (1995:46).

403.   Interview November 21, 1995: Knud Mosekjær Madsen, DEF.

404.   See DN (1995a:6 and 26) and DN (1995b:230). DN's membership is an impressive figure compared to a total Danish population of 5 million.

405.   Interviews November 20 1995 and June 4 1993: Allan Andersen, DN.

## 6.5  EXPLANATIONS

DI has officially asked for 'voluntary agreements' in private industry. Exactly
what this means is not clear. No specific guidelines have been provided by the
regulator for the solution of voluntary $CO_2$ abatement. How and where the
reduction is actually to take place on a voluntary basis is not defined.

The argument here is that $CO_2$ reduction cannot be accomplished by voluntary agreements. Clearly, industry will never pay taxes voluntarily. And no
central organization has the information needed to allocate abatement among
sources in a cost-effective way. Such a proposal would only result in a CAC
setting without sufficient enforcement mechanisms. Therefore, it will be argued
that the request for voluntary agreements is tactical; it serves to delay and
postpone regulation.

The disadvantages of an actual $CO_2$ tax for the target group were clearly
displayed in the political discussions surrounding its implementation. When it
was first introduced as a bill by green interests in February 1991, industry
representatives opposed it strongly on the basis that it would weaken
competitiveness. Several large and energy-intensive firms threatened to move
their production abroad, and it was claimed that the $CO_2$ tax would cost at least
10,000 jobs in Denmark. Written statements to this effect were forwarded to the
Minister of Energy and the Minister for the Environment. The protests succeeded in two ways. First, the tax on industry was lowered to $8 in the final
legislation. (According to the original $CO_2$ tax proposal, industry was to pay the
general rate of tax, that is $16 per ton). Second, the generous refund system was
added for the benefit of industry so that the average $CO_2$ tax at present is
roughly $5. This constitutes a substantial reduction.

Industry representatives estimate that the $CO_2$ tax in 1993 yielded a total
$100 million payment from industry before rebate. The Danish Ministry of
Taxation has calculated that $50 million will be refunded to industry per year.[406]
In other words, the costs for the industry have been lowered from the $200
million implied by the original proposal to $50 million in the final legislation.
The actual $CO_2$ tax is the result of a political clash between organized interests
and the state. In light of this political equilibrium, it will not be possible to
adjust the tax using a trial-and-error procedure, that is to increase the present $8
tax sufficiently to reach the 20% target level.

Electric utilities in Denmark are fully regulated in both production and
distribution. They are allowed to cover all expenses by raising consumer
prices.[407] As such, they have no incentive to minimize production costs.[408]

---

406.   Interview June 25, 1994: Niels O. Gram, DI, and Comments on the $CO_2$ Tax Proposal (1992).

407.   See Svendsen (1991) for more details on the utilities' organization and pricing regulatives.

408.   The Danish Anti-Trust Commission (1993:7) concludes that 'the public Danish energy sector
is characterized by a system where market forces are out of use and replaced by rules and planned
economy'.

Utility representatives' preference for taxation is consistent with the hypothesis that utilities – like players in a centrally planned economy – will share interests with the state and assist it in tax collection.

DEF representatives argue that taxation of consumption (not fuel input) is justified when some of the revenue it generates is earmarked for changing fuel input. Earmarking is effectively CAC regulation, however, and gives sources no economic incentive to engage in cost-effective behaviour or to develop and invest in appropriate new technology.

Nonetheless, public electric utilities may become economically rational actors in the near future. At the moment, the EU is preparing a single market for electricity. This means that production and distribution of electricity will be separated; a Danish distribution company will no longer be forced to buy from the local production company, but may choose any other producer within the EU or Scandinavia.

When competition is introduced to the production link in this way, utilities will no longer be able to cover any expense by raising consumer prices because other and more distant producers may underbid them.[409] Such a development will be similar to the liberalization already taking place in the US electricity market.[410] With more competition in the EU, electric utilities can be expected to react in the same way as private industry, that is to demand low-cost environmental regulation, as is already the case in the US.

Environmental groups have argued strongly for green taxation and the introduction of a $CO_2$ tax in order to achieve environmental improvement. From an earlier focus on CAC regulation, the Danish environmental groups are now evidently and openly advocating the tax solution, according to various statements during the last few years. A historical overview can help to explain the switch.

The market idea was first introduced in 1988 by the Danish Ministry for the Environment and was then sent out for discussion and hearings.[411] The initial reaction from Danish environmental groups was strongly against a 'license to pollute'; this reaction was so strong that all plans concerning the introduction of emissions trading in Denmark were abandoned.[412]

A misunderstanding of how permit markets function led many environmental groups to express a fear that emissions trading would allow firms to increase pollution as they wanted. Concerns regarding the spatial dimension and source

409.    Such a 'contestable' market will give $CO_2$-emitting producers the necessary incentive to minimize cost (see Section 3.6). Concerning competition in the electricity supply industry and the development of a single market. (See Olsen 1995; and Hensel and Svendsen (1995).

410.    See Section 5.6. Production and distribution will be split into two competitive markets and authorities will then be able to leave all arrangements and decisions to buyers and sellers in the free market.

411.    Danish Ministry of the Environment (1988).

412.    Interview October 6, 1993: Karen Årø, Ministry for the Environment. See Svendsen (1991) for a detailed investigation of the arguments put forth by the environmental groups.

location were also raised, but, as declared above, in the case of $CO_2$ only the emitted amount matters.

Danish environmental groups are now powerfully advocating green taxes. This fundamental and recent change in attitude towards economic instruments corresponds to that of the US environmental groups. Traditional arguments against 'licenses to pollute' are now considered invalid. Even the tax solution means that $CO_2$ emissions are paid for.

Because a $CO_2$ market works similarly to a tax but makes industry likely to accept even more stringent environmental goals, Danish environmental groups should promote a potential grandfathered $CO_2$ market. At present, however, DN is approaching this idea with scepticism. This attitude can only be explained as reflecting a lack of knowledge. When adequately informed about the consequences of a permit market, DN may embrace the idea in the same way the US environmental groups have.

## 6.6  $CO_2$ EMISSION SOURCES IN DENMARK

$CO_2$ emission sources in Denmark can be categorized into four sectors: electric utilities, private industry, households and transportation. The electric utilities sector includes all public electric utilities. The industry sector covers private energy production for industrial processes. The household sector includes home heating production not for sale. The transportation sector includes all mobile combustion engines. Table 6.1 opposite describes the sizes and quantity of $CO_2$ emissions from each of these sectors.

The household and transportation sectors contain numerous and small sources. These sectors can therefore, according to Section 2.4.2, be identified as two large groups that will not block taxation.

Furthermore, fuel input to the transportation sector can be taxed at $50 per ton $CO_2$ emitted without raising the prices of fuel above those in Germany. A $50 tax per ton $CO_2$ will raise prices on petrol and diesel roughly by 4 cents per litre.[413] The difference in price level between Denmark and Germany is even higher and leaves plenty of room for a 4 cent increase per litre.[414] Car owners could get the tax revenue refunded in a general way, for example as a lower car tax.

The household and transportation sectors could successfully be taxed whereas electric utilities and industry, as well-organized interest groups, should be targeted in the market to take their interests into account. Therefore, the potential target group for a $CO_2$ market should, at the start, be limited to electric

413.  Interview December 5, 1995: Poul Erik Morthorst, Risø.

414.  Unleaded 98 octane petrol costs 99 cents and 107 cents per litre in Denmark and Germany, respectively, whereas the respective diesel fuel prices are 72 cents and 82 cents. (Prices valid on Wednesday, December 6, 1995.) These data on petrol and diesel prices were collected on December 11, 1995 from Oliebranchens Fællesrepræsentation, Copenhagen.

utilities and private firms. These two groups are organized, large and stationary, and are covered by already existing control systems. Electric utilities are the main polluters, emitting 55% of the total $CO_2$ emissions in Denmark, and industry emits 15%. Together these two sectors contribute 70% of the total $CO_2$ emissions in Denmark. A $CO_2$ market for electric utilities and private industry will be shared proportionately, that is electric utilities will, after grandfathering, hold roughly 80% of the permits and industry will hold roughly 20%.

*Table 6.1: CO₂ emission by source, Denmark 1988*

|  | CO₂ emission | | |
|---|---|---|---|
|  | – mill.ton – | – % of total – | – number – |
| **Electric utilities** | 32 | 55 | 18*) |
| **Industry** | 9 | 15 | 10,000**) |
| **Households** | 9 | 15 | 989,000 |
| **Transportation** | 9 | 15 | 1,304,000***) |
| **Total** | 59 | 100 | 2.3 mill. (approx.) |

*Notes:*
*) Electric utilities larger than 25 MW. In 1989, they produced 99% of the total public energy production based on fossil fuels. The last 1% is produced by 80 small electric utilities with capacity below 25 MW.
**) Private firms approved by Chapter 5 of the Danish Environmental Protection Act.
***) Number of families that own a car. Other transportation facilities, such as aeroplanes, railway trains, trucks, and ferries are not included. This is just to give an impression of the number of actors involved.

*Sources:* Association of Danish Electric Utilities (1990), unpublished estimates from the Danish Environmental Protection Agency, and an unpublished database from Danmarks Statistik, and STO (1995:58).

The Danish Environmental Protection Agency estimates that 10,000 private firms are individually controlled by the Danish Environmental Protection Act with respect to their $SO_2$ and $NO_x$ emissions.[415] This constitutes the number of possible industrial market agents in the target group but many of them are small firms with low energy costs. These small firms may be better off paying a small tax than participating in a market system.

A good indicator of potential participants is found in connection with the $CO_2$ tax refund system. To receive a refund, as described above in Section 6.2, a firm applies for a consultant to perform an energy review. One hundred and thirty-seven energy-intensive firms have applied. These firms may have a strong economic interest in participation in a $CO_2$ permit market.[416]

---

415. Interview June 9, 1993: Erik Thomsen, Danish Environmental Protection Agency.

416. Danish Ministry of Energy (1994a;1994b) and Rasmussen (1995).

Electric utilities are much fewer in number. In 1989, 10 production companies owned 18 electric utilities. The companies are arranged as cooperatives and are split up into the two consortia: ELSAM and ELKRAFT. Due to their relative sizes compared to those of private industry, these two consortia should be kept out of a potential $CO_2$ market, as discussed in the next section.

## 6.7 POTENTIAL MARKET FAILURES

### 6.7.1 Introduction

A $CO_2$ market may fail for two reasons: 1 incomplete competition because of price manipulation in the permit market and impediments to competition in the product market; and 2 a lack of information on market price.

### 6.7.2 Incomplete Competition

#### 6.7.2.1 Price manipulation in the permit market

Potential price manipulation in a grandfathered $CO_2$ market depends directly on the distribution of $CO_2$ emissions across firms. As noted above, ELSAM and ELKRAFT will dominate the market, holding four-fifths of the permits. The permits will be roughly equally divided between them. Clearly they will have market power in the permit market (and in a potential auction), both as sellers and buyers. Price manipulation is, therefore, highly likely.

One way of pushing the public electricity sector into greater competition would be to reorganize it and to establish competition on a production company level. Then, there would be 10 agents rather than two agents in the market. The largest production company would emit 28% of the total $CO_2$ emissions in the electric utility sector. It would not dominate the market because three other companies would each emit more than 10% and five would emit between 5% and 10%.[417] If the role of a large production company is seriously questioned, one may sanction any attempts to manipulate price by excluding the violator from the market. Drop-outs are then required to pay the full \$50 $CO_2$ tax, as suggested by the Danish Economic Council (1993).

However, the single market has not yet come into effect and has not yet created a contestable electricity market. Therefore, at present, a better approach might be to implement something similar to the $SNO_x$ bubble. To lower production costs in preparation for a single market, each consortium could be grandfathered its own $CO_2$ bubble so that it would be allowed to move $CO_2$ quotas internally and to trade quotas with the other consortium.

---

417. Svendsen and Steiner (1997).

### 6.7.2.2 Impediments to competition in the product market

A complication arises when firms participating in permit markets are also competing in the product market. This is the case with electric utilities that produce the same product: electricity. If the permit market is to take place at the production-company level, then production companies are, in a sense, competing. But buying up permits to create a barrier to entry to the product market is in conflict with the Danish anti-trust law.[418] If attempts to manipulate the permit price create or exacerbate barriers in the product market, a rule could be defined that obliges sources to sell permits to other sources indiscriminately. This would force sources with surplus holdings of permits to sell. Another possibility would be to let the regulating authority buy up permits and to sell them to interested sources.

Private electricity producers in Denmark could be used as buffers in a single market in the same way as is done in the US. This solution is, by far, less costly than building new units and installations and gives utilities an incentive to protect small, private producers, rather than to destroy them. If a source outside Denmark tried to buy permits with the purpose of harming a Danish competitor, such attempts could be prohibited by the regulator, or any holding of permits outside the regulated area (Denmark) could be prohibited if held longer than a certain period of time.

In contrast to electric utilities, private firms in Denmark are in general very different with respect to products. They have much less rational interest in harming one another in the product market through the use of strategic action in the permit market. Nevertheless, the open Danish economy ensures strong competition in the product market.

### 6.7.3  Missing Information

The development of brokerage services should be encouraged so that information on permit prices will be easily available. This will help to keep transaction costs low. Public brokerage services could be provided by the Danish Ministry of Energy. An annual, revenue-neutral auction would provide information on permit prices. Banks at which permits are deposited can also advertise or advise potential customers on the availability and prices of permits.

Another possibility for creating better information is through leasing permits. A source can then plan when to use its permits again when the lease terminates. The demand profile of electric utilities appears well-suited for leasing arrangements.[419]

---

418.   Danish Anti-Trust Law, §§11 and 12. See Koktvedgaard (1991:126pp) and Svendsen and Steiner (1997).

419.   Leasing has been used twice under the ETP in the US (Raufer and Feldman 1987:66–67, 108 and 125). Both examples stem from the firm 'International Harvester' in Louisville, Kentucky, which in 1982 and 1983 leased permits to emit organic pollutants.

## 6.8   DESIGN: $CO_2$ MARKET PROPOSAL

It is now possible to recommend a design for a potential $CO_2$ market in Denmark based on the US experience.[420] The design is analytically split up into 5 points, as was the case in the evaluation model: Target level, Target group, Distribution rule, Trade rules and Control system.

### 6.8.1   Target Level

The Danish government has decided that $CO_2$ emissions in Denmark are to be reduced by 20% of the 1988 level by the year 2005. A $CO_2$ market would force emitters to adapt to the fixed number of permits. Over time, the price generated in the $CO_2$ market would automatically adjust to reflect demand and supply. Permits could be devalued after, for example, 8 years, so that the program should run from 1998 to year 2005. The Danish Environmental Protection Act, provides that CAC permits may be devalued every eighth year. According to the rules of the $SNO_x$ bubble for Danish electric utilities, permits may be devalued every fourth year. So, compared to former regulation, an 8-year period should give plenty of time for adjustment.

### 6.8.2   Target Group

Initially, the public electric utility sector should be kept out of the $CO_2$ market. It is not competitive yet and follows the interests of the state, that is, its representatives promote tax collection. The low $CO_2$ tax, state intervention and earmarking of revenue, however, do not provide appropriate incentives. As preparation for a low-cost single market, a more competitive solution for electric utilities would be the creation of two $CO_2$ bubbles, under which permits are devalued after a set period of time. Perhaps a reorganization, whereby the production companies become the recipients of the permits, would make it possible to add these bubbles to the $CO_2$ market in the future. It is important to private industry and its competitiveness that electricity costs are kept low because private industry consumes 30% of the electricity production in Denmark.[421]

The current Danish $CO_2$ tax should be maintained for households and the transportation sector as a general fuel tax. This tax could be gradually raised towards its correct $50 level by the year 2005. The benefits of a permit market for sources in the household and transport sectors would probably be exceeded by the regulatory costs associated with subjecting these sources to an individual control system.

Private industrial sources are already covered by the $CO_2$ taxation system and

420.   This subsection draws heavily on Svendsen (1998b).
421.   Association of Danish Electric Utilities (1995:6).

the related energy reviews.[422] It is important that the control system can be effected by one single and central authority so that local municipalities do not have control responsibility and as such are not tempted to protect their own firms.

The actual permit market should then start up for private industry alone. The Danish Ministry of Energy recently released a dataset to facilitate the study of a potential $CO_2$ market for the Danish manufacturing sector.[423] This dataset contains 1993 data on 2000 $CO_2$-emitting firms that have more than 20 employees each. In total, these 2000 firms emit 4.8 million tons of $CO_2$ per year. A workable experiment could, for a start, incorporate the 200 largest firms, which emit 4.1 million tons of $CO_2$ per year, or roughly 7% of the total $CO_2$ emissions in Denmark. The size of emissions from these 200 firms is shown on an aggregate level in Figure 6.1.

*Figure 6.1: 200 CO₂-emitting firms in the Danish manufacturing sector*

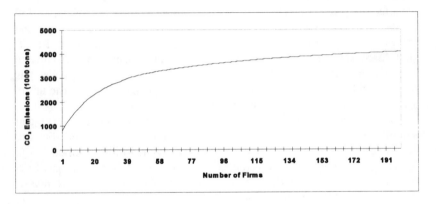

*Note*:  Data base contains only firms with more than 20 employees.

*Source*:  Rasmussen (1995).

As can be seen, one firm is by far the largest: it emits .80 million tons of $CO_2$, or 20% of the total emissions of these 200 firms. The next largest firm emits .14 million tons of $CO_2$, or 3.4%, while the smallest firm emits .003 million, or .1%. Average emissions are .02 million ton $CO_2$.

To survey the potential $CO_2$ market, it is useful to divide the sources into 5

---

422.   In a similar way, the introduction of tradable permits in Denmark for acid rain abatement could be based on the existing regulatory infrastructure in Chapter 5 of the Danish Environmental Protection Act. (See Svendsen 1994e).

423.   All figures are calculated on the basis of Rasmussen (1995). I am grateful to the Danish Ministry of Energy for supplying me with these data which allow an anonymous depiction of a potential $CO_2$ market for the manufacturing sector.

fractions with each group emitting roughly equal amounts of $CO_2$. The largest firm constitutes the first 20% fraction. The second 20% fraction is made up of the next eight firms, which are roughly equal in size. The third 20% contains the next 14 firms. The fourth 20% covers the next 34 firms. And the fifth 20% covers the last 143.

Even though one firm might hold one-fifth of the permits in the initial market, the second, third and fourth fractions have relatively few actors (8, 14 and 34, respectively). As such, permits will be fairly well spread out, and it will be hard for the largest actor to manipulate the market significantly.

Each of these 200 firms should choose whether to participate or not. Any firm that does not participate would be required to pay the tax, which should be refunded to the industry as a whole, for example in the form of a reduced tax contribution to labour market services, or a reduced tax. The refund each firm receives will typically be much lower than its tax payment (if it chooses the tax option) because the refunds are general and benefit the whole industry.

As with the ARP, it should be possible for smaller $CO_2$ emitters in the manufacturing sector and those from other sectors to optin. For example, 450 commercial nurseries have been reviewed for their energy use, and some energy-intensive agricultural firms also exist, such as manufacturers of feed-stuff. Many of these would probably be interested in participation.[424] All private firms should, therefore, be allowed to apply to the system and, perhaps later, this option could even be extended to production companies in the electric utility sector, when the single market for electricity is further developed.

Sources have two options for reducing $CO_2$: increased fuel efficiency and substitution of energy source. There are very slight differences in fuel efficiency across firms. Utilities typically have a 40% utilization ratio of input.[425] The newest coal-fired plants, however, have a 46% ratio, and the modern gas-fired plant has a 58% fuel efficiency.[426] So, there may be some trade due to invest-ments in more efficient fuel burners.

Regarding the second option, the most obvious substitution is from coal to gas. The potential for $CO_2$ emissions reduction here is great. Out of 18 electric utilities, 16 used coal in 1992, whereas only 2 used gas. Shifting from coal to gas can reduce a plant's $CO_2$ emission by 50%.[427]

This shift is not technically problematic. But the associated costs are influ-enced by the geographic location of a source in relation to the gas network. The greater the distance, the longer the pipelines must be. This fact may result in

424.   The different industrial sectors are defined in STO (1995:19).

425.   Fuel efficiencies are calculated from data supplied by the Danish Electricity Association (Svendsen and Steiner 1997).

426.   Interview November 27: Mogens Weel-Hansen, Dk-Teknik. Coal dominates the use of fossil fuels in the public electricity sector. In 1991, coal accounted for 94.8% whereas gas and oil amounted to 2.1% and 3.1%, respectively (Association of Danish Electric Utilities 1992:15).

427.   See Danish Ministry of the Environment 1990:141.

significant differences in marginal reduction costs across sources.[428]

A similar argument can be made regarding bio fuels, wind energy, and other alternative energy sources, which are considered neutral with respect to $CO_2$. The costs will again depend on geographic location. The distance to the resources determines transportation costs, which can be significant.[429]

The variety of substitution options can be presumed overall to encourage trade activity by allowing the exploitation of variations in marginal reduction costs.[430] In Section 6.9, new findings on chemical $CO_2$ reduction technology, which may come into production in the future, will be discussed.

### 6.8.3 Distribution Rule

The distribution rule could be defined for a three-year period, similar to the distribution rule in the ARP. Free distribution could, for example, be based on average fuel input for the period 1995–1997. Firms established after 1997 could apply for a free, initial standard distribution before a certain.

### 6.8.4 Trade Rules

Trade rules are very simple when source location is not a consideration. Permits can be traded one-to-one and can be banked. It is critical that the sources receive full property rights to their permit holdings.

To secure the availability of permits to new sources, the ARP may be used as a model again. One per cent of the permits could be withdrawn every year for direct sale at a price corresponding to an expected market price, initially, for example, at $50 per ton of $CO_2$. These permits could be made available to new entrants before being sold to existing sources.

In addition, to encourage participation of new sources and to give a price signal, a non-discriminative and revenue-neutral auction could be held every year by the Copenhagen Board of Trade. Again, as in the ARP, 2% of the permits could be offered; anybody should be allowed to bid and offer $CO_2$ permits.

### 6.8.5 Control System

Sources could be controlled in the same way as in the ARP and the lead trading program.[431] An annual self-reporting system concerning fuel input would allow

---

428. Svendsen and Steiner (1997). See also Svendsen (1997).

429. See ELSAM (1994:4–5).

430. Morthorst (1994:966–70). A consultant's report, referred to by the Danish Economic Council (1995:85–86), confirms that significant differences in marginal reduction costs are to be found in Danish industry. (See Dansk Energi Analyse 1995.)

431. Claire Schary – one of the leading forces behind the design of the ARP – advises other

the Danish Ministry of Energy, as a central authority independent of local interests, to double check this data (from both buyers and sellers) and the related trade activity, by checking individual energy inputs in different firms.[432]

Even though the CEMS system from the ARP could be applied to $CO_2$ as well, this control system, as discussed in Section 4.5.1.5, is very expensive. An annual cost of $120,000 is doubtless too high for the small manufacturing firms in Denmark. A system based on the indirect measure of fuel input would be less expensive and could build on the already existing administrative infrastructure.

If a source were to exceed its quota, it would automatically be fined and would have to reduce the excess amount in the following year. The level of the fine per ton could, for example, be five times the expected market permit price of $250 per ton.[433] The funds created by collecting fines could perhaps be used to pay administrative costs or to subsidize the entrance of new sources.

Table 6.2 summarizes the recommended design for a $CO_2$ permit market in Denmark.

potential users of permit markets to design the system as simply as possible. She advocates the following 5-step procedure: 1 choose representative years from which to calculate the initial distribution rule; 2 elaborate a detailed list of sources; 3 focus on figures in defining a reduction cap rather than percentage because numbers give less room for interpretation; 4 define formulas for calculating initial distributions to sources that existed in the base year and those that entered after it; and 5 plan early what computerized data systems to use (Interview, November 12, 1994: Claire Schary, Acid Rain Division, EPA).

432.   The need for unambiguous and general rules in sanctioning the environmental norms has been apparent in Denmark (Hjorth-Andersen 1988).

433.   If any doubt arises over figures, the source should have the burden of proof. This is in contrast to traditional Danish criminal law where the prosecution has to prove that a firm has violated the rules. Also, the traditional Danish sanction system has been ineffective because it has been difficult to calculate the profits from violation and as such, the level of a fine or penalty.

*Table 6.2: CO₂ market for the manufacturing sector in Denmark*

| | |
|---|---|
| **Target level** | 20% $CO_2$ reduction from 1988 to 2005 (devaluation takes place in the year 2005). |
| **Target Group** | The 200 most energy-intensive firms in the manufacturing sector with optin possibility for other firms. There are significant variations in marginal reduction costs across firms. |
| **Distribution Rule** | Free, initial distribution based on the average use of fossil fuels in the 3-year period 1995–1997. |
| **Trade Rules** | Transfer of full property right to permits. Allow banking of permits for later use or sale. Withdraw 3% of the permits each year, 1% for direct sale (price fixed at $50 and offered first to new entrants) and 2% for an annual, revenue-neutral auction at the Board of Trade in Copenhagen. The reserve serves to ease the entry of new sources and to give the market a price signal. |
| **Control System** | Annual self-reporting about input of fossil fuels to a central authority, for example the Danish Ministry of Energy, which already controls the target group and which can double-check trade figures. If violations occur, the source should be automatically fined. The violating source should be required to reduce the excess amount in the following year. |

## 6.9 A WORST-CASE SCENARIO

How big are the reduction costs that new or expanding sources may face in a potential Danish $CO_2$ market? What would happen in the worst-case, that is, if the market did not work at all and no price were established? Such a worst-case scenario could be based on the technological maximum price.

Two new Dutch reports investigated the costs of reducing $CO_2$ emissions chemically, including capital and operation/maintenance costs. One pilot project analysed three chosen industries; the other analysed electric utilities.

### 6.9.1 Chemical $CO_2$ Reduction in Industry

Farla et al. (1992) established marginal reduction costs for the three largest $CO_2$-emitting industries in the Netherlands. These costs are presented in Table 6.3.[434]

$CO_2$ reduction in the fertilizer industry is relatively inexpensive because $CO_2$ is already being recovered from the process streams ($CO_2$ would otherwise

434. Depreciation is calculated on the basis of annuity, with a depreciation time of 25 years and a discount rate of 5%. All dollar values are calculated at a 1:1.7 $/Fl exchange rate.

interfere with the production process).

*Table 6.3: Chemical CO₂ reduction costs in three Dutch industries, 1990*

| Industry | Marginal reduction costs ($/ton $CO_2$) |
|----------|:-----:|
| 1. Fertilizer | 8 |
| 2. Iron and steel | 40 |
| 3. Petrochemical | 50 |

*Source:*  Farla et al. (1992).

### 6.9.2  Chemical $CO_2$ Reduction in Electric Utilities

Hendriks et al. (1992) investigated the marginal $CO_2$ reduction costs in electric utilities. The costs amounted to $40 and $45 in coal-fired and natural gas-fired electric utilities, respectively.[435] These costs are in line with marginal reduction costs in the iron and steel industry.

The authors recommended that the recovered $CO_2$ be injected into aquifers. The Dutch subsurface contains a large number of aquifers suitable for storage, that is they satisfy constraints related to aquifer depth, permeability, presence of a seal, and presence of a structural trap.[436] The $CO_2$ gas could then be piped through pipeline systems from the point of removal to the storage site.[437]

The costs of injection are estimated at $0.6 and $1 per ton of $CO_2$ injected, for aquifers above and below 1000 m depth, respectively. Costs will be assumed to be at their highest, that is $1 per ton of $CO_2$, for the remainder of this discussion.[438]

---

435.    A recent Danish research project by ELSAM shows similar results. Here, the removal of $CO_2$ from a modern coal-fired power plant costs $30, whereas the storage costs amount to $13, a total of $43 per ton. Storage costs are based on 30 km transportation of fluent $CO_2$ under a pressure of 40 bar and is to take place in Danish underground aquifers where geological conditions are considered most favourable (Ingeniøren 1995:26). Other storage alternatives are fixed deposition (dry ice) in sea depths greater than 3000 m or by dissolving $CO_2$ in 1000 m deep sea water. The sea is capable of absorbing tremendous amounts of $CO_2$ (*Ibid*). Another obvious possibility would be to use the recovered $CO_2$ as propellant gas when recovering oil and natural gas in the North Sea. When a pocket in the underground is empty and filled with $CO_2$, it can be closed again. No cost estimates have yet been made in this respect.

436.    Hendriks et al. note that total aquifer storage capacity for $CO_2$ in the Dutch aquifers is estimated to be 1.2 billion tons of $CO_2$. A rough estimate for the worldwide storage capacity is about 400 billion. US electric utilities emitted 0.5 billion ton $CO_2$ in 1990 (EIA 1994:table 12.2).

437.    Van der Meer et al. (1992) have simulated the behaviour of $CO_2$ stored in aquifers based on sample reservoirs. They find that $CO_2$ storage in aquifers ('structural traps') is technically feasible. When $CO_2$ is injected into aquifers, it will dissolve in the water. Part of the water already present will be displaced by processes known as 'gravity segregation' and 'vicious fingering'.

438.    Van der Meer et al. (1992). Blok (1993:22) refer to a Japanese study of $CO_2$ storage in aquifers. Here, the technique is somewhat different. Again, $CO_2$ is injected into aquifers, but then

As such, the technological maximum price for $CO_2$ reduction and storage varies between approximately \$10 and \$50 in the two studies. In industries other than those studied, $CO_2$ concentration in the process streams is likely to be lower so chemical reduction costs are probably larger, although no data are available yet.

### 6.9.3 Technological Maximum Price

The technological maximum price in a hypothetical $CO_2$ market will, if the public electricity sector is included, be dominated by the 18 Danish electric utilities. Since the utilities are predominantly coal-fired, the maximum price in the market might stabilize around \$40, corresponding to the technological reduction costs in a modern, coal-fired power plant. However, if it is not possible to deregulate the electric utility sector into competing production companies, for example if the single market does not develop as planned, a market should only be considered for private industry.

This means, given a worst-case scenario, that the most expensive chemical reduction installation must be considered, that is the one from the petrochemical industry. Here, the \$50 price corresponds exactly to the tax level for achieving a 20% $CO_2$ reduction in Denmark established by the Danish Economic Council.

The figures show the total chemical $CO_2$ reduction costs on a one-year basis, so that a corresponding permit would entitle the holder to emit a unit once. Therefore, the maximum technological permit price corresponds to the maximum technological tax. However, if the permits are to be valid for several occasions or more than one year – which will most likely be the case because existing firms will probably ask for permanent permits – the value must be capitalized in relation to a time horizon and a discount factor, as explained in Section 3.5.2. The capitalized value of the permanent or 'infinite' permit with a 5% discount rate is \$1000 per ton in the absence of any technological change that would affect reduction costs during this time period.

An important observation is that even in the worst-case, new entrants would not be any worse off under an inactive permit market than under a corresponding tax, because both the technological maximum price and the correctly set tax have the value of \$50. A \$50 technological maximum price means constant marginal reduction costs. It is therefore possible to calculate the reduction costs for the industry when a 20% reduction is accomplished and to compare this worst-case scenario with costs incurred under the actual $CO_2$ tax.

Industry is obliged to carry out a 20% $CO_2$ reduction by 2005, based on the 1988 levels (9 million tons, see Table 6.1). In total, industry has to reduce

aquifer water is extracted to compensate. Part of this water is injected again together with the $CO_2$ in order to improve the displacement efficiency. The remainder is disposed of in the ocean. Storage costs reported in this study are much higher: \$24/ton of $CO_2$. They estimate the worldwide storage capacity to be 300 billion tons. Because the Dutch research program is the most recent, it has taken the Japanese findings into account, and is the most comprehensive, the results from it are used here.

emissions by 1.8 million tons, which means total reduction costs on a one-year basis of approximately $90 million.

As mentioned in Section 6.5, industry representatives estimate that the $CO_2$ tax in 1993 cost the industry $50 million after rebate. In other words, a grandfathered $CO_2$ market – in the worst-case – would impose net costs on industry equal to $40 million, if emissions were reduced by 20% in one year. The $90 million total cost to industry under the worst-case permit market is low compared to key statistics. The size of this payment is equivalent to just 0.4% of the total 1994 wage costs in the Danish manufacturing sector, or 0.6% of Denmark's 1994 GDP.[439]

## 6.10  THE EU

How should an economic instrument be designed for $CO_2$ reduction in the EU? How can it fit both the institutional structure and the wishes of all individual member states and at the same time preserve competitiveness?

This section takes a closer look at how the tax approach to $CO_2$ regulation has been working in practice. The attempted application of the tax approach has not met with success in the EU. This fact may lead to further consideration of a permit market approach. A decision to implement a permit market might provide a politically acceptable outcome to the current $CO_2$ negotiations.[440]

$CO_2$ emissions are to be stabilized in the EU at the 1990 level by the year 2000. However, the EU Commission expects an 11% increase in the demand for energy between 1990 and 2000.[441] So, unless there is a drastic change in the behaviour of polluters, the target will not be met.[442] In the following section, empirical evidence from $CO_2$ taxation attempts in the EU will be presented and the possibility for introducing a common $CO_2$ market will be sketched.

### 6.10.1  The CO₂ Tax

The concern for competitiveness in the world market has so far prevented the introduction of a common $CO_2$ tax in the EU. When the EU Commission launched a $15 tax directive proposal in May 1992, this proposal was opposed by several member states.[443] Following a meeting on October 5, 1994 between

439.   STO (1995:113 and 119). In Denmark, total energy costs equal about 5% of total wage costs (Danish Economic Council 1995:83).

440.   This subsection draws heavily on Svendsen (1998e).

441.   Fee (1992).

442.   At present, the 15 members of the EU are Austria, Belgium, Denmark, Finland, France, Germany, Greece, Ireland, Italy, Luxemburg, the Netherlands, Portugal, Spain, Sweden and the United Kingdom.

443.   The EU has considered a $CO_2$ tax of $3 ($ 15/ton $CO_2$) on the equivalent of one barrel of oil with an increase to $10 ($50/ton $CO_2$) per barrel by the year 2000. Half this tax would be levied on the use of energy from any source other than renewable ones (which would be excluded) and half

the ministers of the environment in the EU, the Danish minister of the environment stated publicly that the proposed common $CO_2$ tax in the EU was dead.[444]

Great Britain is against common EU taxes in principle and wishes to deal with the $CO_2$ problem on its own.[445] Spain demands the right to increase its $CO_2$ emissions by 25% because its industrial level is lower than that of other EU member states. Portugal and Greece have argued against the $CO_2$ tax for the reason that taxation could slow economic growth. Spain, Portugal and Greece refuse to accept further production costs until they reach an economic level similar to that of the more wealthy northern EU members.[446]

Individual action has so far been taken by four member states. In addition to Denmark, the Netherlands, Finland and Sweden have introduced $CO_2$ taxes. The Netherlands and Finland have $CO_2$ taxes roughly equal to $3 per ton $CO_2$ emitted.[447] However, $3 per ton is much too low to create incentives to change $CO_2$-emitting behaviour.[448] In Sweden, industry must pay a $12 $CO_2$ tax per ton, whereas the rate for other sectors is $47. As in Denmark, special reduction rules exist for industries that have a high ratio of energy use compared to sales revenues. This green tax is a part of the reform of the Swedish tax system. The revenue has enabled the dissolution of the general energy tax and the lowering of income taxes. The idea of refunding green taxes to households in the form of lower income taxes is proposed in this book too.[449]

A $CO_2$ permit market would be more workable in the EU than a $CO_2$ tax for three reasons.[450] First, the substantial revenue from a pure tax approach could not be redistributed to the countries (or individual sources) in a politically acceptable way. Such regulation would always create economic 'losers' who would oppose its introduction.

Second, the institutional structure prevents the use of a common $CO_2$ tax. The EU unanimity rule for fiscal measures – which would apply to the $CO_2$ tax – points to a grandfathered permit market in which no financial transfers between member states and the EU are implied. A permit market has no fiscal character and therefore may be settled upon by majority rule.

Third, the free-rider problem may be overcome by positive inducements to

on carbon emissions.

444.  See Rudisill (1992) and Carraro and Siniscalco (1993).

445.  Interview May 30, 1994: Karsten Laursen, Danish Environmental Protection Agency.

446.  Interview May 27, 1994: Jesper Jørgensen, DG-XI – Task Force, European Environment Agency.

447.  Norway, which is outside the EU, also has a $CO_2$ tax at this $3 level.

448.  See Opschoor (1993). For further criticisms on the design of the Danish $CO_2$ tax, see Danish Economic Council (1993), Jespersen (1992), Svendsen (1993a–b). For a complete review of environmental taxes in Europe, see Howe (1994).

449.  Values are calculated on a 1:6.8 $/Skr exchange rate. Swedish Ministry of the Environment and Natural Resources (1994:25) and Lövgren (1994).

450.  See Hensel and Svendsen (1995) for further evidence on these three arguments.

reluctant member states. A permit market builds on historical emission levels and the status quo. However, reluctant EU members may be persuaded into a common agreement if they are initially allocated a relatively larger number of permits than their historical emission levels qualify them for.

### 6.10.2  The $CO_2$ Market

A design for a potential $CO_2$ market in the EU can, as was the case of Denmark, be based on the US experience. Again, the design can be split up analytically into 5 points: Target level, Target group, Distribution rule, Trade rules, and Control system.

### 6.10.2.1  Target level
The target emission level for a $CO_2$ market can be fixed at its 1990 level in the EU. Initially, each country would get the right to emit its 1990 emission level for free. Member countries or firms would be allowed to trade permits.

### 6.10.2.2  Target group
The permit market could be introduced at both the state and the plant level in the EU. It could be implemented at the state level, requiring each of the 15 member states to agree on a maximum level of $CO_2$ emissions and where only the purchase of permits from another member state would give the right to increase emissions beyond this upper limit. In the EU, member countries are already free to choose in which way they want to accomplish the $CO_2$ target level.

This would allow the individual states to pursue their own environmental policies, and would allow any two states to voluntarily create a common trade area. For example, Germany and Denmark could choose a permit market system, whereas Greece could choose a more traditional CAC approach. Then Germany and Denmark could agree to create a common trade area for $CO_2$ permits among their major, stationary sources.

However, the permit market could also be introduced on a plant level in a way similar to that of the US Acid Rain Program. A workable experiment could, for a start, incorporate all fossil-based electric utilities in the EU with a production capacity greater than 25 MW.[451] These emitters are large and stationary, and are covered by already existing control systems. It should be possible for other $CO_2$ emitters to optin. Firms should choose themselves whether they want to participate or not. If not, they should be regulated by the traditional (and much more expensive) CAC approach.

In a market formed along these lines, permits would probably – as has been the case in the US Acid Rain Program – be fairly well spread out among market participants. It would therefore be hard for the largest participants to manipulate

---

451.  For example, in 1990, a 122 coal-fired power plant consortia existed in the present 15 member states (International Energy Agency 1991:131–147).

the market in a strategic way.

### 6.10.2.3  Distribution rule
Initially, each firm would get the right to match its 1990 emissions for nothing, that is the permits would be 'grandfathered'. The distribution rule could be defined for a three-year period in order to reduce the influence of economic fluctuations. Free distribution could, for example, be based on average fuel input for the period 1990–1992. Utilities established after 1990 could be eligible for a free, initial standard distribution, if they apply before a certain deadline.

To overcome the problem of collective choice, a grandfathered permit market may therefore initially be defined so that a positive inducement can be offered to the most reluctant member countries in the EU, thus introducing a 'selective incentive'.[452] This distribution rule may be tailored to political reality. In this case, the 'bribe' for taking part in the market would be allocation of an extra portion of permits.

### 6.10.2.4  Trade rules
Permits should be tradable on a one-to-one basis, and banking of permits should be allowed. Sources should receive full property rights to their permit holdings.

To secure the availability of permits for new sources, 3% of the permits could be withdrawn every year as a reserve in a procedure identical to that recommended above for a Danish $CO_2$ market. One per cent would be used for direct sale at a price corresponding to an expected market price. These permits would be made available to new entrants before being sold to existing sources. To encourage new sources and to give a price signal, 2% could be auctioned off every year in a non-discriminative and revenue-neutral auction.

### 6.10.2.5  Control system
As recommended for the Danish $CO_2$ market, it is important that the control system is administered by one single and central authority so that local municipalities do not have the control responsibility and as such are not tempted to protect their own firms. An annual self-reporting system concerning fuel input would allow the European Environmental Agency in Denmark, as a central authority independent of local interests, to double check this data (from both buyers and sellers) and the related trade activity, by checking individual energy inputs in different firms. Furthermore, as in the ARP, CEMS monitors could be required. The CEMS would monitor $CO_2$ emissions and enable the European Environmental Agency to enforce property rights. The large electric utilities could, as in the US, afford the annual expenses of running the CEMS. If a source were to exceed its quota, it would automatically be fined and would have to reduce the excess amount in the following year. The level of the fine could, for example, be five times the expected market permit price per ton.

452.  Olson (1965:133), see Section 2.4. See also Steiner and Svendsen (1998).

Table 6.4 summarizes the recommended policy design for a $CO_2$ permit market in the EU.

*Table 6.4: $CO_2$ market for the electric utility industry in the EU*

| | | |
|---|---|---|
| **1 Target Level** | | $CO_2$ emissions are to be stabilized at the 1990 level by the year 2000. |
| **2 Target Group** | | All fossil-based electric utilities in the European Union with a production capacity greater than 25 MW in the EU with optin possibility for other firms. |
| **3 Distribution Rule** | | Free, initial distribution ('grandfathering') based on the average use of fossil fuels in the 3-year period 1990–1992. |
| **4 Trade Rules** | | Transfer of full property right. Allow banking of permits for later use or sale. Withdraw 3% of permits each year; 1% for direct sale and 2% for an annual, revenue-neutral auction at the Board of Trade in Copenhagen. |
| **5 Control System** | | Annual self-reporting about input of fossil fuels to a central authority, for example the European Environmental Agency in Denmark, which can double-check trade figures. Also, the CEMS monitoring system should be applied to avoid any cheating. If violations occur, the source should be automatically fined and required to reduce the excess amount in the following year. |

## 6.11  GLOBAL $CO_2$ MARKET

The US opposes a $CO_2$ reduction policy on the grounds that it would be costly for business and detrimental to the economy. The US instead prefers a policy that limits all greenhouse gases (including ones which are limited under current US law) but allows for increases in $CO_2$ emissions. In contrast, many EU officials have argued that $CO_2$ reductions force greater energy efficiency and therefore will be economical in the long run. This deadlock has so far prevented an agreement for a global, binding $CO_2$ reduction strategy.[453]

As such, $CO_2$ emissions are not controlled jointly among industrialized countries. What can be done? Is it possible to reach any global solutions? Because $CO_2$ reduction can take place much more cheaply in less developed areas, there must be a mutually beneficial solution for both rich and poor nations. The industrialized countries own new technology and are relatively more energy-efficient than developing countries. Therefore, the marginal reduction costs are higher in industrialized states with 'new' technology than in developing countries with 'old' technology. For example, the marginal $CO_2$

---

453.  Rudisill (1992).

reduction costs in Denmark are four times higher than those in Poland.[454] How is it possible to incorporate and reward the poor countries for taking active part in a global effort against global warming?

An interesting proposal has been put forth by Bertram (1992).[455] He suggests that the global dilemma between energy production and environmental protection could be solved by granting each world citizen one $CO_2$ permit. Roughly 5 billion tons $CO_2$ are emitted every year on a global scale. This number equals the world population of 5 billion, so that each world citizen could have a $CO_2$ permit allowing him to emit 1 ton of $CO_2$ per year.[456] The most feasible way of distributing the permits in practice would be to grandfather the 5 billion $CO_2$ permits to the various states in relation to population and not directly to each citizen.

Developing countries would receive an economic reward by participating in such a global $CO_2$ market. In most cases their populations are larger, so their permit allocations would be larger. Furthermore, since the industrialized countries emit more $CO_2$ per capita, they would need to buy permits from the developing countries. In fact, almost half of all permits initially allocated to the developing countries would have to be bought by the industrialized ones if the present profile of energy production across countries were to be maintained.

The payment flow from rich to poor countries would be determined by the price of one $CO_2$ permit in the global market. Several scholars have made guesses on this permit price[457] and concluded that the price would not exceed $40. The annual payment flow from industrialized to developing countries at a permit price of $40 would amount to roughly $100 billion, or twice the present development aid from OECD and OPEC. Total debt in developing countries amounted to $1,265 billion in 1990. Therefore, an annual $100 billion transfer could be a significant step toward solving the debt crisis.[458]

If such a program were initiated, $CO_2$ permits would become a security, like shares or bonds, and could be traded through existing brokerage services. Trade activity could be surveyed by a central computer register. Bertram (1992:429) suggests that this global $CO_2$ market could be controlled best if it were to run in 10-year periods, that is one-tenth of the permits in circulation would expire each year as each state is simultaneously given a new one-tenth, corresponding to the size of its population.

It is possible to devalue these annual distributions, for example to reduce $CO_2$

---

454.  Svendsen (1998c).

455.  See also Bohm (1993;1992), Grubb (1989), Hoel (1991), Chapman and Drennen (1990), Manne and Richels (1991),Young and Wolf (1992), Yu and Kinderman (1991), Morgenstern (1991), Paterson and Grubb (1996), Zhang (1997), Schneider (1994), and Rose and Tietenberg (1993).

456.  Bertram's figures are based on Bolin (1989) and World Bank (1990).

457.  See Bertram (1992:442 pp) for references and more details.

458.  In comparison, the annual military expenditures in OECD and the world, respectively, amounted to $500 and $800 billion in 1990.

emissions by 20% gradually over 10 years. The 10-year periods also make it possible to deter individual states from cheating. In addition to being fined for violations, they could be denied the free distribution of permits.

This idea of a global $CO_2$ market has its appeal. Developing countries and eastern Europe would be given the right to raise living standards in the same way industrialized countries did, that is by fossil-fuel-based energy production. However, four serious objections have been voiced.

First, population growth is rewarded. To prevent the policy from encouraging population growth certain rules would have to be developed to take this matter into account. For example, the distribution rule could be fixed at a base-year level, so that each country would receive the same number of permits every year in the future. However, this would amount to a permanent subsidy to the developing countries. Therefore, other global distribution rules should be evolved based on, for example, GDP or voluntary agreements.[459] Second, industry in the developing countries would be favoured by such a subsidy, which certainly would provoke protests from industry in the developed world. Third, no international authority exists to handle the system, though international trade sanctions, like the retaliation mechanism in the World Trade Organization, could be used for enforcing the rules. The United Nations (UN) could also play an important role as a central, international authority. Fourth, even though cheating countries would be punished by fines or by losing the right to free permit distributions, it could be hard for a central authority to monitor activity and verify official statistics. The world community is perhaps not yet ready for a global market since the necessary administrative enforcement systems remain unprepared.

Still, with more international cooperation, this idea may turn out to be feasible in the future, in particular if the permits are to be renewed. For example, following the voluntary UN climate negotiations in Kyoto, Japan (December 1997) trade among individual countries, such as the US and Russia, could be enforced by the UN if the permits were renewed within a short time period, for example 5 or 10 years. It will not pay to cheat if permits are renewed periodically and if cheating countries are excluded from the program, and forced to miss out on profitable trade in the future.[460]

## 6.12 RECOMMENDATION

$CO_2$ emission taxation has in general failed in the EU. Organized interests have resisted increased costs and have used the argument of competitiveness. The actual Danish $CO_2$ tax is too low, contains a perverse refund system for energy-intensive industry, and taxes electric utilities on electricity consumption (not

---

459.   See Barrett (1992) and Larsen and Shah (1994) for a survey of different scenarios following different distribution rules.

460.   See Svendsen (1998c).

fuel input). Even though the net tax revenue from industry is to be refunded, it is to happen by subsidizing energy savings. This earmarking initiative and heavy state involvement only reinforces the CAC approach. Furthermore, potential winners from the regulation are not easily identified and will, therefore, not compensate potential losers. The losses of the losers are, in this case, much more transparent than the gains of the winners.

$CO_2$-emitting sources in Denmark can be subdivided into four groups: public electric utilities, private industry, households and the transportation sector. Households and the transportation sector are large groups with diffuse costs and benefits and can, therefore, be taxed without political repercussions. For administrative reasons also, these two large groups should be kept out of a permit market. They should, instead, pay a $50 $CO_2$ tax which can be refunded, for example through a lower income tax or a lower car tax. Border trade in relation to transportation does not seem to be a problem with regard to this tax because the resulting 4-cent-per-litre rise in petrol and diesel prices will not raise the Danish price level above the German one.

What kind of regulation would Danish electric utilities prefer? The answer at present is a system of taxation, because the electricity industry at the moment is so heavily regulated that – in return for its monopoly – it follows state interests. This situation may become more competitive if the two consortia are reorganized on the production-company level, or in the future when more competition arises from the introduction of a single market in the EU. However, at present, Danish electric utilities maintain that a $CO_2$ tax is appropriate and that it should be imposed on consumption so that the tax stays neutral with respect to exports.

In Denmark, two $SNO_x$ bubbles are in effect for the two consortia in the electric utility sector, ELSAM and ELKRAFT. Because the participation of two public monopolies would spoil a $CO_2$ market, they should instead be covered by two $CO_2$ bubbles (corresponding to the two $SNO_x$ bubbles) making it possible to transfer permits on an internal basis. To protect exports of electricity, only net numbers should be considered. When net exports are positive, the $CO_2$ surplus should be added to the permit holdings of ELSAM and ELKRAFT.

Danish industry, on the other hand, would prefer voluntary agreements. However, if control is to be stringent and if the target level is to be achieved, then this solution is most unreliable. Compared to a tax solution, Danish industry prefers a $CO_2$ permit market. Danish environmental groups promote the use of taxes, but are, paradoxically, sceptical of the use of permit markets. Even though their argument is based on the fear of hot spots, scepticism remains with regard to $CO_2$. The only rational explanation for this attitude is the lack of knowledge about a new and unfamiliar instrument.

A suitable starting point for a Danish $CO_2$ permit market could be to incorporate the 200 largest firms in the Danish manufacturing sector noted in the new, individual data released by the Danish Ministry of Energy. One firm would hold one-fifth of the permits, but the permits would otherwise be well distributed, making it hard for the largest actor to manipulate the market significantly. The 200 firms should be allowed to choose for themselves whether they want to participate or not. If not, they should continue to pay a $50 tax which could be refunded through, for example, reduced tax contributions to labour market services or reduced corporate taxes.

Other firms or sectors may also be interested in the system if their energy costs are significant. An optin facility should be added to the program so that these other firms subsequently may apply for participation. Also, it should be possible to leave the system and alternatively pay a $50 tax on each emitted unit. As in the ARP, an annual 3% reserve for direct sale and for revenue-neutral auctions should be included.

New sources would have to buy their way into the market. Note, however, that their payments, in a competitive market without market power or strategic behaviour, will not exceed the corresponding tax of $50 per ton. This number, calculated by the Danish Economic Council, equals the worst-case technological maximum price for new Dutch pilot projects in chemical $CO_2$ reduction, which shows that $CO_2$ can now be chemically removed and stored at annual costs varying between $10 and 50 per ton. Over time, the equilibrium price in the $CO_2$ market will probably be lower than $50 due to $CO_2$ reduction capabilities other than chemical recovery and storage.

Hence, for political, economic, and administrative reasons, a mixed design is preferable in Denmark. The $CO_2$ market should be introduced for the private manufacturing sector in Denmark, an administratively set $CO_2$ bubble should be introduced for the public electricity sector, and a $CO_2$ tax should be set at the correct $50 level for households and the transportation sector.

The grandfathering of $CO_2$ permit rights may also be the most politically feasible solution for regulating $CO_2$ in the EU and in the world at large. Within the EU, it may fit both the institutional structure and the wishes of all individual member states, and at the same time, preserve competitiveness. First, no revenue needs to be redistributed. Second, in contrast to taxation, the institutional structure in the EU allows a permit market, as a non-fiscal measure, to be settled on by majority rule. Third, the free-rider problem may be overcome by allocating to those EU members that are reluctant to participate a relatively larger proportion of the permits than their historical emission levels qualify them for. A design similar to that of the US Acid Rain Program could be considered whereby the initial group would be those fossil-based electric utilities in the European Union with a production capacity greater than 25 MW.

A similar $CO_2$ market in the US for the 1,000 electric utilities already covered by the ARP seems an obvious possibility too. If there is to be $CO_2$ regulation in the US, the electric utilities must surely be expected to ask for $CO_2$ emission trading, just as they have promoted $SO_2$ emission trading in the ARP. This incentive is reinforced by the fact that the electric utilities covered by the ARP have invested in the continuous emissions monitoring system (CEMS), which is capable of monitoring both $SO_2$ and $CO_2$ emissions. Therefore, the CEMS monitors already in use can be used in a potential $CO_2$ market as well. In this way, the efficient control system from the ARP can be transferred to the setting of a future $CO_2$ market. Again, it will not be possible to cheat in the system. This market is well-described in relation to $SO_2$, but not in relation to $CO_2$. The fact that $CO_2$ has not been regulated before and the fact that it is much more costly to reduce $CO_2$ will result in an initial distribution of $CO_2$ permits which is different from the initial distribution of $SO_2$ permits. Therefore, it is necessary to check the potential market structure and the concentration of permits among electric utilities following grandfathering and the distribution rule of historical $CO_2$ emissions.

Global $CO_2$ emissions may also be brought under control by grandfathering $CO_2$ permits to all nation states in the future, for example in relation to population, GDP or voluntary agreements. The initial distribution key must be defined so that developing countries are sufficiently rewarded for participation. On the other hand, if developing countries receive too many permits, industrial sectors in the developed countries can be expected to protest against the bias of redistribution to industrial sectors in developing countries. Finally, the world community must agree on establishing an international authority such as the UN, for enforcing the market and for defining permits valid for a shorter period only. For example, the permits could run in 10-year periods to prevent countries from cheating. If a country cheats in one period, it will be excluded from participating in the next.

Future research should focus on the collection of more data on these potential $CO_2$ markets in the US and the EU. It would be useful to describe the market structure more fully and to calculate the expected market price. Such research could help to uncover the risk of strategic behaviour in the potential $CO_2$ market, to estimate potential cost savings, and to identify the level of fines needed to deter violations of quota limitations. The potential $CO_2$ markets for electric utilities in the EU and the US, matching the design of the ARP, have not yet been described or discussed among academics. The task of doing so is a major challenge to social scientists in the near future.

# 7 Conclusion

In a democracy, the public state of affairs is no longer that of stationary banditry. There is no longer an absolute ruler capable of manipulating both the tax rate and the provision of collective goods to his or her own advantage. Things are different because the democratic State represents a majority and because it is counteracted by organized interest groups, which will use lobbyism to influence the actions of political decision-makers. A balance of power exists. Therefore, the democratic State must take into consideration the incentives that drive main interest groups if new policy proposals are not to be blocked or changed beyond recognition by political opposition. The State must now look for politically acceptable policy designs that serve the twin goals of maximizing revenue and providing collective goods at minimum cost.

The fundamental question of this book has concerned the form of regulation to be used in environmental regulation. The book aimed to reveal how well-organized interests influence the choice of policy design in environmental regulation. Economics and politics were not discussed separately in the traditional way but were combined. Literature on this kind of public choice approach, and on the use of it in environmental regulation, has been weak. Economists have not considered political and administrative concerns in the traditional analysis of economic instruments. The approach taken here may, therefore, contribute to the search for the most cost-effective approaches to environmental regulation and diminish the gap between theory and practice. Europe can learn from the actual use of permit markets in the US, whereas the US can learn from the European experience with taxes.

The general conclusion reached here is that a mix of economic instruments would probably achieve the most cost-effective outcome in practice. Political, economic and administrative distortions were considered. Grandfathered permit markets should be used in relation to organized interests whereas taxes should be used in relation to badly organized interests. Permit markets may involve higher economic and administrative distortions than taxes do because well-functioning markets need to be established, but they involve much lower political distortions and are in fact demanded by the main interest groups.

What have been the specific results of mandating $CO_2$ abatement in Denmark and the EU? How could the $CO_2$ target levels be achieved at minimum cost in practice? These issues from Chapter 6 will be reconsidered before the results from Chapters 2, 3, 4 and 5 are summarized and brought into perspective.

Three main distortions affecting the ability to achieve a target level at minimum cost were considered. They were political, economic and administrative distortions. First, policy must be designed in a politically acceptable way so that it is not changed during the political decision-making process. Second, if the permit market is to be used, the market set-up must be competitive and generate price signals. Third, the administration of the policy must take place at low costs with well-defined and enforceable property rights. Reconsider these three points.

The first distortion is political. Organized interests, particularly those representing capital-intensive and privileged firms, tend to resist taxation because of the extra production costs it creates. Organized interests prefer a grandfathered permit market because it creates a barrier to entry for new sources, which have to buy their way into the market. It was noted, however, that heavily regulated industries, such as electric utilities, might act as part of a state-planned economy and, as such, follow State interests by promoting traditional CAC regulation or taxation in return for their monopolies. On the other hand, poorly organized interest groups, such as households and the transportation sector, could be regulated with a tax instrument because they are latent groups and are not able to organize. A correctly set emission tax would be politically feasible in relation to badly organized interests because each taxpayer would only be affected on the margin. That is, the individual benefits from organizing opposition through an interest group would be smaller than the added costs of doing so.

When the Danish $CO_2$ emission tax was introduced in 1992, it was set much too low to accomplish the 20% target emission reduction level. The tax was not imposed on the transportation sector due to concerns about competitiveness with Germany, and it was set lower for industry than for households. A complicated refund system was linked to the program, so that energy-intensive firms were protected. Danish electric utilities, which produce energy based on fossil fuels, were also protected; the tax, in this case, was imposed on production, not on input.

These observations support the hypotheses derived from the stationary-bandit model. First, green taxation is primarily an innovation in tax collection not a behaviour modifier, and therefore, it was rational for a small country like Denmark to be ahead on its own and not wait for big countries, like the US, to act. Second, the $CO_2$ tax was supported by the Danish electric utilities, which followed the interests of the Danish State. As monopolies, they were expected to do this. Third, Danish environmental groups met the possibility of permit markets with surprising scepticism, but fully supported the use of green taxes. This paradox could only be explained by lack of knowledge. Fourth, Danish private industry preferred permit markets to taxes, but promoted foremost the option of voluntary agreements. Voluntary agreements would, however, result in a traditional CAC setting, without enforcement mechanisms.

Three political reasons were found to explain why the Danish $CO_2$ tax rate could not be set sufficiently high with a politically acceptable refund system. First, it is not transparent in the implementation of the $CO_2$ tax exactly who wins, although it is clear who loses (energy-intensive firms). The potential winners are in need of knowing, however, because otherwise they are unable to comply with the relevant rules and cannot apply for subsidies and arrange for visits from energy consultants (who are necessary for approval of refunds). A related problem with this system is that the subsidy is not in cash, but rather earmarked for use on uncertain energy-saving arrangements. This administrative and cumbersome earmarking system equals a throwback to a CAC setting, in which the regulator dictates technology-based standards for each individual firm and discourages the firm from making use of its own information.

Second, the worst-hit $CO_2$-emitters are large and capital-intensive firms, which, as part of a privileged group, are able to protest quickly and with success. This behaviour contrasts with that of the latent group of potential net winners, which are typically numerous and small service firms unable to organize.

Third and relatedly, the privileged group, the losers, claim that they earn only normal profits so a higher tax would result in the loss of jobs. Because of their organizing ability, they can lobby this argument with great enthusiasm. The latent group, the potential winners, however, cannot organize and lobby with the same enthusiasm in support of a corresponding increase in production and jobs following a subsidy. These issues indicate how difficult it will be in the future to tax organized interests at a meaningful level.

Even if the Danish $CO_2$ tax could be designed optimally with regard to level and the general refund system, the ultimate arguments against a tax would not change, even though some of the problem areas listed above would be mitigated. The first problem area, concerning transparency, for example, was linked to the actual design of the $CO_2$ tax and can be resolved with more clarity. However, even if the tax were refunded in a transparent and general way as a monetary transfer, the political opposition against $CO_2$ taxation would probably persist because capital-intensive firms, which are also the most energy-intensive, are normally the largest and can organize for collective action – they may behave as a single collective actor or privileged group. In the Danish case, it was shown that a few large firms were most active in their lobbying efforts. Therefore, the political opposition against $CO_2$ taxation is likely to stay asymmetrically in favour of potential losers. The overall problem is that potential winners cannot organize their lobbying powers to counteract the potential losers in the political decision-making process.

In the EU, several member countries opposed a common $CO_2$ tax proposal on the grounds of its potential to damage competitiveness and increase production costs; this proposal was ultimately rejected. This book has argued for a permit market system as the way to solve the problem of political acceptability and co-operation in the EU. There are three reasons for this. First, there would be no tax revenue to distribute back to member states. Second, the EU unanimity rule for fiscal measures point to a permit market, which could be settled upon by majority rule. Third, the free-rider problem could be overcome by positive inducements to reluctant member states, like Great Britain. For instance, such members could start out with a relatively larger number of permits than that justified by historical emissions. In perspective, such an international market could be expanded to the global level at which permits could be distributed to reward developing countries for participation, for example with extra permits per capita. However, as industry in the developing countries would be favoured by such a subsidy, industry in the developed countries would certainly lobby against this kind of redistribution.

Similar to the argument for the EU and the world, the initial permit distribution rule in Denmark could be defined so that the worst-hit polluters are compensated with relatively more permits than the polluters who would be likely to sell. Energy-intensive Danish firms and strong opponents to taxation could be compensated in this way. This flexibility in the initial distribution rule could, in conclusion, make it possible to reach consensus in the political arena.

The second main distortion to the ability to reach a cost-effective outcome is economic. Concerning Denmark, the book has argued for a $CO_2$ permit market that starts with the 200 largest $CO_2$-emitters in the manufacturing sector and an optin possibility for other, smaller firms. The market could be combined with a reserve of permits for direct sale and for a $CO_2$ auction with a non-discriminative design, so as to ensure the entrance of new sources and a well-defined price signal to the market. This annual price signal would create more information in the market and lower transaction costs.

In future, the single market for electricity in the EU may lead to a more competitive structure so that, for example, Danish production companies may optin too. Until then, the two Danish electricity consortia should be covered by two administrative $CO_2$ bubbles, within each of which it should be allowable to move $CO_2$ permits. A $CO_2$ tax that is high enough to secure the target level should then be applied to firms not wishing to take part in the permit market. It should also be applied to the multiple and poorly organized sources in the household and transportation sectors. New sources would also have to pay the tax or, if they are VAT-registered firms, they may choose to buy themselves into the market.

Important indicators for the size of these entry costs were the recent findings on $CO_2$ scrubbers. Here, a worst-case scenario showed that, even without trade or reduction options other than buying a $CO_2$ scrubber, the technological maximum price could not supersede the correctly set $50 tax. So, a new entrant to the market would never be worse off than if it were required to pay a correctly set tax. It was also shown that the worst possible cost scenario for the 200 manufacturing firms, representing half of total $CO_2$ emissions from Danish private industry, would entail permit-related costs that are only a small fraction of the total costs incurred by these firms.

A similar $CO_2$ market in the US for the 1,000 electric utilities already covered by the US Acid Rain Program (ARP) seemed an obvious possibility too. Likewise, a design similar to that of the ARP could be considered in the EU, so as to include all fossil-based electric utilities with a production capacity greater than 25 MW. Research concerning these $CO_2$ markets for the electricity sectors in the US and the EU, should be conducted in the future. Finally, on a global scale, it was discussed how the approximately 250 countries could trade at the state level.

The third main distortion involves the administration of the policy. Households and the transportation sector should be taxed, not just for political reasons but also on administrative grounds as both these sectors contain numerous and small sources. It is easy to define property rights to $CO_2$ permits because source location can be ignored. The two Danish electricity consortia and the 200 Danish manufacturing firms considered for participation in the proposed permit market are already controlled by the regulator. The manufacturing sector has already reported its use of fossil fuels to the Danish Ministry of Energy, and would therefore be relatively easy to control. Also, the sector is covered by the present $CO_2$ taxation system. It is important that one central authority runs the control systems so that local competition and strong free-rider incentives among municipalities does not undermine enforcement of the rules. The permits should be devalued by 20% in the year 2005 so as to achieve the target level.

In the EU, a similar model could be developed. The already existing institutional structure should make the enforcement of a permit market possible. At the international level, each country would be responsible for not violating its quota and could choose for itself how to reach its target, for example by using CAC regulation nationally, or by participating in a permit market system on a plant level, or on a member-state level in the EU. The emission level for a $CO_2$ market in the EU could in this way be fixed at its 1990 level. The suggestion was made, as in the ARP, to use the electric utility sector in the EU as target group. This $CO_2$ market could be linked to the single market for electricity. It was also suggested that the central authority running the market should be the European Environmental Agency in Copenhagen. A $CO_2$ market in the US for the 1,000 electric utilities already covered by the ARP seems a reasonable possibility as well. Again, as in the ARP, this market could be run by the EPA. In the case of both the EU and the US, the enforcement of property rights to permits should be based on the accurate ARP control system, the so-called continuous emissions monitoring system (CEMS), which is capable of monitoring both $SO_2$ and $CO_2$ emissions. All affected electric utilities must pay for and install the rather costly CEMS themselves.

The world community has not yet developed sufficient enforcement systems for handling a global $CO_2$ market. The world community must agree on establishing an international authority such as the United Nations, for enforcing the market and for defining permits valid for a short period only. For example, the permits could run in 10-year periods to prevent countries from cheating. If a country cheated in one period, it would be excluded from participating in the next. Trade sanctions could be considered as well.

The findings in Chapter 6, as reconsidered above, were based on the theory and empirical evidence presented in the previous four chapters. Theoretically, the book is based on public choice theory (Chapter 2) and environmental economics (Chapter 3). Empirically, the book is based on evidence from the US experience with permit markets (Chapters 4 and 5).

Chapter 2 first discussed the public choice approach by comparing the disciplines of economics and political science. A presentation and discussion was made of economically rational behaviour, the choice of political arena and the method of economics, and then each in turn was argued to be justified in this setting. The method chosen in this book was a combination of both deductive and inductive elements. The deductive approach, based on the economic rationality of the agent, allowed theory to be used in both an explanatory and a predictive way so as to explore the potential for new and more cost-effective policies in future environmental regulation. The inductive approach from political science meant that the structure of reality was kept in mind. This combination gave an important interplay between theory and reality, because it assured that theory was appropriate for solving a problem based in reality.

To understand the logic that drives the economic behaviour of the State and interest organizations in environmental regulation, the origins of organization were traced from the times of roving banditry to those of stationary banditry (autocracy) to those of majority banditry (democracy). The roving bandit discovered that settling down, defining property rights, and imposing taxation rather than confiscating property was more profitable. Also, it is rational for the stationary bandit to channel resources into the military and to expand his territory and tax base. Following this logic, the State can be seen to have an incentive to provide collective goods in spite of free-rider incentives, both in autocracies and democracies, in order to maximize tax revenue. The stationary bandit would redistribute to himself, whereas the democratic leader would redistribute to the majority. Both kinds of leaders would consider their constituency's share of the national income when calculating the optimal tax rate and the amount of collective goods to provide.

Because the majority in a democracy earns a significant share of national income, it is rational to tax less and provide more collective goods. For this reason, collective goods, such as a peaceful order and environmental improvements, are provided. In the same way, interest groups gradually evolve with the help of entrepreneurs and organize to influence policy making in a direction favourable for them. Successful lobbyism by special interest groups in modern democracies was finally explained by the notion of rational ignorance. It is not economically rational for a voter to take part in public affairs, and this clears the road for plausibility arguments and propaganda in favour of new redistributive arrangements.

The assumption that both the State and the main political actors are rational in an economic sense was used to advance hypotheses on their political behaviour with regard to environmental regulation. The State prefers the use of green taxes to maximize its revenue. Public electric utilities, because they are monopolies, support the State in its revenue-maximizing efforts. Private industry representatives prefer permit markets where historical pollution rights are distributed free of charge among existing sources and potential competitors are forced to buy their way into the market.

Chapter 3 compared the static and dynamic properties of the tax and the permit system and showed how a tax and a permit market have very different financial consequences for sources. A permit market is politically more attractive to the polluters than a tax due to the possibility of a free, initial distribution (grandfathering). If the marginal reduction cost curve for $CO_2$ were assumed to be linear, the permit market would cost the sources one-ninth as much as a tax without refund would. As such, Danish industry would save one-third of its actual tax payments and, consequently, improve competitiveness. Similarly, the ARP aims to reduce $SO_2$ emission by 50%. Because permits have been grandfathered, the polluters only have to pay for the 50% reduction. In this case, a tax solution (without refund) would be expected to be three times more costly to the polluters than the grandfathered permit market.

Another important feature connected to the permit market is the potential capability of incorporating source location. However, existing theories and administrative trade rules are too complex to be used for the creation of well-functioning markets at present. The definition and enforcement of property rights to permits cannot take place at low costs yet.

Finally, the comparative method chosen was that of the experiment. Each case study was viewed as an independent experiment, and each allowed the researcher to focus on the variables pointed to by theory. Since the number of variables that needed to be taken into account was reasonable, US experience could be transferred to European ground and vice versa. The political, economic and administrative distortions in the US experience with permit markets were then tested in Chapters 4 and 5 against the evaluation model developed in Chapters 2 and 3.

Chapter 4 focused on economic and administrative distortions and systematically evaluated eight main permit market programs in the US. It explained why the early experience with permit markets was not successful whereas recent experience has been. Market failure and economic costs due to incomplete competition seem not to have been a problem. However, high transaction costs were created in some programs for two administrative reasons. First, in early programs, such as the Emissions Trading Program (ETP), the concern for source location and creation of hot spots led to too many time-consuming approval procedures. Second, regulatory uncertainty occurred as a result of the many attempts to reduce emission ceilings; permits could be confiscated in an arbitrary way and trade-ratios could be redefined without notice. This regulatory uncertainty occurred because the administrative rules were not clearly defined and enforced.

In the most recent programs, such as the ARP, these two administrative problems disappeared and property rights to permits were well-defined. First, it was possible to trade without risking hot spots, so the location of sources was ignored. Second, the period of time over which permits were valid and the amount and rate by which emission ceilings would be reduced became clearly defined. Further, the annual $SO_2$ auction linked to the ARP succeeded: it both lowered transaction costs (by giving price signals to the market) and served as an extra option for new sources to buy their way into the market. However, the design should be changed from a discriminative to a non-discriminative one to give a single rather than two price signals to the market.

The ARP was very effectively enforced by the CEMS and run by the EPA as a central authority, independent of local interests. The CEMS is a computer-controlled bookkeeping system which gives the EPA accurate data on tons emitted and makes it possible to run the ARP effectively from the federal level. All affected utilities had to pay for the CEMS themselves. The CEMS was combined with an efficient penalty system. If an electric utility superseded its permit, a fine of $2000 per ton $SO_2$ was imposed, and the extra tons emitted had to be reduced the following year. Due to the CEMS, high fines and computer controls, it was not profitable to cheat.

Chapter 5 gave a political explanation for these different choices of policy designs. All three main political actors in the US (environmental groups, private industry and electric utilities) were found to prefer permit markets over other instruments. This result was to be expected for private industry, which strives to reduce costs and create barriers to entry. This is a new attitude among environmental groups though; these groups recently learned from experience that the cheaper regulation could be for industry, the greater the reductions in emissions that industry would be ready to accept. Environmental groups need results to present to their members if they want to maintain voluntary contributions. Chapter 5 also discussed the former, traditional opposition from environmental groups to licenses to pollute and the maintenance of a goal of zero pollution. This position led environmental groups in the past to lobby against well-defined property rights to permits, which reinforced administrative problems in the early stages of the US permit market programs. With respect to the US electric utility sector, the recent rise of competition in that sector gave even these traditional monopolies an incentive to prefer permit markets over traditional and complex CAC regulation.

The empirical evidence showed how the US programs were influenced by lobbyism. New firms had to buy their way into the market and, furthermore, they had to comply with more stringent emission standards in all eight programs. Even the $SO_2$ auction was designed only to allocate 2% of the total permits in circulation and to redistribute as much as possible from new to existing firms in a discriminative and pay-what-you-bid setting. Therefore, it is important to ensure, that new sources have no trouble in buying their way into the market. Consequently new sources should therefore not face more stringent emission standards than those applied to already existing sources. Also, a special permit reserve should be taken out of the total number of permits in circulation, reserved for direct sale at a fixed price and for an annual non-discriminative auction. Both arrangements would serve the purpose of limiting barriers to entry in the permit market.

These US experiences are most useful in guiding the design of a potential $CO_2$ market in Denmark, Europe, the world and the US itself. In this way, political, economic and administrative distortions could be minimized in relation to well-organized interests. The initial distribution rule of grandfathering made the permit market politically attractive. At the same time, the recent programs had competitive market structures and were easy to administrate because source location could be ignored and because accurate emission-monitoring equipment was available.

In conclusion, the democratic State may very well serve its own interests best by using a mix of environmental policies selected to avoid distortion by organized interests in the political arena. This recommendation can be useful for reaching new and even more stringent environmental target levels in days to come. If a country develops successful permit markets, its industrial sector may even gain a competitive advantage and it may increase exports relative to other countries that use more expensive instruments. This increase in production will consequently raise tax revenue. Green taxation can provide a double dividend when applied to households and the transportation sector: first, it can provide the collective good of environmental improvement; and second, the revenue could be used to lower distortive income taxes and as such increase production. This would fulfill the State's objective to increase its tax collections. So, even though theory suggests that a small country like Denmark will have an incentive to free-ride on $CO_2$ abatement undertaken by large countries, $CO_2$ taxation may be economically rational in this sense.

As the stationary bandit was also interested in increased production and, therefore, produced collective goods, so innovative permit markets and green taxation enables the democratic leader to collect more taxes for redistribution and for the purchase of new support. As the roving bandit learned that settling down and becoming a stationary bandit was more profitable, so the democratic State can learn that the use of permit markets and green taxes can work to its own – and society's – benefit.

# Bibliography

Ackerman, B.A. and Hassler, W.T. (1981), *Clean Coal/Dirty Air, or How the Clean Air Act Became a Multibillion-Dollar Bail-out for High Sulfur Coal Producers and What Should Be Done About It*, New Haven: Yale University Press.

Aidt, T.S. (1997), 'Cooperative Lobbying and Endogeneous Trade Policy', *Public Choice*, **93**, 455-75.

Andersen, P. (1987), 'Miljøøkonomi – samfundsøkonomiske principper for miljøregulering', ('Environmental Economics and National Economics'), in Basse, E.M. (red.), *Erhvervsmiljøret*, Copenhagen: G.E.C. Gad, pp. 261–312.

Andersen, P. (1984), 'Miljøpolitik og markedskræfterne', ('Environmental Policy and Market Forces'), *Politica*, **2**, pp. 131–46.

Anderson et al. (1990), *The Use of Economic Incentive Mechanisms in Environmental Management*, Research paper #051, June. American Petroleum Institute.

APPA (1994), 'American Public Power Association', *Brochure*, Washington D.C.: American Public Power Association

APPA (1991), 'Comments of American Public Power Association on Proposed Auction and Direct Sale Rule for Acid Rain Emissions Allowances', *EPA Public Hearing*, June 28, Docket No. A–91–32.

Association of Danish Electric Utilities (1995), 'Danish Electricity Supply in 1994', Copenhagen.

Association of Danish Electric Utilities (1992), 'Danish Electricity Supply in 1991', Copenhagen.

Association of Danish Electric Utilities (1990), 'Danish Electricity Supply in 1989', Copenhagen.

Atkinson, A.B. and Stiglitz, J.E. (1980), *Lectures on Public Economics*, Maidenhead, Berkshire, England: McGraw-Hill.

Atkinson, S.E. (1994), 'Tradable Discharge Permits: Restrictions on Least Cost Solutions', in Klaassen, G., and Førsund, F.R. (eds.), *Economic Instruments for Air Pollution Control*, Boston: Kluwer Academic Publishers, pp. 3–21.

Atkinson, S.E. and Tietenberg, T.H. (1991), 'Market Failure in Incentive-Based Regulation – The Case of Emissions Trading', *Journal of Environmental Economics and Management*, **21**, pp. 17–31.

Atkinson, S.E. and Tietenberg, T.H. (1987), 'Economic Implications of Emissions Trading Rules for Local and Regional Pollutants', *Canadian Journal of Economics*, **20**, pp. 370–86.

Atkinson, S.E. and Tietenberg, T.H. (1984), 'Approaches for reaching Ambient Standards in Non-Attainment Areas: Financial Burden and Efficiency Considerations', *Land Economics*, **2**, pp. 149–59.

Atkinson, S.E. and Tietenberg, T.H. (1982), 'The Empirical Properties of Two Classes of Designs for Transferable Discharge Permit Markets', *Journal of Environmental Economics and Management*, **9**, pp. 101–21.

Barrett, S. (1992), *Negotiating a Framework Convention on Climate Change: Economic*

*Considerations*, Paris: OECD.

Bartfeld, E. (1992), *Point/Nonpoint Source Trading: Looking Beyond Potential Cost Savings*, Master thesis at University of Michigan.

Baumol, W.J. and Oates, W.E. (1988), *The Theory of Environmental Policy*, 2. ed., New York: Cambridge University Press.

Baumol, W.J., Panzar, J.C., and Willig, R.D. (1982), *Contestable Markets and the Theory of Industry Structure*, New York: Harcourt Brace Jovanovich.

Becker, G.S. (1983), 'A Theory of Competition Among Pressure Groups for Political Influence', *Quarterly Journal of Economics*, **XCVIII**, pp. 371–400.

Begg, D., Fischer, S. and Dornbusch, R. (1984), *Economics*, London: McGraw-Hill.

Bertram, G. (1992), 'Tradeable Emission Permits and the Control of Greenhouse Gases', *The Journal of Development Studies*, **28**, pp. 423–46.

Bierbaum, R. and Friedman, R.M. (1992), 'The Road to Reduced Carbon Emissions', *Issues in Science and Technology*, **8**, pp. 58–65.

Blok, K. (1993), *Final Report of the Integrated Research Programme on Carbon Dioxide Recovery and Storage*, Report no. 92063, The Netherlands: Department of Science, Technology and Society, Utrecht University.

Bohi, D.R. (1993), 'Utilities and State Regulators are Failing to Take Advantage of the Benefits of Trading Emission Allowances', *Working Paper*, Resources For the Future, October.

Bohi, D.R. and Burtraw, D. (1992), 'Utility Investment Behavior and the Emission Trading Market.' *Resources and Energy*, **14**, pp. 129–53.

Bohi, D.R. and Burtraw, D. (1991), 'Avoiding Regulatory Gridlock in the Acid Rain Program', *Journal of Policy Analysis and Management*, **10**, pp. 676–84.

Bohi, D.R. et al. (1990), *Emissions Trading in the Electric Utility Industry*, Discussion Paper QE90–15, Resources for the Future.

Bohm, P. (1993), 'Incomplete International Cooperation to Reduce $CO_2$ Emissions: Alternative Policies', *Journal of Environmental Economics and Management*, **24**, pp. 258–71.

Bohm, P. (1992), 'Distributional Implications of Allowing International Trade in CO2 Emission Quotas', *World Economy*, **15**, pp. 107–14.

Bohm, P. and Russel, C. (1985), 'Comparative Analysis of Alternative Policy Instruments' in A.V. Kneese og J.L. Sweeney (eds.), *Handbook of Natural Resource and Energy Economics*, **Vol.1**, Amsterdam, North-Holland, pp. 395–460.

Bolin, D.W. (1989), 'Preventive Measures to Slow Down Man-Induced Climate Change', *Mimeo*, University of Stockholm.

Bolwig, N.G. and Jeppesen, S.E. (1973), *Synspunkter på anvendelsen af økonomiske virkemidler i forureningsbekæmpelsen (Viewpoints on the Use of Economic Instruments in Pollution Abatement)*, Copenhagen: Danish Environmental Protection Agency.

Bonner, R. (1993), *At the Hand of Man – Peril and Hope for Africa's Wildlife*, New York: Alfred A. Knopf.

Bradford De Long, J. and Shleifer, A. (1993), 'Princes and Merchants', *Journal of Law and Economics*, October, pp. 671–702.

Brimblecombe, P. (1976), 'Attitudes and Responses Towards Air Pollution in Medieval England', *Journal of the Air Pollution Control Association*, **26**, pp. 941–45.

Broadbent, J.P. (1993), 'The South Coast Air Basin Regional Clean Air Incentives Market', South Coast Air Quality Management District, Diamond Bar, CA.

Broadman, H.G. and Kalt, J.P. (1989), 'How Natural is Monopoly?', *Yale Journal on Regulation*, **6**, pp. 181–208.

Bromley, D.W. (ed.) (1995), *The Handbook of Environmental Economics*, Cambridge, Massachusetts, USA: Blackwell Publishers.

Brundtland Report (1987), *Our Common Future*, United Nations' World Commission on Environment and Development.

Buchanan, J.M. and Tullock, G. (1976), 'Polluters' Profits and Political Response: Direct Controls Versus Taxes: Reply', *American Economic Review*, **65**, pp. 983–84.

Buchanan, J.M. and Tullock, G. (1975), 'Polluters' Profits and Political Response: Direct Controls Versus Taxes', *American Economic Review*, **65**, pp.139–47.

Burtraw, D. (1996), 'The $SO_2$ Emissions Trading Program: Cost Savings Without Allowance Trading.' *Contemporary Economic Policy*, 14, 79-94.

Burtraw, D. and Swift, B. (1996), 'A New Standard of Performance: An Analysis of the Clean Air Act's Acid Rain Program.' *Environmental Law Reporter*, 26, 10411-23.

Carlin, A. (1992), 'The United States Experience With Economic Incentives to Control Environmental Pollution', *230–R–92–001*, Policy, Planning and Evaluation (PM–223X), EPA.

Carraro/Siniscalco (1993), *The European Carbon Tax: An Economic Assessment*, Dordrecht, The Netherlands: Kluwer Academic Publishers.

Cason, T.N. (1995), 'An Experimental Investigation of the Seller Incentives in the EPA's Emission Trading Auction', *The American Economic Review*, **4**, pp. 905–22.

Cason, T.N. (1993), 'Seller Incentive Properties of EPA's Emission Trading Auction', *Journal of Environmental Economics and Management*, **25**, pp. 177–95.

Chalmers, A.F. (1990), *What Is This Thing Called Science?* Second Edition, Open University Press.

Chapman, D. and Drennen, T. (1990), 'Equity and Effectiveness of Possible $CO_2$ Treaty Proposals', *Contemporary Policy Issues*, **8,** pp. 16–28.

Christensen, J. (1995), 'Forklaringsmuligheder for dispariteten mellem 'Willingness To Pay' og 'Willingness To Accept' værdiansættelser af miljøgoder', ('Explanations for the disparity between 'Willingness To Pay' and 'Willingness To Accept' in Relation to Environmental Goods'), Master thesis, Institute of Economics, University of Aarhus.

Coase, R.H. (1974), 'The Lighthouse in Economics', *Journal of Law and Economics*, **17**, pp. 357–76.

Coase, R.H. (1960), 'The Problem of Social Cost', *Journal of Law and Economics*, **3**, pp. 1–44.

Congleton, R.D. (ed.) (1996), *The Political Economy of Environmental Protection. Analysis and Evidence.* Ann Arbor, The University of Michigan Press.

Cook, B.J. (1988), *Bureaucratic politics and regulatory reform: The EPA and emissions trading*, New York: Greenwood.

Crocker, T.D. (1966), 'The Structuring of Atmospheric Pollution Control Systems', in Harold Wolozin (ed.), *The Economics of Air Pollution*, New York: W. W. Norton.

Cropper, M.L. and Oates, W.E. (1992), 'Environmental Economics: A Survey', *Journal of Economic Literature*, **XXX**, pp. 675–740.

Dales, J.H. (1968a), *Pollution Property and Prices*, Toronto: University Press.

Dales, J.H. (1968b), 'Land, Water and Ownership', *Canadian Journal of Economics*, **1**, pp. 797–804.

Danish Anti Trust Commission (1993), *Undersøgelse af energiområdet, (Report on*

*Energy Production),* Copenhagen.

Danish Economic Council (1995), *Danish Economy,* Autumn 1995, Copenhagen.

Danish Economic Council (1993), *Danish Economy,* May 1993, Copenhagen.

Danish Ministry of Energy (1994a), 'Resultaterne af de udførte energisyn', ('The Results from the Energy Reviews Carried Out'), *note,* January 7, 10. kontor.

Danish Ministry of Energy (1994b), 'Erfaringerne fra de første energisyn', ('The Experiences from the First Energy Reviews'), *note,* September 3, 10. kontor.

Danish Ministry of Energy (1990), *Energy 2000: A Plan of Action for Sustainable Development,* Copenhagen.

Danish Ministry of the Environment (1990), *Tal om Natur og Miljø, (Figures on Nature and Environment),* Copenhagen.

Danish Ministry of the Environment (1988), *Enkelt og effektivt, (Simple and Effective)* Copenhagen.

Danish Ministry of Finance (1994), *Grønne afgifter og erhvervene, (Green Taxes and Industry),* Copenhagen.

Dansk Energi Analyse (1995), *Det teoretiske potentiale for energibesparelser i erhvervslivet, (The Theoretical Potential for Energy Savings in Industry),* Copenhagen.

David, E.L. and Downing, D. (1992), 'Marketable Water Pollution Permits as Economic Incentives: Point Source Trading in Wisconsin', State of Wisconsin, Madison: Department of Natural Resources.

David, M. and Joeres, E. (1983), 'Is a Viable Implementation of TDPs Transferable' in Joeres, E. and David, M. (eds.) (1983), *Buying a Better Environment: Cost–Effective Regulation through Permit Trading,* Land Economics Monograph Number 6, Madison: Univ. of Wisconsin Press.

Davidson, R. (1998), 'California Goes Competitive', *Windpower Monthly,* **14,** pp. 32–37.

Demsetz, H. (1968), 'Why Regulate Utilities?', *Journal of Law and Economics and Management,* **11,** pp. 55–65.

Dennis, J.M. (1993), 'Smoke for Sale: Paradoxes and Problems of the Emissions Trading Program of the Clean Air Act Amendments of 1990', *Ucla Law Review,* 40, pp. 1101 –44.

Dijkstra, B. (1998), *The Political Economy of Environmental Policy: A Public Choice Approach to Market Instruments,* New Horizons in Environmental Economics Series, Edward Elgar Publishing Limited, Aldershot, England, forthcoming.

DN (1995a), *1995,* Copenhagen: Danish Society for Conservation of Nature.

DN (1995b), *DN-Håndbog, (Organization Guide),* Copenhagen: Danish Society for Conservation of Nature.

Dowie, M. (1995), *Losing Ground – American Environmentalism at the Close of the Twentieth Century,* Cambridge, Massachusetts: The MIT Press.

Downs, A. (1957), *An Economic Theory of Democracy,* New York: Harper & Brothers Publishers.

Driesen, D.M. (1993), 'Trade as a Technique, Not a Religion', Washington D.C.: Natural Resources Defense Council,

Drexel, J. (ed.) (1991), *Encyclopedia of the 20th Century,* New York: Facts on File Inc.

Dwyer, J.P. (1993), 'The Use of Market Incentives in Controlling Air Pollution – California Marketable Permits Program', *Ecology Law Quarterly,* **20,** pp. 103–17.

EDF (1994), 'Annual Report 1994 – 1995', New York: Environmental Defense Fund.

EEI (1994a), 'Statistical Yearbook of the Electric Utility Industry 1993', Published October 1994/Number 61, Washington D.C.: Edison Electric Institute.

EEI (1994b), 'Edison Electric Institute. The Association of Investor-Owned Electric Utilities', *Brochure*, Washington D.C.: Edison Electric Institute.

Eheart, J.E., Joeres, E.F. and David, M.H. (1980), 'Distribution Methods for Transferable Discharge Permits', *Water Resources Research*, **16**, pp. 833–43.

EIA (1994), *Annual Energy Review 1993*, Washington D.C.: Energy Information Administration.

Elman et al. (1992), 'Economic Incentives Under the New Clean Air Act', *92–176.05*, May 1, Regulatory Innovations Branch, EPA.

Ellerman, D.A. et al. (1997), 'Emissions Trading under the U.S. Acid Rain Program: Evaluation of Compliance Costs and Allowance Market Performance.' Center for Energy and Environmental Policy Research, MIT, Ninth draft, 08/19/97.

ELSAM (1994), 'Halvdelen af ELSAMs forskning retter sig mod vedvarende energi', *ELSAM-posten*, 05/94.

EPA (1997a), 'Developments in Allowance Trading.' *Acid Rain Update*, 3, 14-02-97, US Environmental Protection Agency.

EPA (1997b), 'Trading Activity Breakdown.' http://www.epa.gov/acidrain/ats/chart.html.

EPA (1994a), 'Auction Results', Fax of printout file from EPA, December 2, 1994 (Claire Schary, Acid Rain Division).

EPA (1994b), 'Acid Rain Program: Update No. 1', *EPA 430–K–94–012*, September.

EPA (1993), 'Protection of Stratospheric Ozone: Proposed Rule', *40 CFR Part 82*, U.S. Environmental Protection Agency.

EPA (1992a), 'Incentive Analysis for Clean Water Act Reauthorization: Point Source/Non-Point Source Trading for Nutrient Discharge Reductions', Office of Water and Office of Policy, Planning and Evaluation, U.S. Environmental Protection Agency.

EPA (1992b), 'Guidance for the Stratospheric Ozone Protection Program', U.S. Environmental Protection Agency.

EPA (1992c), 'Acid Rain Program: Allowance Auctions and Direct Sales', *EPA430/ F–92/017*, December.

EPA (1991), 'Auctions, Direct Sales and Independent Power Producers Written Guarantee Regulations', 56 Fed. Reg. (proposed May 23). U.S. Environmental Protection Agency.

EPA (1987), 'Water Quality Program Highlights', Office of Water Regulations and Standards, Monitoring and Data Support Division, U.S. Environmental Protection Agency, July.

EPA (1986), 'Quarterly Reports on Lead in Gasoline', Field Operations and Support Division, Office of Air and Radiation, March 21, May 23, July 15, U.S. Environmental Protection Agency.

EPA (1985a), 'Quarterly Reports on Lead in Gasoline', Field Operations and Support Division, Office of Air and Radiation, July 16. U.S. Environmental Protection Agency.

EPA (1985b), 'Costs and Benefits of Reducing Lead in Gasoline', *230–05–85–006*, U.S. Environmental Protection Agency.

EPA (1985c), 'Quarterly Reports on Lead in Gasoline', Field Operations and Support Division, Office of Air and Radiation, July 16.

Farla, J. et al. (1992), *Carbon Dioxide Recovery From Industrial Processes*, Report no. 92076, The Netherlands: Department of Science, Technology and Society, Utrecht University.

Fee, D. (1992), 'A New Proposal in the Framework of the 'Save' Programme to Limit Carbon Dioxide Emissions by Improving Energy Efficiency', *Energy in Europe*, **20**, pp. 19–22.

Ferrall, B.L. (1991), 'The Clean-Air Act Amendments of 1990 and the Use of Market Forces to Control Sulfur-Dioxide Emissions', *Harvard Journal on Legislation*, **28**, pp. 235–52.

Findley, R.W. and Farber, D.A. (1992), *Environmental Law*, Third Edition, St Paul, Minesota: West Publishing Co.,

Foster, C.D. (1993), *Privatization, Public Ownership and the Regulation of Natural Monopoly*, Oxford UK & Cambridge USA: Blackwell.

Foster, V. and Hahn, R. (1994), 'ET in LA: Looking Back to the Future', *P–94–01*, Project 88 – Round II, Center for Science & International Affairs, JFK School of Government, Harvard University.

Franciosi et al. (1993), 'An Experimental Investigation of the Hahn-Noll Revenue Neutral Auction for Emission Licenses', *Journal of Environmental Economics and Management*, **24**, pp. 1–24.

Frederiksson, P.G. (1997), 'The Political Economy of Pollution Taxes in a Small Open Economy', *Journal of Environmental Economics and Management*, **33**, pp. 44–58.

Freeman, A.M. (1994), 'The Measurement of Environmental and Resource Values: Theory and Methods', Washington D.C.: Resources for the Future.

Frey, B.S. (1994), 'Direct Democracy: Politico-Economic Lessons from Swiss Experience. Papers and Proceedings', *American Economic Review*, **84**, pp. 338–43.

Fromm, O. and Hansjürgens, B. (1996), 'Emission Trading in Theory and Practice: An analysis of RECLAIM in Southern California.' *Environment and Planning C: Government and Policy*, **14**, 367–84.

GAO (1994), 'Air Pollution: Allowance Trading Offers an Opportunity to Reduce Emissions at Less Cost', *GAO/RCED–95–30*, United States General Accounting Office, December.

GAO (1986), 'Vehicle Emissions', *GAO/RCED–86–182*, United States General Accounting Office.

GAO (1982), 'A Market Approach to Air Pollution Control Could Reduce Compliance Costs Without Jeopardizing Clean Air Goals', *GAO/PAD–82–15*, United States General Accounting Office.

Geddes, R.R. (1992), 'A Historical Perspective on Electric Utility Regulation', *Regulation*, Winter, pp. 75–82.

Georg, S. (1993), *Når Løsningen Bliver Problemet (When the Solution Becomes the Problem)*, Copenhagen: Samfundslitteratur.

Goffman, J. (1994), 'Testimony of Joseph Goffman, Senior Attorney, Environmental Defense Fund', *before the Subcommittee on Energy and Power Committee on Energy and Commerce, United States House of Representatives*, October 5, 1994.

Goodin, R.E. (1994), 'Selling Environmental Indulgences', *Kyklos*, **47**, pp. 573–96.

Goulder, L.H. (1995), 'Environmental Taxation and the Double Dividend: A Readers Guide', *International Tax and Public Finance*, **2**, pp. 157–183.

Green, D.P. and Shapiro, I. (1994), *Pathologies of Rational Choice Theory: A Critique of Applications in Political Science*, Yale University.

Grossman, G.M. and Helpman, E. (1994), 'Protection for Sale', *American Economic Review*, **84**, pp. 833–50.

Grubb, M. (1989), *The Greenhouse Effects – Negotiating Targets*, London: Royal

Institute of International Affairs.

GUC (1994), *Tar-Pamlico NSW Implementation Strategy: Phase II*, December 5, North Carolina: Greenville Utilities Commission, Tar-Pamlico Association.

Hahn, R.W. (1990), 'The Political Economy of Environmental Regulation: Towards a Unifying Framework', *Public Choice*, **65**, pp. 21–47.

Hahn, R.W. (1989a), *A Primer on Environmental Policy Design*, New York: Harwood Academic Publishers.

Hahn, R.W. (1989b), 'Economic Prescriptions for Environmental Problems: How the Patient Followed the Doctor's Orders', *The Journal of Economic Perspectives*, **3**, pp. 95–114.

Hahn, R.W. (1989b), 'Market Power and Transferable Property Rights', *The Quarterly Journal of Economics*, November, pp. 753–65.

Hahn, R.W. (1983), 'Designing Markets in Transferable Property Rights: A Practitioner's Guide', in Joeres, E.F. and David, M.H. (eds.), *Buying a Better Environment: Cost-Effective Regulation Through Permit Trading*, Madison, Wis.: University of Wisconsin Press.

Hahn, R.W. and Hester, G.L. (1989a), 'Marketable Permits – Lessons for Theory and Practice', *Ecology Law Quarterly*, **16**, pp. 361–406.

Hahn, R.W. and Hester, G.L. (1989b), 'Where did all the Markets Go? An Analysis of EPA's Emission Trading Program', *Yale Journal of Regulation*, **6**, pp. 109–53.

Hahn, R.W. and Hester, G.L. (1987), 'The Market for Bads. EPA's Experience with Emissions Trading', *Regulation*, **XI**, pp. 48–53.

Hahn, R.W. and McGartland, A.M. (1989), 'The Political Economy of Instrument Choice: An Examination of the U.S. Role in Implementing the Montreal Protocol', *Northwestern University Law Review*, **83**, pp. 592–611.

Hahn, R.W. and Noll, R.G. (1983), 'Barriers to Implementing Tradable Air Pollution Permits: Problems of Regulatory Interaction', *Yale Journal on Regulation*, **1**, pp. 63–91.

Hahn, R.W. and Noll, R.G. (1982a), 'Designing a Market for Tradable Emission Permits', in W.A. Magat (ed.), *Reform of Environmental Regulation*, Cambridge, Mass.: Bal-linger.

Hahn, R.W. and Noll, R.G. (1982b), 'Designing an Efficient Permits Market' in Cass, G.R. et al. (eds.), *Implementing Tradeable Permits for Sulfur Oxide Emissions: A Case Study in the South Coast Air Basin*, **Vol.II** Main Text. Environmental Quality Laboratory of the California Institute of Technology (June), pp. 102–134.

Hahn, R.W. and Stavins, R.N. (1993), 'Trading in Greenhouse Permits: A Critical Examination of Design and Implementation Issues', *Faculty Research Working Paper Series*, R93–15, John F. Kennedy School of Government, Harvard University.

Hahn, R.W. and Stavins, R.N. (1992), 'Economic Incentives for Environmental Protection: Integrating Theory and Practice', *American Economic Review*, **82**, pp. 464–68.

Hahn, R.W. and Stavins, R.N. (1991), 'Incentive-Based Environmental Regulation: A New Era from an Old Idea?', *Ecology Law Quarterly*, **18**, pp. 1–42.

Hansen, S. et al. (1995), 'Greens 1996', Copenhagen: Forlaget Børsen.

Hansjürgens, B. (1998), 'The Sulfur Dioxide ($SO_2$) Allowance Trading Program: Recent Developments and Lessons to be Learned', *Environment and Planning C: Government and Policy*, forthcoming.

Hansjürgens, B. and Fromm, O. (1994), 'Erfolgsbedingungen von Zertifikatemodellen in der Umweltpolitik – am Beispiel der Novelle des US–Clean Air Act von 1990',

*Zeitschrift für Umweltpolitik und Umweltrecht*, **17**.

Hardin, G. (1968), The Tragedy of the Commons, *Science*, **162**, pp. 1243–48.

Hardin, R. (1982), *Collective Action*, Resources For the Future, Baltimore, Maryland: The Johns Hopkins University Press.

Hausker, K. (1992), 'The Politics and Economics of Auction Design in the Market for Sulfur-Dioxide Pollution', *Journal of Policy Analysis and Management*, **11**, pp. 553–72.

Hecq, W. and Kestemont, B. (1991), 'A Model of Emission Trading for Minimizing the Cost of Air-Pollution Control from Belgian Power-Plants', *Journal of Environmental Management*, **32**, pp. 367–82.

Heggelund, M. (1991), *Emissions Permit Trading: A Policy Tool to Reduce the Atmospheric Concentration of Greenhouse Gases*, Canadian Energy Research Institute.

Hellevik, O. (1980), *Forskningsmetode i sosiologi og statsvitenskap*, **4. utgave**, Oslo: Universitetsforlaget.

Helm, D. (ed.) (1991), *Economic Policy Towards the Environment*, Blackwell Publ.

Helm, D. and Pearce, D. (1990), 'Assessment: Economic Policy Towards the Environment', *Oxford Review of Economic Policy*, **6**, pp. 1–16.

Hendriks et al. (1992), *Verwijdering en Opslag van $CO_2$ bij elektriciteitsopwekking*, Report no. 92035, The Netherlands: Department of Science, Technology and Society, Utrecht University.

Hensel, J. and Svendsen, G.T. (1995), 'Collective Action and $CO_2$ Taxation in the European Union', Draft.

Hesse, M. (1989), Letter from Martha O. Hesse, Chairman, Federal Energy Regulatory Commission, to Honourable John D. Dingell, Chairman of Committee on Energy and Commerce, House of Representatives, 26th September.

Hillman, A.L. and Ursprung, H.W. (1992), 'The Influence of Environmental Concerns on the Political Determination of Trade Policy', in Anderson, K. And Blackhurst, R. (eds.), *The Greening of the World Trade Issue*, New York, pp. 195–220.

Hjorth-Andersen, Chr. (1989), 'Omsættelige forureningstilladelser', ('Tradable Permits'), *Samfundsøkonomen*, **5**, pp. 23–30.

Hjorth-Andersen, Chr. (1988), 'Miljøbøder: Danske erfaringer', ('Environmental Fines: Danish Experiences'), *Miljøøkonomi i Norden*, **1**, pp. 5–8.

Hjorth-Andersen, Chr. (1982), 'Miljøøkonomi', ('Environmental Economics'), Niels Haarløv (red), *Miljøforvaltning*, pp. 43–69, Copenhagen: DSR-Forlag,.

Hjorth-Andersen, Chr. (1975), *Forureningsøkonomi, (Economics of Pollution)*, Ph.D. dissertation, Department of Economics, University of Copenhagen.

Hoel, M. (1991), 'Efficient International Agreements for Reducing Emissions of $CO_2$', *Memo*, no. 397, Economics Department, University of Oslo.

Hoffmann, M.C. (1994), 'The Future of Electricity Provision', *Regulation*, **3**, pp. 55–62.

Holcombe, R.G. and Meiners, R.E. (1981), 'Corrective Taxes and Auctions of Rights in the Control of Externalities: A Reply', *Public Finance Quarterly*, **9**, pp. 479–84.

Holcombe, R.G. and Meiners, R.E. (1980), 'Corrective Taxes and Auctions of Rights in the Control of Externalities', *Public Finance Quarterly*, **8**, pp. 345–49.

Houston, D.A. (1992), 'User-Ownership of Electric Transmission Grids. Towards Resolving the Access Issue', *Regulation*, Winter, pp. 48–57.

Howe, C.W. (1994), 'Taxes *Versus* Tradable Discharge Permits: A Review in the Light of the U.S. and European Experience', *Environmental and Resource Economics*, **4**, pp. 151–69.

Hume, D. ([1739] 1984), *A Treatise of Human Nature*, New York: Penguin Books.
ICF (1992), *Regulatory Impact Analysis of the Final Acid Rain Implementation Regulations*, Washington: ICF Incorporated, EPA, Acid Rain Division.
ICF (1989), *Economic Analysis of Title V (Acid Rain Provisions)*, Washington: ICF Incorporated, EPA, Acid Rain Division.
Ingeniøren (1995), 'Dyrt at slippe af med drivhusgassen', ('Expensive to get rid of $CO_2$'), **20**, May 19.
Ingham, A. and Ulph, A. (1991), 'Market-Based Instruments for reducing $CO_2$ Emissions – The Case of UK Manufacturing', *Energy Policy*, **19**, pp. 138–48.
International Energy Agency (1991), *Coal Information*, Paris: OECD/IEA.
Jespersen, J. (1992), '$CO_2$-afgift', ('$CO_2$ Tax'), *Samfundsøkonomen*, **3**, pp. 33–37.
Jespersen, J. og Brendstrup, S. (1994), *Grøn Økonomi, (Green Economics)*, Jurist- og Økonomforbundets Forlag.
Jochem, E. (1991), 'Reducing $CO_2$ Emissions – The West-German Plan', *Energy Policy*, **19**, pp. 119–26.
Joeres, E.F. and David, M.H. (eds.) (1983), 'Buying a Better Environment: Cost-Effective Regulation through Permit Trading', *Land Economics Monograph Number 6*, Madison: University of Wisconsin Press.
Johnston (1994), 'Pollution Trading in LA LA Land', *Regulation*, **3**, pp. 44–54.
Jones, G. (1984), *A History of the Vikings*, New York: Oxford University Press.
Joskow, P.L. (1997), 'Restructuring, Competition and Regulatory Reform in the U.S. Electricity Sector', *Journal of Economic Perspectives*, **11**, pp. 119–138.
Joskow, P.L. (1992), 'Expanding Competitive Opportunities in Electricity Generation', *Regulation*, Winter, pp. 25–37.
Joskow, P.L. and Schmalensee, R. (1996), 'The Political Economy of Market-Based Environmental Policy: The U.S. Acid Rain Program', Massachusetts Institute of Technology, Center for Energy and Environmental Policy, *MIT-CEEPR*, 96–003, Boston.
Klaassen, G. (1996), *Acid Rain and Environmental Degradation*. New Horizons in Environmental Economics. Cheltenham, UK: Edward Elgar and IIASA.
Klaassen, G. and Nentjes, A. (1997), 'Sulfur Trading Under the 1990 CAAA in the US: An Assessment of First Experiences.' *Journal of Institutional and Theoretical Economics*, 2, 384–410.
Kete, N. (1992), 'The U.S. Acid Rain Control Allowance Trading System', in *Climate Change: Designing a Tradable Permit System*, Paris: OECD.
Koktvedgaard, M. (1991), *Lærebog i konkurrenceret, (Rules on Competition)*, Copenhagen: Jurist- og Økonomforbundets Forlag.
Kort, P.M. (1992), 'The Effects of Marketable Pollution Permits on the Firms Optimal Investment Policies', *Working Paper*, no. 9242, The Netherlands: Tilburg University, Economics Department.
Koutstaal, P. (1997), *Economic Policy and Climate Change: Tradable Permits for Reducing Carbon Emissions*, New Horizons in Environmental Economics Series, Edward Elgar Publishing Limited, Aldershot, England.
Krupnick, A.J. et al. (1990), 'Emissions Trading in the Electric Utility Industry', *Resources*, Summer, pp. 10–13.
Krupnick, A.J. and Burtraw D. (1994), Critique of Johnston (1994), 'Pollution Trading in LA LA Land', Regulation, **3**, pp. 44–54, *Letter forwarded to editor.*
Krupnick, A.J., Oates, W.E. and Van de Verg, E.V. (1983), 'On Marketable Air-Pollu-

tion Permits: The Case for a System of Pollution Offsets', *Journal of Environmental Economics and Management*, **10**, pp. 233–47.

Larsen, A. et al. (1993), *Virkemidler og elbesparelser, (Instruments and Electricity Savings)*, Copenhagen: AKF.

Larsen, B. and Shah, A. (1994), 'Global Tradeable Carbon Permits, Participation Incentives and Transfers', *Oxford Economic Papers,* **46**, pp. 841–56.

Lee, B. (1991), 'Highlights of the Clean-Air Act Amendments of 1990', *Journal of the Air & Waste Management Association*, **41**, pp. 16–19.

Levitas, S.J. and Rader, D.N. (1993), 'Point/Nonpoint Source Trading: A New Approach to Reducing Nutrient Pollution', *Environmental Permitting*, Winter, pp. 5–19.

Lijphart, A. (1975), 'The Comparable-Cases Strategy in Comparative Research', *Comparative Political Studies*, **8**, pp. 158–77.

Lindahl, E. (1919), 'Positive Lösung Die Gerechtigkeit der Besteuerung', translated as 'Just Taxation – a Positive Solution', in Musgrave, R.A. and Peacock, A.T. (eds.), *Classics in the Theory of Public Finance*, London: Macmillan.

Linderoth, H. (1993), *Oliemarkedet og Saudi Arabiens Oliepolitik, (The Oil Market and the Oil Policy of Saudi Arabia)*, Ph.D. thesis, The Aarhus School of Business.

Liroff, R.A. (1980), *Air Pollution Offsets: Trading, Selling and Banking*, Washington D.C.: Conservation Foundation.

Lohmann, A. S. (1994), 'Incentive Charges in Environmental Policies: Why are they White Ravens?', in Faure, M. et al. (eds.), *Environmental Standards in the European Union in an Interdisciplinary Framework*, Apeldoorn, pp. 117–33.

Ludwig, F.L., Javitz, H.S., and Valdes, A. (1983), 'How Many Stations are Required to Estimate the Design Value and the Expected Number of Exceedances of the Ozone Standard in an Urban Area?', *Journal of the Air Pollution Control Association*, **33**, pp. 963–67.

Lundquist, L. (1980), *The Hare and the Tortoise: Clean Air Policies in the United States and Sweden,* Ann Arbor, University of Michigan Press.

Lyon, R.M. (1989), 'Transferable Discharge Permit Systems and Environmental Management in Developing-Countries', *World Development*, **17**, pp. 1299–1312.

Lyon, R.M. (1986), 'Equilibrium Properties of Auctions and Alternative Procedures for Allocating Transferable Permits', *Journal of Environmental Economics and Management*, **13**, pp. 129–52.

Lyon, R.M. (1982), 'Auctions and Alternative Procedures for Allocating Pollution Rights', *Land Economics*, **58**, pp. 16–32.

Lövgren, K. (1994), 'Economic Instruments for Air Pollution Control in Sweden', in Klaassen, G., and Førsund, F.R. (eds.), *Economic Instruments for Air Pollution Control,* Boston: Kluwer Academic Publishers, pp. 107–21.

Maaløe, E. (1993), 'The Explorative-Integrative Approach to Case Research', Paper presented at the 10'th World Association for Case Method Research and Case Method Application in Bratislawa, July 4–7.

Majone, G. (1976), 'Choice Among Policy Instruments for Pollution Control', *Policy Analysis*, **2**, pp. 589–613.

Major, M.J. (1992), 'A Trading Market for Pollution', *Public Power*, July–August, pp. 34–38.

Maloney, M.T. and Brady, G.L (1988), 'Capital Turnover and Marketable Pollution Rights', *Journal of Law and Economics*, **31**, pp. 203–26.

Manne, A.S. and Richels, R.G. (1992), *Buying Greenhouse Insurance: The Economic*

*Costs of Carbon Dioxide Emission Limits*, Cambridge, The MIT Press.

Manne, A.S. and Richels, R.G. (1991), 'International Trade in Carbon Emission Rights: A Decomposition Procedure', *American Economic Review*, **81**, pp. 135–39.

March, J.G. and Olsen, J.P. (1989), *Rediscovering Institutions – the Organizational basis of Politics*, New York: The Free Press.

McGartland, A.M. and Oates, W.E. (1985), 'Marketable Permits for the Prevention of Environmental Deterioration', *Journal of Environmental Economics and Management*, **12**, pp. 207–28.

McGuire, M. and Olson, M. (1996), 'The Economics of Autocracy and Majority Rule – The Invisible Hand and the Use of Force', *Journal of Economic Literature*, March 1996, XXXIV, 72–96.

Michaels, R.J. (1992), 'Deregulating Electricity. What Stands in the Way', *Regulation*, Winter, pp. 38–47.

Mitnick, B. (1980), *The Political Economy of Regulation*, New York: Colombia University Press.

Montgomery, D. (1974), 'Artificial Markets and the Theory of Games', *Public Choice*, **18**, pp. 25–40.

Montgomery, W.D. (1972), 'Markets in Licences and Efficient Pollution Control Programs', *Journal of Economic Theory*, **5**, pp. 395–418.

Morgenstern, R.D. (1991), 'Towards a Comprehensive Approach to Global Climate Change Mitigation', *American Economic Review*, **81**, pp. 140–45.

Mortensen, J.B. (1992), 'Incitamenter og regulering på miljøområdet', ('Incentives and Regulation of the Environment'), *Nationaløkonomisk Tidsskrift*, **130**, pp. 215–223.

Mortensen, J.B. og Andersen, P. (1990), 'Økonomisk regulering – betydningen af ufuldkommen og asymmetrisk information', ('Economic Regulation – the Importance of Incomplete and Asymmetrical Information'), in *Regulering og styring II*, Ellen Margrethe Basse (ed.), København: Gad.

Mortensen, J.B. og Olsen, O.J. (1991), *Privatisering og deregulering, ('Privatization and Deregulation')*, Copenhagen: Jurist- og Økonomforbundets forlag.

Mortensen, J.B. og Sørensen, P.B. (1991), *Økonomiske styringsmidler i miljøpolitikken, (Economic Instruments in Environmental Policy)*, Miljøministeriet.

Morthorst, P.E. (1994), 'Constructing $CO_2$ reduction cost curves: The case of Denmark', *Energy Policy*, **22**, pp. 964–970.

Mueller, D.C. (1989), *Public Choice II*, Cambridge University Press.

Nannerup, N. (1995), *Strategic Environmental Policy and International Trade*, PhD Thesis, C 64, The Aarhus School of Business.

Nelson, R. (1995), 'Sustainability, Efficiency, and God: Economic Values and the Sustainability Debate, *Annual Reviews of Ecological Systems*, **26**, pp. 135–54.

Nelson, R.H. (1990), 'Unoriginal Sin: The Judeo-Christian Roots of Ecotheology', *Policy Review*, **53**, pp. 53–59.

Nentjes, A. and Dijkstra, B. (1994), 'The Political Economy of Instrument Choice in Environmental Policy', in Faure, M. et al. (eds.), *Environmental Standards in the European Union in an Interdisciplinary Framework*, Apeldoorn, pp. 197-216.

NIEP (1994), 'The Competitive Power Revolution: Independent Energy's Expanding Role in Electricity Generation', *National Independent Energy Producers*, October. Washington D.C.

Nordhaus, W.W. (1991), 'A Sketch of the Economics of the Greenhouse Effect', *American Economic Review*, **81**, pp. 146–150.

North, D.C. (1991), 'Institutions, Ideology, and Economic Performance', *Cato Journal*, **11**, pp. 477–88.

Novotny, G. (1986), 'Transferable Discharge Permits for Water Pollution Control in Wisconsin', *Mimeo*, December 1, Madison, Wisconsin: Department of Natural Resources.

NRCA (1993), 'The G & Ts', *Brochure*, Washington D.C.: National Rural Electric Cooperative Association.

NRDC (1994), 'The Power of Law, The Power of Science, The Power of People, In Defense of the Environment', *Brochure*, New York: Natural Resources Defense Council.

Nussbaum, B.D. (1992), 'Phasing Down Lead in Gasoline in the U.S.: Mandates, Incentives, Trading, and Banking', in *Climate Change: Designing a Tradeable Permit System*, Paris: OECD.

Oates, W.E. (1995a), 'Green Taxes: Can We Protect the Environment and Improve the Tax System at the Same Time?' *Southern Economic Journal*, **4**, pp. 915–22.

Oates, W.E. (ed.)(1995b), *The Economics of Environmental Regulation*, Aldershot: Edward Elgar.

Oates, W.E. (ed.)(1994), *The Economics of the Environment*, Aldershot: Edward Elgar.

Oates, W.E. (1984), 'Markets for Pollution Control', *Challenge*, May–June, pp. 11–17.

Oates, W.E. (1981), 'Corrective Taxes and Auctions of Rights in the Control of Externalities: some further thoughts', *Public Finance Quarterly*, **9**, pp. 471–78.

Oates, W.E. and Portney, P.R. (1992), 'Economic Incentives and the Containment of Global Warming', *Eastern Economic Journal*, **18**, pp. 85–98.

Oates, W.E. and Schwab, R.M. (1988), 'Economic Competition Among Jurisdictions: Efficiency Enchancing or Distortion Inducting?', *Journal of Public Economics*, **35**, pp. 333–54.

OECD (1992a), *Climate Change: Designing a Tradeable Permit System*, Paris.

OECD (1992b), *Climate Change: Designing a Practical Tax System*, Paris.

OECD (1991), *Recommendation of the Council on the Use of Economic Instruments in Environmental Policy*, Paris.

OECD (1989), *The Application of Economic Instruments for Environmental Protection*, Paris.

Oehmke, J.F. (1987), 'The Allocation of Pollutant Discharge Permits by Competitive Auction', *Resources and Energy*, **9**, pp. 153–62.

Olsen, O.J. (ed.)(1995), *Competition in the Electricity Supply Industry – Experience from Europe and the United States*, Copenhagen: DJØF Publishing.

Olson, M. (1993a), 'Dictatorship, Democracy, and Development', *American Political Science Review*, **87**, pp. 567–76.

Olson, M. (1993b), 'Why Is Economic Performance even Worse after Communism Is Abandoned?', *Ninth Annual Virginia Political Economy Lecture*, Fairfax, Virginia: George Mason University.

Olson, M. (1992), *Foreword* in Sandler, T., *Collective Action: Theory and Applications*, Ann Arbor, University of Michigan Press.

Olson, M. (1991), 'Rational Ignorance, Professional Research, and Politician's Dilemmas', in Robinson, W.H. and Wellborn, C.H. (eds.), *Knowledge, Power, and the Congress*, Washington D.C.: The Congressional Quarterly.

Olson, M. (1988), 'The Productivity Slowdown, the Oil Shocks, and the Real Cycle', *Journal of Economic Perspectives*, **2**, pp. 43–69.

Olson, M. (1982), *The Rise and Decline of Nations*, New Haven: Yale University Press.

Olson, M. (1965), *The Logic of Collective Action*, Cambridge: Cambridge University Press.

Olson, M. and Zeckhauser, R. (1967), 'Collective Goods, Comparative Advantage, and Alliance Efficiency', in R. McKean, ed., *Issues in Defense Economics*, New York: National Bureau Econ.Res.

O'Neil, W., David, M., Moore, C. and Joeres, E. (1983), 'Transferable Discharge Permits and Economic Efficiency: The Fox River', *Journal of Environmental Economics and Management*, **10**, pp. 346–55.

Opschoor, J.B. (1993), 'Trends in the Use of Economic Instruments in OECD Member Countries', Paper presented at the International IIASA Conference 'Economic Instruments for Air Pollution Control', October 18–20 1993 in Laxenburg, Austria.

Opschoor, J.B. and Vos, H.B. (1989), *The Application of Economic Instruments for Environmental Protection in OECD Countries*, Paris: OECD.

Ordeshook, P.C. (1993), 'The Development of Contemporary Political Theory', in Barnett, W.A., Hinich, M.J., and Schofield, N.J. (eds.), *Political Economy: Institutions, Competition and Representation*, Cambridge, USA: Cambridge University Press.

Paldam, M. and Svendsen, G.T. (1998), 'An Essay on Social Capital: Reflections on a Concept Linking Social Sciences', *Working Paper No. 1998-8*, University of Aarhus, Denmark.

Palmer, A.R. et al. (1980), *Economic Implications of Regulating Chlorofluorocarbon Emissions from Nonaerosol Applications*, Report No. R–2524–EPA prepared for the US Environmental Protection Agency by the Rand Corporation, June.

Parry, I.W.H. (1995), 'Pollution Taxes and Revenue Recycling', *Journal of Environmental Economics and Management*, **29**, S–64–S–77.

Paterson, M. and Grubb, M. (eds.)(1996): *Sharing the Effort: Options for Differentiating Commitments on Climate Change*, The Royal Institute of International Affairs, London.

Pearce, D.W. and Turner, R.K (1990), *Economics of Natural Resources and the Environment*, Harvester Wheatsheaf.

Pigou, A. (1920), *The Economics of Welfare*, London: Macmillan.

Polesetsky, M. (1995), 'Will a Market in Air Pollution Clean the Nation's Dirtiest Air? A Study of the South Coast Air Quality Management District's Regional Clean Air Incentives Market', *Ecology Law Quarterly*, **22**, pp. 359–411.

Portney, P.R. (1990), 'Policy Watch: Economics and the Clean Air Act', *Journal of Economic Perspectives*, **4**, pp. 173–81.

Project 88 (1988), *Harnessing Market Forces To Protect Our Environment: Initiatives For The New President*, A Public Policy Study sponsored by Senator Timothy E. Wirth, Colorado, and Senator John Heinz, Pennsylvania. Washington D.C.

Project 88 – Round II (1988), *Incentives for Action: Designing Market-Based Environmental Strategies Initiatives*, A Public Policy Study sponsored by Senator Timothy E. Wirth, Colorado, and Senator John Heinz, Pennsylvania, Washington D.C.

Rasmussen, U. (1995), 'Emission af $CO_2$ beregnet på grundlag af industritællingen 1993', ('$CO_2$ Emission Calculated From Count on Industry in 1993'), *Paper produced for this book*, December 13, Danish Ministry of Energy.

Raufer, R.K. (1992), 'Market-Based Environmental Development', *Natural Resources Forum*, **16**, pp. 111–16.

Raufer, R.K. and Feldman, S.L. (1987), *Acid Rain and Emissions Trading: Implementing a Market Approach to Pollution Control*, Rowman & Littlefeld.

Raufer, R.K., Hill, L.G. and Samsa, M.E. (1981), 'Emission Fees and TERA: Evaluation of Policy Alternatives in the Twin Cities', *Journal of the Air Pollution Control Association*, **31**, pp. 839–45.

Rico, R. (1995), 'The U.S. Allowance Trading System for Sulfur Dioxide: An Update on Market Experience.' *Environmental and Ressource Economics,* 5, 115–29.

Rico, R. (1993), 'United States' Experience in Designing and Implementing an Emission Trading System for Sulfur Dioxide', Paper presented at the international IIASA conference *Economic Instruments for Air Pollution Control* in Laxenburg, Austria, 18–20 October 1993.

Roberts, M.J. (1982), 'Some Problems of Implementing Marketable Pollution Right Schemes', in Wesley A. Magat (ed.), *Reform of Environmental Regulation*, Mass.: Balling.

Roberts, M.J. and Spence, M. (1976), 'Effluent Charges and Licenses Under Uncertainty', *Journal of Public Economics*, **5**, pp. 193–208.

Roberts, P.C. (1991), 'Privatization Solves All', *Cato Journal*, **11**, pp. 405–08.

Rose, M. (1973), 'Market Problems in the Distribution of Emission Rights', *Water Resources Research*, **9**, pp. 1132–44.

Rose, A. and Tietenberg, T.H. (1993), 'An International System of Tradeable $CO_2$ Entitlements: Implications for Economic Development', *Journal of Environment & Development*, **2**, pp. 348–83.

Rose-Ackerman, S. (1977), 'Market Models For Water Pollution Control: Their Strengths and Weaknesses', *Public Policy*, **25**, pp. 383–406.

Rosencrantz, A. (1981), 'Economic Approaches to Air Pollution Control', *Environment*, **23**, pp. 25–30.

Rubin, J. and Kling, C. (1993), 'An Emission Saved Is an Emission Earned: An Empirical Study of Emission Banking for Light-Duty Vehicle Manufacturers', *Journal of Environmental Economics and Management*, **25**, pp. 257–74.

Rudisill, C. (1992), 'Decreasing Carbon Dioxide Emissions', U.S. Environmental Protection Agency, MD–12.

Russel, C. S. (1981), 'Controlled Trading of Pollution Permits', *Environmental Science and Technology*, **15**, pp. 1–5.

Russel et al. (eds.) (1994), *National Trade and Professional Associations of the United States*, Washington D.C.: Columbia Books, Inc.

Samuelson, P. (1954), 'The Pure Theory of Public Expenditure', *Review of Economics and Statistics*, Nov., pp. 387–89.

Sandler, T. (1992), *Collective Action: Theory and Applications*, Ann Arbor, University of Michigan Press.

SCAQMD (1993), 'RECLAIM: Socioeconomic and Environmental Assessments', Volume 3, South Coast Air Quality Management District, Diamond Bar, California.

Schaerer, B. (1993), 'Use of Economic Instruments in Germany in Air Pollution Control', Paper presented at the international IIASA conference *Economic Instruments for Air Pollution Control* in Laxenburg, Austria, 18–20 October 1993.

Schelling, T.C. (1992), 'Some Economics of Global Warming', *American Economic Review*, **82**, March, pp. 1–14.

Scherer, F.M. and Ross, D. (1990), *Industrial Market Structure and Economic Performance*, Third Edition, Houghton Mifflin Company.

Schmalensee, R. (1989), Testimony of Richard Schmalensee, Member, Council of

Economic Advisors, before the Subcommittee on Energy and Power of the Committee on Energy and Commerce, U.S. House of Representatives, 11th October.

Schneider, F. (1994), 'Ecological Objectives in a Market Economy: Three Simple Questions, but no Simple Answers?', in Faure, M. et al. (eds.), *Environmental Standards in the European Union in an Interdisciplinary Framework*, Apeldoorn, pp. 93–116.

Schumpeter, J.A. ([1943] 1994): *Capitalism, Socialism & Democracy*, London: Routledge.

Schwartz and Turner (eds.)(1995), *Encyclopedia of Associations (1995)*, National Organizations of the U.S., Volume 1, 29th Edition, Washington D.C.: Gale Research Inc.

Segerson, K. and Tietenberg, T. (1992), 'The Structure of Penalties in Environmental Enforcement: An Economic Analysis', *Journal of Environmental Economics and Management*, **23**, pp. 179–200.

Seligman, D.A. (1994), 'Emissions Trading: Opportunity or Scam? A Guide for Activists', The Sierra Club, Center for Environmental Innovation. Understanding Green Markets Project, Washington D.C.

Seskin, E.P., Anderson, Jr. and Reid, R.O. (1983), 'An Empirical Analysis of Economic Strategies for Controlling Air Pollution', *Journal of Environmental Economics and Management*, **10**, pp. 112–24.

Shapiro, M. and Warhit, E. (1983), 'Marketable Permits: The Case of Chlorofluorocarbons', *Natural Resource Journal*, **23**, pp. 577–91.

Sierra Club (1994), 'Save America's Last Wild Lands', *Brochure*, San Francisco: Sierra Club,

Skou Andersen, M. (1994), *Governance by Green Taxes. Making Pollution Prevention Pay*, Manchester: Manchester University Press.

Skou Andersen, M. (1989), 'Omsættelige forureningskvoter', ('Tradable Permits'), *Nordisk Administrativt Tidsskrift*, **2**, pp. 124–32.

Smith, A. ([1776] 1991), *The Wealth of Nations*, New York: Everyman's Library, Alfred A. Knopf, Inc.

Snow, D. (1992), *Inside the Environmental Movement – Meeting the Leadership Challenge,* Washington D.C.: The Conservation Fund, Island Press.

Stavins, R.N. (1995), 'Transaction Costs and Tradeable Permits', *Journal of Environmental Economics and Management*, **29**, pp. 133–148.

Stavins, R.N. (1989), 'Harnessing Market Forces to Protect the Environment', *Environment*, **31**, pp. 4–7 and pp. 28–35.

Stavins, R.N. and Hahn, R.W. (1993), 'Trading in Greenhouse Permits: A Critical Examination of Design and Implementation Issues', *Faculty Research Working Paper Series*, R93–15, John F. Kennedy School of Government, Harvard University.

Stavins, R.N. and Whitehead, B.W. (1992), 'Pollution Charges for Environmental Protection: A Policy Link Between Energy and Environment', *Annual Reviews (Energy and Environment)*, **17**, pp. 187–210.

Steiner, U. and Svendsen, G.T. (1998), 'The Use of Permit Markets for Incorporating Source Location: The Case of Acid Rain in Europe.' Working Paper 97-10, Department of Economics, The Aarhus School of Business.

Stigler, G.J. (1971), 'The Theory of Economic Regulation', *Bell Journal of Economics and Management Science*, **2**, pp. 2–21.

Stigler, G.J. (1968), *The Organisation of Industry*, Richard D. Irwin, Homewood.

STO (1995), 'Statistical Ten-Year Review', Copenhagen: Danmarks Statistik.

Strøjer Madsen, E., Nielsen, J.U.-M., and Pedersen, K. (1986), *Økonomisk Teori i internationalt perspektiv, (Economic Theory in International Perspective)*, Jurist- og Økonomforbundets Forlag.

Svendsen, G.T. (1998a), 'The US Acid Rain Program: Design, Performance and Assessment', *Environment and Planning C: Government and Policy*, forthcoming.

Svendsen, G.T. (1998b), 'A General Model for $CO_2$ Regulation: The Case of Denmark', *Energy Policy,* **26**, 32–44.

Svendsen, G.T. (1998c), 'Kyoto: Heros or Scoundrels? The Idea of Global $CO_2$ Trade' Draft. May 12.

Svendsen, G.T. (1998d), 'US Interest Groups Prefer Emission Trading: A Public Choice Perspective', *Public Choice*, forthcoming.

Svendsen, G.T. (1998e), 'Towards a $CO_2$ Market for the EU: The Case of Electric Utilities', *European Environment* **8**, forthcoming.

Svendsen, G.T. (1997), '$CO_2$-regulering i Danmark: Marked, kvotelov og afgift.' ('$CO_2$ Regulation in Denmark: Market, Bubble and Tax.') *Nationaløkonomisk Tidsskrift (Journal of the Danish Economic Association)*, **135**, 98–103.

Svendsen, G.T. (1995a), 'Hvordan bortauktionere $CO_2$-tilladelser i Danmark? – de amerikanske erfaringer giver svaret!', (How to Design Auctions for $CO_2$ Permits in Denmark), *Nationaløkonomisk Tidsskrift, (Journal of the Danish Economic Association)*, **133**, pp. 148–158.

Svendsen, G.T. (1995b), 'California Shows the Future of Electricity Production in the Single Market', *Energy Policy*, **10**, pp. 857–59.

Svendsen, G.T. (1995c), 'Den Stationære Bandit – og Lobbyisme', (The Stationary Bandit and Lobbyism), *Økonomi & Politik*, **3**, pp.24–31.

Svendsen, G.T. (1994a), 'Kvotemarked og kildeplacering', ('Permit Market and Spatial Dimension'), *Nationaløkonomisk Tidsskrift, (Journal of the Danish Economic Association)*, **132**, pp. 209–15.

Svendsen, G.T. (1994b), '$CO_2$ Taxation in the EU', Paper prepared for presentation at the 12th Annual Association of Management Conference, August 10–13, 1994, Dallas, Texas, USA, Working paper C 62, Department of Economics, The Aarhus School of Business.

Svendsen, G.T. (1994c), 'Experience in the United States on Tradable Permits', Paper presented at the International Conference 'Tradable Permits', April 13, 1994, Danish Fuels and Combustion Society, Copenhagen, Denmark, Working paper C 61, Department of Economics, The Aarhus School of Business.

Svendsen, G.T. (1994d), 'Omsættelige $SO_2$-kvoter i USA', ('Acid Rain Program'), *Samfundsøkonomen*, **5**, pp. 9–13.

Svendsen, G.T. (1994e), 'Kvoter og syreregn', ('Quotas and Acid Rain'), *Økonomi & Politik*, **1**, pp. 33–39.

Svendsen, G.T. (1994f), 'Globalt $CO_2$-marked', ('Global $CO_2$ Market'), *Fremtidsorientering*, **1**, pp. 35–36.

Svendsen, G.T. (1993a), 'The Danish $CO_2$ Tax and Emissions Trading', Paper presented at the International IIASA Conference 'Economic Instruments for Air Pollution Control', October 18–20 1993 in Laxenburg, Austria, Working paper C 60, Department of Economics, The Aarhus School of Business.

Svendsen, G.T. (1993b), 'Fordele ved et marked for $CO_2$-kvoter', ('Advantages in $CO_2$ Emissions Trading'), *Samfundsøkonomen*, **7**, pp. 5–9.

Svendsen, G.T. (1992), 'Omsættelige forureningstilladelser i USA', ('Emissions Trading in the USA'), *Samfundsøkonomen*, **3**, pp. 26–31.

Svendsen, G.T. (1991), *Indførelse af tilladelsesmarkeder i Danmark? – med normstyrede energiproducenters udledning af $CO_2$, $SO_2$ og $NO_x$ som eksempel, (Emissions Trading in Denmark? – $CO_2$, $SO_2$ and $NO_x$ Emitted by Norm Regulated Energy Producers)*, Thesis in Political Science, University of Aarhus, Denmark.

Svendsen, G.T. and Steiner, U. (1997), 'Omsættelige $CO_2$-kvoter i den danske elsektor' ('Transferable $CO_2$ Quotas in the Danish Electricity Sector'). Draft.

Swann, D. (1988), *The Retreat of the State: Deregulation and Privatisation in the UK and US*, New York: Harvester.

Swedish Ministry of the Environment and Natural Resources (1994), *The Swedish Experience – Taxes and Charges in Environmental Policy*, Stockholm.

Taylor, S.R. (1992), 'Tradeable Credits: Variants for the Transport Sector' in *Climate Change: Designing a Tradeable Permit System*, Paris: OECD.

Thatcher, J. (1994), 'United States Partnership Approach to Climate Change Mitigation', Washington D.C.: Center for Clean Air Policy.

Tietenberg, T.H. (1996), *Environmental and Natural Ressource Economics*, Fourth Edition, Harper Collins College Publishers.

Tietenberg, T.H. (1995), 'Economic Instruments for Pollution Control When Emission Location Matters: What Have We Learned?' *Environmental & Resource Economics*, **5**, pp. 95–113.

Tietenberg, T.H. (ed.) (1992), *Innovation in Environmental Policy: Economic and Legal Aspects of Recent Developments in Environmental Enforcement and Liability*, Ashgate.

Tietenberg, T.H. (1990a), 'Economic Instruments for Environmental Regulation', *Oxford Review of Economic Policy*, **6**, pp. 17–33.

Tietenberg, T.H. (1990b), 'Using Economic Incentives to Maintain Our Environment', *Challenge*, **33**, pp. 42–46.

Tietenberg, T.H. (1989a), 'Acid Rain Reduction Credits', *Challenge*, **32**, pp. 25–29.

Tietenberg, T.H. (1989b), 'Marketable Emission Permits in the U.S.: A Decade of Experience', in Karl W. Roskamp (ed.), *Public Finance and the Performance of Enterprises*, Detroit, MI: Wayne State University Press.

Tietenberg, T.H. (1985), *Emissions Trading: An Exercise in Reforming Pollution Policy*, Washington, D.C.: Resources for the Future.

Tietenberg, T.H. (1980), 'Transferable Discharge Permits and the Control of Stationary Source Air Pollution: A Survey and Synthesis', *Land Economics*, **56**, pp. 391–416.

Tietenberg, T.H. (1974), 'The Design of Property Rights for Air Pollution Control', Public Policy, **22**, pp. 275–92.

Torvanger, A. (1991), 'Manufacturing Sector Carbon–Dioxide Emissions in 9 OECD Countries, 1973–87 – A Divisia Index Decomposition to Changes in Fuel Mix, Emission Coefficients, Industry Structure, Energy Intensities and International Structure', *Energy Economics*, **13**, pp. 168–86.

Tripp, J.T.B and Dudek, D.J. (1989), 'Institutional Guidelines for Designing Successful Transferable Rights Programs', *Yale Journal on Regulation*, **6**, pp. 369–91.

Tschirhart, J.T. (1984), 'Transferable Discharge Permits and Profit-Maximizing Behavior', in Crocker, T.D. (ed.), *Economic Perspectives on Acid Deposition Control*, pp. 157–71, Boston: Butterworth Publishers.

Ursprung, H.W. (1991), 'Economic Policies and Political Competition', in Hilman, A.

(ed.), *Markets and Politicians*, Boston, pp. 1–41.

Van der Meer, L.G.H. et al. (1992), *Investigations Regarding the Storage of Carbon Dioxide in Aquifers in The Netherlands*, Delft, The Netherlands: TNO Institute of Applied Geoscience.

Van Dyke, B. (1991), 'Emissions Trading to Reduce Acid Deposition', *Yale Law Journal*, **100**, pp. 2707–26.

Varian, H.R. (1987), *Intermediate Microeconomics*, London: Norton.

Weck-Hannemann, H. and Frey, B.S. (1995), 'Are incentive Instruments as Good as Economists Believe? Some New Considerations', in Bovenberg, L. and Cnossen, S. (eds.), *Public Economics and the Environment in an Imperfect World*, Boston.

Vickrey, W. (1961), 'Counterspeculation, Auctions, and Competitive Sealed Tenders', *Journal of Finance*, **16**, pp. 8–37.

Wilson, J.Q. (1980), 'The Politics of Regulation', in Wilson, J.Q. (ed.), *The Politics of Regulation*, New York: Basic Books.

Vogel, D. (1987), *National Styles of Regulation – Environmental Policy in Great Britain and the United States*, London: Cornell University Press.

World Bank (1990), *World Development Indicators 1990*, Washington, D.C.

WQCC (1984), 'Regulations for Control of Water Quality in Dillon Reservoir', Water Quality Control Commission, June 21, State of Colorado: Department of Health.

Yandle, B. (1978), 'The Emerging Market in Air Pollution Rights', *Regulation*, July/August, pp. 21–29.

Yin, R.K. (1989), Case Study Research: Design and Methods, Newbury Park, California: Sage Publications Inc.

Young, H.P. and Wolf, A. (1992), 'Global Warming Negotiations: Does Fairness Matter?', *Brookings Review*, **10**, pp. 46–51.

Yu, O.S. and Kinderman, E.M. (1991), 'Energy-Technology Efficiency-Improvements – Capital Requirements, Energy-Cost Savings, and Global CO2-Emission Reduction', *Energy*, **16**, pp. 1503–17.

Zander, B. (1991), 'Nutrient Trading – in the Wings: The Phosphorus Club Recommended the Dillon Bubble', *EPA Journal*, November/December, pp. 47–49.

Zhang, Z.X. (1997), *The Economics of Energy Policy in China: Implications for Global Climate Change*, New Horizons in Environmental Economics Series, Edward Elgar Publishing Limited, Aldershot, England.

# Interviews

1993
October 6     Karen Årø, Danish Ministry of the Environment.
June 16       Mogens Weel-Hansen, Dk-Teknik
June 9        Erik Thomsen, Danish Environmental Protection Agency.
June 4        Allan Andersen, DN

# Subject Index